Dear Reader:

The book you are about to read is the latest bestseller from the St. Martin's True Crime Library, the imprint the *New York Times* calls "the leader in true crime!" Each month, we offer you a fascinating account of the latest, most sensational crime that has captured the national attention. St Martin's is the publisher of bestselling true crime author and crime journalist Kieran Crowley, who explores the dark, deadly links between a prominent Manhattan surgeon and the disappearance of his wife fifteen years earlier in THE SURGEON'S WIFE. Carlton Smith's COLD BLOODED details the death of a respected attorney—and the secret, sordid life of his wife. In Edgar Award-nominated DARK DREAMS, legendary FBI profiler Roy Hazelwood and bestselling crime author Stephen G. Michaud shine light on the inner workings of America's most violent and depraved murderers. In the book you now hold, VANISHED, veteran true crime scribe Carlton Smith examines the details surrounding the sudden disappearance of a former California state senator's daughter—was her husband guilty?

St. Martin's True Crime Library gives you the stories behind the headlines. Our authors take you right to the scene of the crime and into the minds of the most notorious murderers to show you what really makes them tick. St. Martin's True Crime Library paperbacks are better than the most terrifying thriller, because it's all true! The next time you want a crackling good read, make sure it's got the St. Martin's True Crime Library logo on the spine—you'll be up all night!

Charles E. Spicer, Jr.
Executive Editor, St. Martin's True Crime Library

VANISHED

Carlton Smith

St. Martin's Paperbacks

VANISHED

Copyright © 2005 by Carlton Smith.

Cover photo of van © Bruno Ehrs/Photonica; Photo of Bruce Koklich © AP Photo/Gary Friedman; Photo of Paul Carpenter © AP Photo.

ISBN: 0-312-98609-2
EAN: 9780312-98609-4

Printed in the United States of America

St. Martin's Paperbacks edition / August 2005

St. Martin's Paperbacks are published by St. Martin's Press, 175 Fifth Avenue, New York, NY 10010.

10 9 8 7 6 5 4

LAKEWOOD,
CALIFORNIA

AUGUST 18, 2001

Where's Bruce?

It was late, maybe half past midnight, and when Nini turned her car onto her friend Jana's street, both of them noticed that all the lights were off at Jana's house.

"Where's Bruce?" Nini wondered aloud, and Jana said she had no idea.

Nini pulled her car alongside the curb to let Jana out. They'd had a great time at the Eric Clapton concert at the Staples Center in Los Angeles, but both of them had an early day ahead. Nini, perhaps a bit more cynical than her friend, or maybe wiser in the unhappy ways of the real world, suggested that Jana take care when she got inside her house: Who knew what may be lurking in the dark on the other side of the threshold?

"When you get inside," Nini said, "flash the lights on and off, and open and close the door a few times, so I know everything's okay."

Jana said she would do that, and she got out of Nini's car, clutching the tee-shirt she'd bought at the concert. Nini watched as Jana opened the front door with her key and went in. Nini waited, then saw the lights flash on and off four times. She guessed that everything must be all right, so she put her car in gear and headed home.

That was the last time anyone—except Jana's presumed killer—ever saw her. It was early in the morning of August 18, 2001.

After that, it was as if Jana Carpenter Koklich, a 41-year-old multimillionaire real estate tycoon, and the wife of 42-year-old real estate maven Bruce David Koklich, simply vanished. And while the nation wondered that same summer about the fate of Chandra Levy, or the next spring about Utah's Elizabeth Smart, or the winter after that about Laci Peterson, or the winter of the next year about North Dakota's Dru Sjodin, or the spring after that about Salt Lake City's Lori Hacking, all of them were eventually found, either living or dead. But Jana Carpenter Koklich is still out there, somewhere, lost to the world.

Her husband, Bruce David Koklich, however, is serving 15 years to life for her murder—even though no trace of Jana Carpenter Koklich's body has ever been found.

Going missing: the idea that someone can simply vanish without a trace, leaving loved ones behind to grapple with an agonized confusion that has no end, no resolution, no answer, no explanation—this is today's unspoken nightmare, the modern equivalent of voracious wolves in the forest for the people of the Middle Ages, or involuntary possession by evil spirits in still earlier times. As an unquantifiable danger beyond human control, it is the very absence of information, the utter lack of something solid to grip, anything in the way of some glimmer, any idea of what happened, that makes the unexpected disappearance an undefined universe of the worst of all fears. Over the abyss of silence, the darkest imagination reigns supreme.

For all the weeks or months that Chandra Levy, Elizabeth Smart, Laci Peterson, Dru Sjodin or Lori Hacking were missing, one thing was as clear as it was unmentioned by the major news outlets across the country: as vanished women, though each was the subject of hours upon hours of national publicity, they were hardly alone. They were, in fact, the example, not the definition of the problem: for every missing person who became the subject of Larry King's nightly gabfest, hundreds, probably thousands, of other young women never got the *de rigueur* fifteen minutes (or sometimes much more) of fame, or really, tragedy, as it was encapsulated by an appearance of the grieving relatives on national television.

There were simply too many of them, of the missing; and unless one was very lucky, or had influential friends—enough to get airtime on one of the national networks—too few really cared. These infamous disappearances—Levy, Peterson, Smart, Sjodin and Hacking—became symbols of what some would call an epidemic of violence against women throughout America, even if they represented only the tiniest fragment of the true dimensions of the problem.

No one knows how many people are reported missing every year in the United States, but it must be in the tens, possibly hundreds of thousands. A great many of these missing people are women, significantly over half. The vast majority soon turn up, however—revealed to be only temporarily missing as a result of some misunderstanding, or less frequently, voluntarily absent because of some difficulty with family or money or other such immediately pressing trouble.

Every police department in the country has a protocol for dealing with missing people: if the vanished person is a competent adult, and if there is no reason to suspect foul play, generally nothing is done. After all, there is no law against someone leaving the places and people he or she might know, simply because things have gotten out of hand. Over and over, police agencies have taken missing persons reports from frantic friends and relatives, only to discover that the person reported has simply taken a break from routine, or at worst, has relocated to another part of the country, to start over. The advent of inexpensive systems of long-distance transportation, interstate highways, jet aircraft—a hallmark of the industrial and post-industrial ages—has made the unexpected disappearance a phenomenon of the developed world, and a relatively recent one at that.

There are, however, some types of missing persons reports that *do* get police action, and quickly. Small children almost always prompt police action, as do elderly people who might reasonably be seen to be at risk. And there are those whose disappearances cry out, almost from the start, that something untoward has happened, like those of Chandra Levy, Elizabeth Smart, Dru Sjodin and Lori Hacking.

Such was also the case with Jana Carpenter Koklich, who went inside her house early on the morning of August 18, 2001, and was never seen again. But there were a number of aspects of Jana's disappearance that made her case even more peculiar than those of the networks' Famous Five. While those cases got most of the public attention, indeed hours of exposure on the American village that cable television has created, it was only because of the peculiar circumstances surrounding the timing of Jana Carpenter Koklich's disappearance that her name never became a household word even larger than the others. Because, only a little over three weeks after Jana vanished, terrorists struck New York and Washington, D.C., with airplanes laden with fuel and people, and from that point forward, the news reporters had many other things to talk about than one missing woman.

But Jana's disappearance, when compared to those of

the far more publicized disappearances, was even more unusual.

For one thing, Jana Carpenter Koklich was the daughter
of Paul B. Carpenter, formerly one of the state of California's most controversial political figures, and also a man
who once pulled off a stunning vanishing act of his own.

And for another, there was all the money at stake in
Jana's disappearance—around $6 million in hard assets,
and maybe millions more, in potential future income. That
someone might have a nefarious interest in seeing Jana
Carpenter Koklich disappear, permanently, seemed obvious. It was the unrelated destruction of three American
landmarks that shoved Jana's disappearance off the screen,
and off the front pages; otherwise, she might have been
more of a household name than any of the others.

But whether known or obscure, Jana's untimely disappearance still meant there were three big questions:

First, if she was dead, who killed her?

Second, was Jana Carpenter Koklich really and truly
dead?

And third, if she *wasn't* dead, what the hell was going
on?

But to get a grip on these questions requires a brief side
trip into the often sordid world of California politics, and
how it directly affected the life of Jana Carpenter Koklich,
missing person. It's only when one understands the conditions that made Jana's vanishing unique that one can begin
to understand the final, tragic mystery that makes her case
one of the saddest, by far, of all of those which over the
past few years have captivated the public eye.

So let's turn back the clock a bit, and take a look at the
milieu that lay behind Jana's mysterious disappearance.

PAUL AND JANA
BRUCE AND CHRIS

Shenanigans

Controversial as Paul B. Carpenter's life and career were, he was hardly the first in California politics to have been shipwrecked by the twin sirens of ambition and power. The enduring question, as far as Jana Carpenter Koklich is concerned, is whether the force of her father's colorful personality shaped the reticence of Jana's own—whether, in fact, the rise and subsequent demise of her father played a central role in Jana's uncertain fate.

As one of the largest states in the nation, and as a place that for most of its history has served as a magnet for people from other places, California has long had a reputation as a haven for colorful political rogues, and this holds particularly true for the state's capital, Sacramento.

Located in the north-central portion of the state, Sacramento was, in the earliest years of California, one of the major jumping-off points for the booming gold-fields of the Sierras. Steamboats coming up the Sacramento River from San Francisco discharged millions of tons of cargo, not least the construction materials used for the first transcontinental railroad in the years after the Civil War. As a major focal point for the growing state's commerce, Sacramento by 1854 emerged as the logical place to permanently seat the state government.

Because California was such a large state—nearly 800 miles in length, from the far northwestern corner near Crescent City to the Mexican border in the southeast, near Yuma, Arizona—almost from the start the California Legislature was composed primarily of men (and later women) living far away from home. In these new surroundings, the temptation to re-invent oneself was strong. Unobserved by the ordinary forces of moral suasion such as wives, children, mothers and ministers, the usual patterns of behavior all too often fell by the wayside, as newly elected legislators made their way to the distant capital.

Once they got to town, lionized and feted as they were, many of the electorally anointed were only too willing to indulge their previously repressed, often more carnal appetites. The temptations on offer in California's capital were from the very start varied and plentiful. It was not for nothing that the very first California lawmaking session in 1849 became known as the "Legislature of One Thousand Drinks," because of "hospitality rooms," well-liquored dives—canvas tents, mostly—that were quickly established for purposes of entertaining and influencing the newly anointed officials by job-seeking opportunists.

After free booze came women, some paid by economic interests for purposes of influencing the elected and appointed, others arriving strictly as volunteers attracted to the new center of power. But the real corruptor was the usual: money. Lots and lots of money.

The California State Legislature spent most of the second half of the 19th century in the pocket of the railroad interests, puppets who danced to the tunes called by Collis Huntington and the Central Pacific, later called the Southern Pacific. Bribery and extortion were common political tools. Any politician who balked at the demands of "the

Octopus," as muckraking novelist Frank Norris called the railroad in 1901, soon found himself out of the Legislature, and often, even out of a job. By the turn of the century, the Southern Pacific controlled virtually all of the trackage in the state, which allowed it to set whatever shipping rates it chose, and to extort subsidies from local taxpayers almost at whim. The railroad controlled the Legislature from top to bottom—going so far as to cause it to pass one law that made political cartoons illegal, and almost passing another that made the murder of any journalist accused of libel justifiable homicide.

Still, the railroad's success in dominating the scene contained within it the seeds of its own demise. As other interests—agriculture, mining, commerce—improved their own positions on the coattails of the railroad's prosperity, they began to gain strength—enough strength, in fact, to eventually join forces and push through a reform movement just before World War I. These Progressives, as they were called, managed to enact legislation permitting the initiative, referendum and recall procedures, which, at least initially, had the effect of greatly reducing the corruption practiced in the capital. There were other reforms as well: the nation's first workmen's compensation insurance program; child labor laws; laws regulating hours and wages for women; regulation of public utilities; and direct primary election, known as "cross filing," in which candidates could run on any party's ticket—all of them efforts to drive the railroad out of the control of politics. At least at first, all of these had the effect of letting air and sunshine into the political system. They had a secondary impact as well, which was to reduce the power of political parties, thus opening up the system to maverick candidates—people who could make their own deals with the special interests, if they chose to do so.

But graft has a way of surviving, particularly when it

emanates from the vices, and if the Progressives had any blind spot, it was about the vices—gambling, booze, prostitution. Not long after the Progressives installed their reforms, the graft was back, aided enormously by that most infamous of the Progressive reforms, Prohibition. By the mid-1930s, the state and the legislature were again awash in corruption, this time even harder to ferret out because it was less ideological than it was venal. Thus began the heyday of Artie Samish, who eventually became known across the nation as the "boss" of all of California, although he never received a single vote.

Arthur H. Samish was a huge man—well over 6 feet tall, and in excess of 300 pounds. At the height of his power, in the late 1940s, he virtually controlled all politics in California, Republican as well as Democrat. U.S. Senator Estes Kefauver once referred to him as "a combination of Falstaff, Little Boy Blue, and Machiavelli, crossed with an eel."

A lobbyist, Samish would later explain how he worked: first, he had a "Gestapo," as he called it, a staff of clandestine operatives who reported to him on everything that was going on in Sacramento—personal as well as political. Samish carefully recorded everything in little black books, everything from how a legislator voted to which gambler the legislator owed money to, or which bordello he favored. When vested interests wanted something done in Sacramento, they hired Samish, who, for a hefty fee, would line the legislators up to vote for or against any proposal, often manipulating the rules of legislative committees to keep the hand of control hidden. Samish wasn't ideological; he was in it for the money.

"Throughout the day," Samish would later recall, "I received visitors both big and small: legislators and state executives, brewery owners and bartenders, newspaper publishers and bootblacks. All received the same Samish hospitality. A buffet served lobster, shrimp, caviar and other goodies. I ran the best stocked bar in Sacramento."[1]

By the late 1930s, Samish was so powerful that he virtually ran the state, representing the liquor industry, racetracks, truckers, bus lines, railroads—just about anything that moved, or could be smoked, drunk or eaten. That was when the reformist governor, Culbert Olson, commissioned a former FBI agent to investigate Samish. Using wiretaps, Howard Philbrick traced the mechanisms of Samish's spiderweb, and showed that he was in fact the real governor—"the secret boss of California," as he referred to himself. Philbrick's report was presented to the legislature, which promptly destroyed it. To this day, the Philbrick report remains one of California's most suppressed public documents.

Samish continued to run the state throughout the 1940s—even after Governor Earl Warren, probably the most widely respected chief executive the state ever had, empaneled an organized crime commission. In 1948, that body issued a report that demonstrated how Samish had an iron grip on the politics of the state, and how he used the state attorney general's office to protect entrenched gambling and prostitution interests from San Diego on the southern border to Mendocino County in the north. By that point, Samish's activities had attracted the interest of the national press; Samish didn't seem to care. In the summer of 1948, he was profiled in *Collier's* magazine and even jovially posed for a photograph with a ventriloquist's dummy on his knee.

"That's the way I lobby," Samish said. "That's my legislature. That's Mr. Legislature. 'How are you today, Mr. Leg-

---

[1] Arthur Samish and Bob Thomas, *The Secret Boss of California*, Crown Publishers, New York, 1971, p. 80.

islature?' "[2] Samish said if he'd had a ladder long enough, *Collier's* could have taken a picture of him unscrewing the gold dome from the Capitol's cupola.

In part because of his braggadocio, Samish finally got his comeuppance in 1953, when a federal court jury found him guilty of eight counts of tax evasion, and he departed for the less rarefied climes of a federal prison.

If the Southern Pacific had run California's politics for its second and third generations, and Samish for its fourth, a new arrangement began to emerge in the wake of Samish's conviction. In this incarnation—having learned how to do it from Artie—the legislators began to act as lobbyists themselves, amassing huge stockpiles of cash from interest groups, and using it to make sure that the "right" people were elected: those who also supported the incumbents' point of view. Probably the most famous—or infamous—of these legislator-lobbyists was Jesse Marvin Unruh—"Big Daddy," as many referred to him in his heyday of the 1960s, in wry reference to the character in the Tennessee Williams play *Cat on a Hot Tin Roof*.

Born in Oklahoma, Jesse M. Unruh was the quintessential poor boy who'd made good. By the early 1960s, representing a legislative district just west of Los Angeles, he had become Speaker of the California Assembly, the most powerful job in the state legislature. Sporting expensive Italian suits and shoes, a styled haircut, a large pinkie ring, puffing on large hand-rolled stogies, Unruh simply exuded crass political power.

"We . . . saw him as three hundred pounds of cigar-smoking, booze-guzzling, Machiavellian rapacity," a newly

[2] *The Nation,* August 1949, "The Guy Who Gets Things Done," Carey McWilliams.

elected member of the California Assembly, James R. Mills, eventually a loyal admirer of Unruh, later recalled.[3] "And God knows he looked it. His features were as heavily sensual as a champion English bulldog's." Unruh's sartorial elegance screamed money, Mills recalled—"new money."

Where did the money come from? Some of it, it seemed, came from Unruh's heretofore unrivaled ability to put the arm on lobbyists. Unruh was unabashed about his capacity to squeeze dollars from interest groups.

"If you can't eat their food, drink their booze, screw their women, take their money and then vote against them, you don't belong up here," Unruh was said to have proclaimed.

That was one of three well-publicized Unruh dicta in the 1960s, along with "Money is the mother's milk of politics," and, borrowing from then–Green Bay Packers football coach Vince Lombardi, "Winning isn't everything, it's the only thing."

Unruh achieved his success in much the same way that Artie Samish did, by controlling the legislative process. If an interest group wanted something enacted into law, it had to get its checkbook out. The money, controlled by Unruh, was in turn doled out to candidates across the state who would owe their allegiance to him. The political party was essentially irrelevant to the cult of Unruh's personality. Those who wanted to be elected, or reelected, had to toe Big Daddy's line.

"If I had stayed away from the lobbyists," Big Daddy explained, "I would have been ineffective. If I take their money and do nothing for it, I am a cheat. If I do their bidding, I could be cheating the public. I find myself rationalizing what I have done."[4] By taking the lobbyists' money,

[3] *A Disorderly House,* James R. Mills, Heyday Books, Berkeley, 1987, p. 5.

Unruh said, he could beat them at their own game, even if it tarnished his own reputation along the way.

With Unruh's ascendancy, the power switched from the forces outside the legislature to those on the inside.

But eventually, just like the Southern Pacific, just like Artie Samish, Unruh's very success as an operator generated its own successors. As Samish had demonstrated that the elected could control politics by taming the interest groups, now Unruh's example demonstrated to other legislators that they could free themselves from his control by out-Unruhing Unruh. By the end of the 1960s, a number of legislators had begun establishing themselves as money centers, both collecting and doling out contributions in order to establish their own rival power centers in the legislature. One of those who understood this lesson perfectly well was a tall, inscrutable young man from Sioux City, Iowa: Paul Bruce Carpenter.

[4] *A Disorderly House*, p. 14.

The Skinner Man

Later, much later, after everything that happened, people who'd seen the whole ugly smashup come down would scratch their heads in puzzlement. No one, it seemed, really knew Paul Carpenter. Like a riverboat gambler from another century, Paul Carpenter held his cards close to his watch chain; and it was said his steely gaze could freeze a lobbyist in his tracks at a hundred paces.

A common observation in the political world is that when it comes to psychological motivation, every candidate is animated by one of the "Three Ms"—manipulation, money, or messianism. And while it's no longer possible to stretch Paul Bruce Carpenter out on the psychiatric couch to find out what made him tick, an argument can be made for the proposition that it wasn't the money or the desire to be the heroic savior that motivated him, but rather the thrill of manipulating others to do what he wanted them to do. One important question is whether that stoic taciturnity that was at the root of Paul Carpenter's power to manipulate others had somehow affected Jana Carpenter Koklich, leaving her strangely incapable of asserting and protecting herself, at least when it came to manipulation by demanding men.

Born in 1928, Paul Carpenter grew up in the shadow of the Great Depression in the Midwest, a time of farm foreclosures and widespread economic misery. After World War II and an enlistment in the Navy, he attended the University of Iowa and earned a bachelor's degree in psychology, a master's from the University of Missouri, and a doctorate from Florida State. His studies were centered on the controversial theories, largely Pavlovian in origin, of behaviorist B. F. Skinner, who devised a simple box with reward levers and colored lights to test his conditioned response theories on animals such as mice and rats.

As a behaviorist, Carpenter's own doctoral dissertation owed its origins to Skinner's theories; it was titled "The Effects of Sensory Deprivation on Behavior in the White Rat." In those days, most of the money for psychological research was invested in behaviorism, which promised human efficiency in industry.

By the late 1950s, just as he was entering his thirties, Paul had a job working as an industrial psychologist for Hughes Aircraft in southern California and was on his second marriage, this one to Janeth Turner, known to her friends and family as Janie, a fellow doctorate in psychology, and also a psychologist at Hughes. There was a daughter from the first marriage, Julie, who would soon be joined by a half-sister, Jana, born on New Year's Day of 1960. Jana would be the only child of Paul and Janeth Turner Carpenter.

By all accounts Paul was an extremely smart person, possessor of a lightning-quick brain capable of calculating odds with precision. He was a gifted card player, blessed with the capacity to keep his face utterly blank. His taciturnity and unblinking stare could be unnerving to those more accustomed to wearing their hearts on their sleeves. Some thought him unfathomable, almost a cipher.

But if there was any key to Paul, it lay in his ambition. Exactly why he chose politics as his arena was never quite clear, at least publicly. The hidden underside of Paul's personality, the inveterate gambler who enjoyed taking risks, may have been drawn to an endeavor in which results are almost immediately discernible, and even quantifiable.

In 1964, he ran for a seat in the U.S. Congress from a district that stretched from Orange County through eastern San Diego County to the Mexican border. As a Democrat in a district that was substantially Republican, and an unknown to boot, he generated a lot of press attention by walking from the northern end of the district all the way to the Mexican line. Although he lost, the stunt propelled him into the public eye.

Ten years later, he did win election to the California Assembly, and two years after that, in 1976, he won a seat in the California State Senate. In 1979 he gained more public attention by organizing a rally at the Los Angeles Coliseum, in which the Ayatollah Ruholla Khomeini, then the *bête noire* of the news media, was burned in effigy in protest of the occupation of the U.S. Embassy in Tehran. This was a second prominent aspect of Paul's personality: a penchant for performing outrageous political stunts that attracted public attention. It was as if, at some level, Paul saw himself as the star of a 1930s Capraesque political melodrama, a sort of Jimmy Stewart whose stare could kill.

During his career as a state senator, Paul carved out a populist niche for himself on the right wing of the Democratic Party. Not for him were the bleeding hearts of the liberal wing of the party; his constituents were blue-collar union workers who had mostly voted for Ronald Reagan four different times. Like the behavioral scientist he was, Paul put his constituency into a political Skinner box, stimulating voters with visceral issues like taxes or outrage over perceived unfairnesses, in order to make them pull the correct voting levers.

As a conservative Democrat, Paul was virtually forced to create his own fund-raising machinery, since the mainspring of the Democratic Party considered him unreliable, even demagogic. Of course, there were still many interest groups donating political money who were only too glad to give to Paul, since he enabled the donors to claim they were bipartisan, and best of all, they thought, Paul believed in lowering everyone's taxes, even those of big business.

Soon Paul became a locus for political money, just as Samish and Unruh had been before him. "The money he obtained from lobbyists went into campaign accounts for other members [of the Legislature]," Charles Bloodgood, who would later defend Paul on criminal charges, recalled. "He didn't spend one dime for his own benefit. And we're talking about hundreds of thousands of dollars."

By acting as a conduit for this political money, Paul hoped to do two things: get more people who thought like him elected to the legislature, which would in turn make him more and more powerful; and second, cause a growing number of candidates, even those who didn't agree with him, to be beholden to him for campaign money, just as Unruh had done fifteen years earlier. That was the pathway to power in a democracy, it seemed clear.

In 1982, Paul felt strong enough to move further up the political ladder. He challenged incumbent Jerry Brown for the Democratic Party nomination for governor. That was when a political consultant warned him that Jerry Brown had 100 percent name recognition.

"So does Charlie Manson," Paul cracked. His wit notwithstanding, Paul was crushed in the primary.

While Paul's principal motivation for being in politics was psychological—he enjoyed the power—that predilection in no way prevented him from taking personal advantage of the income opportunities that his increasing power afforded him. A quick review of his annual economic interest disclosure statements, a sort of biopsy of office holders' personal financial condition that had to be filed every year with the state's Fair Political Practices Commission, showed a steady gain in both income and speaking fees for Paul throughout the 1980s, all in addition to his full-time legislator's salary.[6] By 1984 Paul reported substantial holdings in real estate and in two privately held corporations, Pacific Point-to-Point Communications, Inc., and Janaco Investments, Inc.

The latter, doubtless named after daughter Jana, was described by Paul in his annual filings as a company he'd formed with Janie to pursue opportunities in "consulting and international trade." This company was formed in December of 1983, and was valued by Paul as being worth between $10,000 and $100,000 by the end of that year. (The California Secretary of State had no record of "Pacific Point-to-Point Communications, Inc.")

Exactly what made Janaco Investments, Inc., worth that amount less than a month after it was formed wasn't clear in the reports, but it appeared that Janie's non–Hughes Aircraft consulting income the following year was directed through the new firm, according to Paul's state filings, so there may have been some tax advantage in its formation. Over the following years, Janaco Investments held stocks valued between $50,000 and $500,000, according to Paul's filings (the state's forms were notorious for the elastic quality of their disclosure categories).

As he continued to ascend the political ladder, Paul also

[6] Paul Carpenter, California Fair Political Practices Commission filings, 1976–1991.

began earning larger and larger honoraria as a speaker. Where in the late 1970s, he might get a free dinner and a pen-and-pencil set worth $25 for speaking to members of some trade association, by the mid-1980s he was frequently receiving speaking fees of $500 and $1,000 a speech. This money was eligible to go into Paul's pocket as personal income, in contrast to campaign money, which had to be spent for electioneering.

Paul also received all-expenses-paid junkets to different parts of the world financed by well-heeled lobbying groups, including a $2,000 trip to Washington, D.C., in 1983; a $6,450 trip to Baghdad, Iraq (paid for by none other than Saddam Hussein's government), in 1984; $3,000 trips to Portugal, the Caribbean and Saudi Arabia in 1985; $1,200 to go to the Philippines in 1986; and a $12,500 trip to Ireland, England and France in 1988.

By 1984, Paul and Janie had separated. Paul's increasing preoccupation with events and distractions in Sacramento and elsewhere had brought alienation to the marriage. Paul soon began living with his long-time legislative aide, Doris Morrow, in Sacramento. The bitterness from the break-up was intense, and continued for years afterward.

By the mid- to late 1980s, Paul had emerged as one of the major players in Sacramento, mostly because of his mastery in raising and distributing campaign funds. Stories circulated about his icy demeanor. A lobbyist seeking his support, for example, might visit him in his office. Maintaining his poker face, Carpenter would punch at a computer keyboard, and stare at the computer screen, laconically observing that the lobbyist's client had given more money to his opponent. That seemed to pry loose a still larger donation from the lobbyist for Paul or one of his supporters.

Others recalled that Paul had a penchant for staring directly into the eyes of those who spoke to him, and speaking in a slow, almost robotic tone; all recalled it as eerie, even intimidating.

Then there were the tales about the card games: an inveterate gambler (one fellow politician recalled that Paul played his politics the way he played poker—deadpan, with consummate bluffing), Paul often found himself playing for high stakes at such venues as the posh Balboa Bay Club in Newport Beach, usually with those who wanted or needed to do business with the state. Somehow, the big boys always managed to lose a lot of money to Paul, but no one complained.

But as the stories about the Southern Pacific, Samish and Unruh illustrate, for everything and for everyone, there is a season. By 1986, even as Paul was running to become a member of the state's Board of Equalization—a powerful statewide agency that operated to ensure fair tax assessment practices, and therefore a lucrative post for someone whose forte was raising campaign contributions—he had become a target of a federal corruption investigation in Sacramento.

In this investigation, the FBI devised a fictitious business, Gulf Shrimp Fisheries, and then went trolling for legislators thought susceptible to accepting bribes. Paul was one of those caught in the net. Just like Howard Philbrick had with Artie Samish decades earlier, the FBI snared Paul on a wiretap, this one provided by Paul's own chief aide.

By the time he was indicted by a federal grand jury in 1990, Paul had already served almost a full term on the five-member equalization board. Paul was charged with taking money as a state senator to fix appointments to state jobs, and to influence legislation. He denied doing anything wrong. While he admitted taking the cash, he said he believed that as long as he'd done nothing to actually fulfill the desires of those who provided the money, he was within legal bounds just as Unruh had said years earlier. But, said the federal government, doing nothing didn't mean that extortion hadn't taken place. To get extortion, you don't have to give anything but pressure.

At the end of 1990, after being reelected to a second four-year term on the Board of Equalization, Paul was convicted of the extortion charges, kicked off the board, stripped of his state pension and sentenced to serve a term of 12 years in federal prison. It was a shattering fall for a man, then 63 years old, who had once gambled for high stakes, but had finally lost in the biggest game of his life.

Paul went to prison for one day; then he was released on appeal. Subsequently, the conviction was thrown out by the appeals court because of improper jury instructions. But that wasn't the end of troubles for Paul Carpenter. No sooner had his first conviction been wiped out than he was indicted once more, this time on mail fraud and money-laundering charges: The government claimed that Paul, again while still a state senator, had allowed himself to be used as a conduit for what appeared to be a bribe from an insurance industry lobbyist to another state senator. The worst of it was, the end recipient of the money, the state senator who had been Paul's friend, turned around and became a witness for the government against Paul.

This time, three years later, the conviction stuck, and it appeared that Paul was fated to spend a number of years in prison. Then, just before he was due to be sentenced on the new charge, he fled the country.

Now 66 years old, Paul had already discovered that he

was suffering from prostate cancer. Given that he might expect to receive a significant sentence from the federal court, he feared he might die in prison. He wanted to get an experimental treatment for his cancer, and for that he had to go outside the United States. Paul left a note for the sentencing judge: "I find my drive for survival stronger than my sense of legal obligation to your legal system."

Three months later, in April 1994, the FBI found Paul in a suburb near San Jose, Costa Rica, where he had gone directly, using the name Paul Bruce. While there, he had grown a beard, climbed some mountains and generally lived the life of a laid-back expatriate American. According to Charles Bloodgood, his attorney, Paul had fled the country with less than $8,000 in cash, and without any prospect of gaining any other funds. Most of his assets had been previously consumed by legal fees, according to Bloodgood.

Thinking that no one was looking for him very hard, Paul made the mistake of entering the country's national bridge tournament with a Canadian he'd met on a hiking trip, using his own real name. To their mutual surprise, the two men won the tournament. When Paul's full name was published as one of the winners, the FBI tracked him down, arresting him while he was on his way to sign up for the country's national health care program.

"I was arrogant," Paul later admitted.

Jailed in Costa Rica while waiting for the legal extradition process to go forward, Paul believed that the generally unpredictable Costa Rican legal system might prevent his quick return to face his sentencing. At one point, apparently concerned that he might try to escape, Costa Rican authorities had him tied to a hospital bed with two steel straps. Meanwhile, Paul tried to get the Costa Rican courts to agree that he was a "political prisoner," and therefore should not be extradited, but eventually most of that claim was dismissed. His long-time aide, Doris Morrow, came to Costa Rica to be with him.

In late November of 1994, Paul was returned to the United States and lodged in the Sacramento County Jail, less than a mile from where he had once reigned as one of the Capitol's high rollers. In an interview he gave to a *Los Angeles Times* reporter, Paul said he'd left the country because, with his cancer, a lengthy prison term meant, "in effect, they were going to give me a life sentence." But by the time of his extradition, his cancer had gone into remission.

Being at large and undetected in Costa Rica, even if only for a few months, seemed to have mellowed Paul, some thought. From the driven, intense personality who had wanted to win at all costs, the post–Costa Rica Paul was far more relaxed, almost philosophical about his predicament. He was, he said, even prepared to do his time in prison, now that his cancer prognosis was favorable. Bloodgood, for one, thought he had become almost a different person, far more tolerant. But that didn't mean that Paul could be pushed around, or even that he couldn't take what was coming to him. Paul prided himself on being the proverbial stand-up guy.

"I think it's fair to say that I'm tough," he told a reporter for the *Times*. "I'm an adapter. I'm a survivor. I've been on some tough mountains before."

On January 17, 1995, Paul was criticized by the judge and the U.S. attorney who prosecuted him as "calculating and manipulative," and was sentenced to serve 7 years and 3 months in a federal penitentiary for his conviction on eleven counts of obstruction of justice, mail fraud and money laundering. The judge gave him the high end of the incarceration range, primarily because of his decision to vanish before the sentencing.

"It could have been a lot worse," said Charles Blood-good. "I think it was a fair sentence."

With that, Paul went off to federal prison. In all, he served just over 4 years. On his release in 1999, Paul moved in with Doris Morrow in San Antonio, Texas. His pension forfeited, and with no prospects for gainful employment, he was virtually broke, a sad end for one of the biggest wheeler-dealers in California history.

Moving In, Moving Up

Being the child of a politician, especially a controversial one, is never easy. One quickly learns to be wary, especially of outsiders: who knows when an innocent remark or a foolish mistake might be seized upon by a parent's political opponents? So one keeps to oneself, learning to smile pleasantly no matter the provocation, and keep internal thoughts hidden.

For Jana Carpenter Koklich, this normal reticence was doubtless reinforced by her father's own inscrutable personality. In short, Paul Carpenter was a very controlled person, and his life's work was centered on controlling others. It is plainly true that children tend to replicate the personalities of their parents, often in unconscious ways. In Paul, Jana had a powerful example of someone who habitually kept his emotions in check, who cultivated an air of icy reserve. In light of this, it's no surprise that even her closest friends would later remark that they rarely had any idea of what was going on inside Jana.

"She was a very, very private person," people would say, over and over.

There's a second aspect to this: in having a father who

was so controlled and distant, it's more than likely that when Jana began dating, she looked for a man who displayed similar character traits. This sort of behavior was, after all, what she associated with successful masculinity, and what she felt most comfortable with, in the sense that she instinctively understood it.

The earliest public image of Jana is one of a young, somewhat shy teenager hanging around the edges of her father's political circle, someone proud of her father, yet largely an afterthought in his run up the political ladder. Trying to make sense of the artificial world of the hangers-on who lionized her father, Jana learned to play the subordinate role of the dutiful daughter, someone who felt most comfortable in the background.

Jana was 14 when her father won his first election, 16 when he went on to the California State Senate, 19 when he pulled his Khomeini-effigy burning stunt, and 20 when the triumph of Ronald Reagan validated her father's conservative blue-collar populism, propelling him into the center of the political action in Sacramento. By 1982, Jana was attending college at California State University, Fullerton, and working jobs at Disneyland and in the law office of one of her father's close political advisors. It was in that year that she first met Bruce David Koklich, a little less than one year older than she was, while dancing at the Red Onion restaurant in Huntington Harbor, an upscale residential and shopping development in Orange County.

At about 5 feet, 10 inches, and 165 pounds, Bruce was a compactly built young man with dark hair and nerdy eyeglasses. He looked as if he might have been a small-town druggist, or an accountant. Yet he had an air about himself that told observers that he was very smart, as well as intensely driven to succeed. These may have been character traits that attracted Jana to him; in some respects, she may have seen something of her distant, always striving father in Bruce.

But while there were many similarities between Paul Bruce Carpenter and Bruce David Koklich, there was one very important difference: While Paul may have wanted money to get power, Bruce wanted power to get money.

Bruce was born on the last day of March in 1959, in Cocoa Beach, Florida, the second son of John and Naomi Koklich. John Koklich was a skilled metallurgist. In the early 1960s, the Koklich family moved to Sunnyvale, California, where John got a job in the aerospace industry. Subsequently, the family moved to the Sierra Nevada town of Columbia, not far from Sonora, where John Koklich opened his own shop, "The Goldsmith," as an artisan in custom gold jewelry.

In 1964, John and Naomi Koklich divorced, with John assuming the primary custody of Bruce and his older brother, Michael. From this time forward, John Koklich was the primary caregiver for his two sons. A U.S. Marine veteran of Iwo Jima, John believed in tough love with both of his sons: no blubbering allowed.

"My dad's life revolved around me and my brother," Bruce would recall. "He was the best. No matter what, he always made time for us, took us on vacations, camping trips, gold mining in the mountains . . . we did everything together. Because he raised us by himself, Michael and I had to assume a lot of responsibility for our everyday needs, but we accepted this and ran with it. We all worked together. I have nothing but the absolute best memories of my childhood."

Bruce was gifted with a sharp if unrefined intelligence. He was not attracted to intellectual pursuits, but was very focused on practical matters. By the late 1970s, after graduating from Sonora High School, he began working in a local garage as an auto mechanic. He bought a new pickup truck, and then, a year later, traded the truck for a house in Sonora. After remodeling the basement for use as an apartment, he moved in and rented the upper floor to tenants; his career in real estate had begun.

In 1979, after learning that the Powerine Oil Company in Long Beach was hiring mechanics, Bruce left Sonora and moved south, taking a series of jobs with the company, including one in which he maintained pumping derricks. This gave him some familiarity with the locations of various oil fields in and around the city of Long Beach—a circumstance that would later seem significant to those who would blame Bruce for Jana's disappearance.

After his experience acquiring the rental house in Sonora, Bruce was attuned to the prospects offered in the real estate business, particularly with distressed property.

"I was renting a house near the beach," he recalled, "but kept my eyes on the newspapers for available houses. I read about a 'fixer-upper' I thought I could afford, and went to the real estate office which had listed the home." While there, he overheard a real estate agent telling another man about the company's training program. Bruce enrolled, and, studying part-time while still working in the oil fields, eventually obtained a real estate sales license.

This was in 1982, about the same time that he met two people who would have a powerful effect on the course of his life. One was real estate investor Harry Parrell, who would be Bruce's mentor in the ins and outs of the property game for the next eight years. The other was Jana Carpenter Koklich.

Who can say for sure what attracts one person to another? The magic of love is like a spark that somehow ignites; if the fuel is ready, it combusts and burns steadily, faithfully warming and illuminating the soul for years, even decades.

In Bruce, Jana found a young man who seemed brash, confident and capable, clearly someone on his way up in the world. And in Jana, Bruce found a tall, beautiful blonde girl who seemed as anxious to please him as she was smart. Nor did it hurt at all that Jana's father, a candidate for governor at the time, was a very important person in Sacramento. Best of all, both Bruce and Jana were interested in the same thing: making a lot of money in real estate.

Later, friends and associates of Jana would describe her as the brains of the operation; that wasn't entirely fair to Bruce, who, if he lacked a formal education, was nevertheless blessed with a native shrewdness, especially about people's vulnerabilities. But while Jana was quiet, self-effacing, and detail-oriented—she would take charge of all the paperwork for the many real estate deals they would conclude over the next two decades—Bruce was most comfortable when he was engaged with people, either clients or adversaries. Jana was Ms. Inside, Bruce Mr. Outside.

In 1984, after dating for almost two years, Jana and Bruce moved in together, occupying a house in Long Beach. Jana had transferred from Fullerton to California State University, Long Beach, where she graduated with a degree in business, and soon passed her own real estate exam. Later that year, she joined the same firm that employed Bruce.

Bruce, meanwhile, had begun a business, with Harry Parrell, the more experienced real estate investor. Parrell decided to deal in "distressed" properties.

A distressed property was usually one that was in foreclosure—the owners, for whatever reason, had been unable to make the mortgage payment. The forecloser, often the bank or savings and loan, had taken back the property, and was usually wanting to get rid of it to recoup at least some of the loss. By paying a small amount down and investing some paint and elbow grease, Bruce and Harry could often salvage the underlying equity in the property, sometimes at a significant profit. This is exactly the sort of strategy that "You, Too, Can Be a Millionaire" mavens advertise on late-night television. In Bruce, an experienced mechanic familiar with tools, as well as someone with a small pool of capital to draw on, Parrell had found an ideal partner.

"I just got my broker's license," Parrell said later. "I was undergoing a change in career, and Bruce had a part-time real estate license [in 1982], and he took an interest in what I was doing in real estate. In his eagerness to learn, we started to purchase distressed properties together, rehab them . . . and market them—sell them. And then we started to list properties from banks and savings and loans together, and then I convinced Bruce to quit his job in the oil fields, and we became equal partners in a corporation."

Here was the key to Bruce's success, shown to him by Harry Parrell: They began to package the distressed properties for other investors, acting as the agent for the banks and loan companies, who after all, were in the business of making loans, not managing real estate. In effect, Parrell and Bruce had gone wholesale.

At the same time, Bruce and Parrell kept some properties back for themselves, seeing them as excellent rental opportunities. In other cases, Bruce enlisted friends to act as straw men for purchases.

Throughout the rest of the 1980s, while Paul Carpenter continued his political rise, Bruce, Jana and Harry Parrell continued their real estate activities, eventually generating a substantial income, and accumulating significant holdings in real property. By the end of the 1980s, Jana was also investing in real estate with Bruce, and the Parrell–Koklich corporation was "dissolved," as Harry put it later. Instead, in 1989, Bruce and Jana formed their own corporation, Spring Financial Services, Inc. Then, only a

few months later, Paul Carpenter was indicted on the
bribery charges flowing out of what some Sacramento
wags began referring to as "Shrimpgate," and all of Jana's
father's troubles began.

In June of 1990, even as Paul was fighting off his first in-
dictment, Jana and Bruce were married. Perhaps significantly, each signed a pre-nuptial agreement that listed
their separate property. On paper, it appears that Bruce
came into the marriage with far more assets than his
bride: seventeen separately owned pieces of real estate,
two vehicles, forty-eight gold coins worth $13,200, an-
other $13,200 in cash in a safety deposit box at a bank in
Long Beach, a checking account with $22,000 on deposit,
his mechanic's tools and equipment, a $38,963 interest in
"K.C. [for Koklich–Carpenter] Financial Profit Sharing
Plan" (the couple had incorporated their own businesses,
Spring Financial Services and K.C. Financial in 1989),
and his father's antique gun collection. Jana had only her
1984 Honda, and several pieces of jewelry, along with a
$6,000 interest in the K.C. Profit Sharing Plan.

The bride and groom also held joint interests in four
other pieces of real estate, and—curiously—a great many
shares in a company called Life Protecting Services, Inc.
This appeared to be a company that Bruce had started in
1987. Exactly what it did wasn't clear, although it may
have been connected with the sale of vitamins; within a
few years it was suspended as a corporation by the California Secretary of State's office. Bruce did not claim his
211,250 shares as part of his holdings when, much later,
he would pledge most of his assets to get out of jail,
which suggests that the shares by then were worthless.

One thing was clear: Bruce was intent on getting rich.
Later, many of their friends would observe that he was
nearly compulsive about business, working late at night,

early in the morning, and on weekends and holidays. He always seemed to be on the telephone, and when cellular phones became commonplace, never went anywhere without one, even while on vacation.

"I don't classify it as work," Bruce once said. "We enjoy it . . . I mean, it's my profession, I enjoy it."

Bruce was so focused on the opportunities he saw in the real estate market that even when his father John died in 1988, he was back at his desk within hours after the funeral. Harry Parrell was surprised to see him. "He and Jana drove up to northern California to bury his dad, and Monday morning—this was on the weekend—and Monday morning, he was back at work at his regular time, and it surprised me. What was shocking to me—at least in my culture, when a loved one passes away, we mourn and we cry and cover the TVs and cover the mirrors and talk about life . . . so when Bruce came back to work on Monday, I remember asking him, 'Don't you want to go home?' He said, 'No, I'd rather be here at work.' And he didn't show any emotion. He didn't show much sorrow or sadness. He just wanted to work, and his grief is much different from what I'm used to."

In one respect, Bruce's intense focus on work to the exclusion of ordinary emotions was a legacy of the disciplined life he had experienced as a child of a single male parent, where the emphasis was on taking responsibility for oneself, and doing the things that had to be done. Emotions such as grief or sadness or unhappiness were seen as self-indulgent wastes of time, not the sort of thing that real men engaged in. Later, this personality trait would come back to haunt Bruce, when numerous people observed that he wasn't displaying the proper demeanor for someone whose beloved wife had mysteriously gone missing.

Of the two, Jana was seen by most who knew the couple as the more socially adept—at least among the tight circle of friends whom she trusted the most. This group included Kathy Ensign, who had known Jana since the fourth grade; Patty and John Endley; Jan Baird, who had once worked for Paul, and her husband, Jeff, a lawyer who still represented Jana's father; and a woman named Carmen Myrben, who used the professional name Nini Angelini in her work as a Long Beach skin care specialist. Later, Nini—a generation older than Jana—would become a key witness against Bruce. So, too, would Nini's friend Dean Costales, a workout trainer who would help Jana shed some twenty-five pounds in the months before her disappearance.

One of the most striking things about the retrospective look at the Koklichs' marriage—the one that would come into focus after Jana disappeared—was that so few of their mutual friends other than Harry Parrell really liked Bruce. It was Jana whom they all said they were friends with, not Bruce. And indeed, there is even a sense, at least among their women friends, that Bruce tended to be bossy, controlling over Jana—even to the extent of telling her how to fix her hair, what clothes to wear, where to go, what to do. Jana seemed to accept this far too docilely, some thought.

Nini, in particular, thought Bruce was much too domineering. She kept encouraging Jana to be more assertive, to change her look, to step out and enjoy life more. But Jana would say she'd have to check with Bruce first. At one point, Nini invited Jana and Bruce to go on a river-rafting trip. Jana seemed interested in going until she checked with Bruce, and when she learned that he didn't want to go, told Nini she wouldn't be able to go either. Later Nini asked Bruce why he wouldn't let his wife go on a one-night rafting trip, and while he said that Jana could do whatever she wanted to do, Nini thought that wasn't the case at all—that Bruce had stopped Jana from going, since he wouldn't be along, too.

Bruce was similarly controlling when it came to spending money, Jana's friends thought. Once, when Jana wanted to buy a new car—this at a time when the couple's income exceeded $200,000 a year—Bruce told her she didn't need a new car, so she dropped the idea. About the only thing Jana did spend money on was clothes—she had several closets packed with dresses, suits, shoes, some items only worn once. But even this indulgence generated sarcastic comments from Bruce, Jana's friends later remembered.

At the same time, Jana sometimes seemed like a servant for Bruce. She made it a point to go home for lunch, friends remembered, usually returning to the office with his lunch—and his vitamins. Bruce was insistent that he get his vitamins.

Bruce was so obviously the dominant partner in the marriage, and Jana so deferential to him, that few if any of her friends sought to inquire as to how their marriage was holding up. Jana's reserve about intimate details of her life with Bruce was all-encompassing, a barrier that friends seldom crossed. When Nini, for instance, once asked Jana about her sex life with Bruce—in the way women friends often confide with one another—Jana drew back, shocked. She would never discuss such things. They were too personal.

Over and over again, as the investigation into Jana's disappearance unfolded in late 2001, her friends and acquaintances would say that she was very private about her inner feelings—so much so that few knew what she was really thinking and feeling, particularly about Bruce.

Nevertheless, as Paul Carpenter's troubles with the law mounted in the early 1990s, Jana managed to achieve something of a reconciliation with her father. In the wake of her parents' separation, and Paul's relationship with

Doris Morrow, father and daughter grew more distant, but by the time Paul was standing trial for the second time, Jana seemed to have made her peace with her father's decision to separate from her mother. Charlie Bloodgood, who represented Paul in the second case, the one alleging money laundering, recalled that Jana frequently called to cheer up Paul, and to check with Bloodgood on how things were going. But if Jana ever had a strong opinion about what had befallen her father, her friends did not later recall it, at least publicly. "I don't think there were any of her friends who even knew that about her," Nini said later. It was something Jana simply would not discuss.

Jana continued to be very close to her mother, Janie, however, as did Bruce. On one occasion, just before Paul was released from prison, Jana, Janie and Bruce all took a vacation to Switzerland together. When Janie had to have a hip replacement early in 2001, Jana and Bruce spent a great deal of time helping to take care of her. Janie, for her part, believed that Bruce doted on Jana. Like others, she was very impressed with his loyalty to Jana, and with his drive to succeed in business.

That drive, however, had already earned Bruce a number of enemies in Long Beach real estate circles. Competing real estate firms saw him as ruthless and unprincipled, always ready to cut a corner if there was more profit to be made. It didn't help that Bruce could be bombastic in his attitude toward his competition, sometimes belittling them as stupid, or lazy, or sloppy. By 2001, in fact, there were any number of other real estate people in the Long Beach area who were only too ready to call the police with negative stories about Bruce, once Jana turned up missing.

In 1994, Bruce and Jana bought a house in one of the tonier sections of Lakewood, California, a bedroom community just north of Long Beach. Backed up against a golf course, the split-level house had three bedrooms and a recreation room, as well as a den. Not long after buying the house, Bruce and Jana began trying to have a child. But as the next few years unfolded, it appeared that Jana was unable to conceive. At one point, they attempted to use *in vitro* fertilization procedures, to no avail. Later, they attempted to find a surrogate mother, but this attempt resulted in a miscarriage. By 1999 they had begun to investigate adoption, and had even contacted a northern California lawyer who specialized in private placements. This effort, too, came to naught, and eventually the couple abandoned their plans. Jana's friends later said that this was the first time they had ever heard her express disappointment about Bruce—that he had given up on the idea of adoption.

But by then, Bruce had in mind another type of offspring—a computer software business that he hoped would make the couple millions of dollars, maybe even tens of millions. And it was this cybernetic child, called AMOS, that would come to play a central role, or so Bruce himself thought, in the fate of Jana Carpenter Koklich.

AMOS

Later, the antecedents of AMOS—an acronym for Asset Management and Origination Systems—and its hurriedly conceived stepbrother, AAMOS, would be a bit murky. Bruce incorporated the first company, AMOS, in March of 1997, in Delaware. Sixty million shares of stock were authorized, 21 million of them held by Bruce and Jana. There were thirteen other stockholders, including several of the couple's business associates.

The plan, according to Bruce, was to develop AMOS as a computer software program that would help banks and other lenders keep track of their foreclosed real estate; it would also help match potential buyers (mainly individual investors and pools of investors) with packages of foreclosed properties. Once the software was perfected, Bruce thought he could sign up a raft of major banks as clients for the software. Nor would there be any shortage of potential buyers for the banks' property, who could do one-stop shopping to cash in on dormant equities, and spread the risk around the country to boot. In effect, the program would automate and computerize what he and Harry Parrell had done in earlier years. Bruce had visions of going national with the programming, building up a virtual empire on the broken dreams of those unfortunates who had been foreclosed on.

Oddly, Bruce wasn't the only one with both the idea and the name of AMOS. Eight months later, a Florida bank holding corporation, Ocwen Financial Corporation, acquired a similar real estate management company that had been formed in Connecticut. This company, too, was named AMOS, and did essentially the same things as Bruce's AMOS did. The most peculiar thing about Ocwen, however, was that it had taken over the assets of a failed Florida savings and loan, Berkeley Federal Savings, which had gone bust in the great S & L collapse of the late 1980s; and further, that Bruce had done some business with Berkeley Federal before it went broke. Bruce said it was there, in fact, that he first made the acquaintance of a man named Christopher Settimo Botosan; and by the time the whole Koklich mess would finally be over, in the spring of 2004, Botosan would be one name Bruce would thoroughly wish he'd never, ever heard of.

Like the roots of AMOS, Chris Botosan's origins would be somewhat murky, despite the strenuous efforts of Bruce's lawyers to later implicate him in the disappearance and probable murder of Jana Carpenter Koklich. Based on anecdotal information from those who knew him, it appears that Chris grew up in the southeastern portion of Los Angeles County, principally near the suburbs of Downey and Bellflower, not far from Lakewood and Long Beach. (It is not for nothing that Los Angeles was once described as seventy-seven suburbs in search of a city—the swath of so many often indistinguishable yet separate towns in one wide arc of nearly identical geography has baffled Easterners and Midwesterners for generations.)

Born on December 13, 1955, Chris had an artistic bent, as well as a highly sensitive nature, according to those who knew him. "He was very, very nervous," Bruce's stepbrother, Dave Titchenal, would later recall. By the early 1980s, Chris was involved in computer graphics, particularly animation programs that could be used by children. It does not appear, at least anecdotally, that he graduated from any college or university. Chris eventually claimed to have been involved in helping to computerize security at the 1984 Olympic Games in Los Angeles, that he consulted with "Special Forces Command" at Homestead Air Force Base in Florida and that he had been invited to accompany former President Bill Clinton to China in the late 1990s.

In the mid-1980s Chris lived in Santa Clara County, where he was briefly married to a photographer. Then, by the late 1980s, he had gravitated to Florida, where he wrote some computer programs for the ill-fated Berkeley Federal Savings and Loan, and where he was initially introduced to Bruce Koklich.

From the public record, it appears that during the 1990s, Chris held jobs in northern California in connection with software development. Certainly Bruce, at least, believed he had worked as a software engineer for Intel at one point in the 1990s.[7]

By the year 2000, Chris was working as the Internet director for Union Rescue Mission in Los Angeles. The charity had apparently provided Chris with a Macintosh computer for this endeavor. Sometime after the first of the year, Chris was reacquainted with Bruce Koklich through a mutual friend, Mike Bowden, a Florida businessman who had known both of them for more than a decade.

---

[7] Intel did not respond to an inquiry as to whether Chris Botosan was ever an Intel employee.

Sitting over drinks in a southeast Los Angeles County nightclub, Bruce explained his plans for AMOS, and within a few days, invited Chris to join the effort as a program developer. Bruce agreed to pay Chris $1,000 a month for his consulting services, and to give him 100,000 shares of AMOS stock. If the program ever did go national, both Chris and Bruce agreed, Chris would get another 100,000 shares of AMOS stock for every bank he managed to get signed up for the program, up to 1 million shares.

As the spring of 2001 unfolded, both Bruce and Chris had gigantic expectations for AMOS. Once it got going nationally, Chris would later tell investigators from the Los Angeles County Sheriff's Department and Los Angeles County District Attorney's Office, the program could be worth as much as $600 million. It was a potential platinum mine, he said.

But first, they had to sell it.

By that same spring of 2001, Paul Carpenter was out of prison and living in San Antonio with Doris Morrow. After four years in federal custody, he was completely broke. Worse, his cancer had returned.

His body wracked with pain, Paul entered an experimental treatment program, trying desperately to stave off imminent death with drastic chemotherapy. The disease and the treatment devastated his immune system, and it appeared that he might die at any time.

Since his release from prison, Jana and Bruce had been sending Paul $400 a month to help cover some of his living expenses. Even so, money was so tight, Doris Morrow recalled later, that Paul couldn't afford to make unanswered long-distance calls to Jana and Bruce; ordinarily he called and quickly hung up if no one answered, rather than be charged for leaving a message on an answering machine.

If Paul, in his heyday, had had a somewhat distant relationship with his youngest child, after his release from prison, father and daughter grew much closer. There had been something of an early strain between Jana and Doris, but after Paul's trials, they grew closer; Jana appreciated Doris for her loyalty to Paul, even if she was the "other woman" in his life.

In the spring of 2001, with Paul at risk of imminent death, Jana made an effort to visit him in San Antonio as often as she could get away, sometimes accompanied by Bruce.

Like his former wife Janie, Paul liked Bruce. He admired him for his self-discipline, and for his ambition. As far as Paul could tell, Bruce seemed completely dedicated to his marriage to Jana, and appreciative of her as someone central to his life and work. But Paul had also become far less driven himself, almost philosophical, as he saw the end approaching. He still had the gambler's mentality, however, the taste for long odds, which was one reason why he'd agreed to the experimental treatment of his cancer. And at the same time, when Bruce described his brainchild, AMOS, Paul was intrigued with its potential for big profit.

Later, some confusion would arise about Paul's interest in the AMOS project. Some would claim that sometime in the spring of 2001, Jana asked Paul for a loan of $5,000 to help underwrite development costs. Paul had $3,800, and got another $1,200 from Doris, to give to Bruce and Jana. Prosecutors would later point to this, asserting that Bruce had made his wife squeeze $5,000 from her own dying father to help pay for AMOS, and suggesting that the costs of its development had made Bruce and Jana desperate for cash in the summer of 2001. Implicit in this was the notion that Bruce was so cynical and self-centered that he'd robbed a dying man to get the money.

But when the roots of the incident are excavated, Bruce

and Jana appeared to be well-fixed, financially speaking. Based on records and testimony later presented in court, the couple owned real estate worth about $4.5 to $5 million, including their house in Lakewood, and cash and investments of another $310,000, and as much as another $270,000 in available credit, should they have chosen to borrow money. Just why, then, Bruce and Jana would have needed to borrow $5,000 from Paul Carpenter wasn't at all clear, leading to the notion that this money was less a loan by Paul to his daughter than it was an investment by Paul in Bruce's AMOS scheme. Indeed, Paul seems to have had a strong interest in Bruce's efforts to arrange financing for the project's national development, an effort that would eventually be mounted through Chris Botosan.

Besides the real estate and cash, Bruce and Jana had one other potential source of cash—twin $1 million life insurance policies on each other. These policies would pay off, of course, only in the event of death. Each was the beneficiary of the other, and since they had no children, Jana and Bruce made their respective surviving parents the contingent beneficiaries. That meant, if Bruce and Jana *both* died, Bruce's mother, Naomi, would receive $1 million from his policy, and Paul and Janie Carpenter would split $1 million from Jana's. Altogether, these policies and holdings made the separate estates of Bruce and Jana each worth a bit over $3 million each.

Money isn't everything, of course, and Jana's friends thought she was less than content as the late spring turned into summer in 2001. Some thought it had to do with a decision, by Bruce alone, most believed, to forgo adoption. Early that spring, Jana had shown her mother, Janie, a brochure about the adoption process, and seemed very committed to going ahead with it. But by June it was off. In a conversation with Jan Baird, Jana said she and Bruce had decided there would be no adoption.

"I asked her why," Baird said later, "and she just kept repeating adamantly that there would be no adoption. When I encouraged her that it could still happen, that maybe a baby would come up tomorrow, she said, 'There will *be* no adoption.' She [said it] very adamantly. Almost angrily" and seemed upset, Baird said.

Other friends of Jana had similar observations—that she seemed disappointed, even angry at the decision not to adopt. Some thought it was because Bruce was insistent that she keep on working, and even he gave support to that notion when he observed that having a child would tie them down, make it more difficult for them to take vacations whenever they wanted to. Some thought the disagreement over adoption was a major issue between Bruce and Jana, although Jana would never say so specifically—it simply wasn't her way to discuss whatever difficulties she might be having in her private life with others, even her closest friends.

All of this was later to convince most of Jana's friends that what Bruce really valued with Jana—indeed, that he demanded of her—was her contribution to the business as the paperwork maven who managed all of his deals.

It *was* true that as they reached their forties, Bruce became increasingly focused on building their business. Several years earlier, in fact, he had hired a housemaid, Consuelo Lopez, in part so that Jana could spend more time at the office. As Bruce rather inelegantly put it later, he'd "bought" Consuelo so Jana didn't have to be burdened with housework along with all of her other duties.

That the office was the center of Bruce and Jana's lives by the summer of 2001 seemed beyond dispute to everyone who knew them. Located on a commercial stretch of Atlantic Avenue in the gentrifying Bixby Knolls section of north Long Beach, it was almost unnoticeable from the sidewalk. But that was because Bruce and Jana rarely dealt with individual home purchasers and sellers. The bulk of their business was with the banks, particularly Wells Fargo, which had its own mortgage brokerage in the same building.

Owing to its prior incarnation as some sort of storefront clinic—or, some thought, a pawnbroker's office—the Koklich business had a bulletproof glass partition in the front. Not that it made much difference to the clientele—virtually everyone who came to the business entered and left through the rear door, which led up to an asphalt parking lot. Three other businesses adjoined the office to the immediate south, including a hair salon and a party supplies emporium.

Because the business was almost exclusively centered on packaging foreclosures, both Koklichs often ventured into economically depressed, sometimes dangerous areas, to inspect seized property. For that reason, both Jana and Bruce carried pistols—each had a matching SIG Sauer .380 semiautomatic. Jana, at least, kept hers in her car, a 1996 white Nissan Pathfinder SUV. The couple also kept other loaded pistols under the mattress at home in case someone seeking revenge for a property seizure might break in. Moreover, Bruce had a sawed-off shotgun at the Lakewood house, as well as his deceased father's extensive antique gun collection. As he later would tell Chris Botosan, "I'm a gun nut." Bruce said both he and Jana trained in marksmanship at a local firing range, and Bruce took pride in his proficiency with his weapons. Neither of the Koklichs was licensed to carry a concealed weapon, however.

But Bruce did have another sort of equalizer: a badge from the Long Beach Police Department that showed he was an honorary member of that agency, which was always useful in a pinch, if it wasn't inspected too closely. He also had a bona fide deputy sheriff's badge from the Los Angeles County Sheriff's Department, which he kept in the glove compartment of his car. He'd found the badge in a house he'd acquired, Bruce later explained, and never bothered to return it to the sheriff's department, although its possession by an unsworn person was clearly a violation of the law.

As their business had prospered in the 1980s and 1990s, the Koklichs had added a number of employees. By the summer of 2001, these included Barbara Hauxhurst, a woman who had just turned 70, who was the office's escrow coordinator, and devoted to Bruce; Rosa Canedo, an administrative assistant to both Koklichs, who had been with the company for about a decade; Cynthia Correa, 30, a buyer's agent; Paula Klem, a 19-year-old receptionist who had known Jana since she was 6 years old; Laura Roman, 30, an evaluation coordinator whose job it was to give the banks an idea of what the foreclosed property might be worth; and Jim Rivas, a friend of Bruce's, who helped him put together the property packages for the prospective buyers.

As the office was configured, the south half of the building was used by the Koklich business, while the north half was sublet to the Wells Fargo operation, which was run by another friend of Bruce's, Larry Garcia. In addition to overseeing the bank's mortgage operation, Garcia was also a partner with Bruce in several real estate properties. It appears he may also have been an investor in AMOS as well. Garcia's operation also employed several women, including Sandra Baressi, Marty Ontiveros and Mickey Jumapao, all of whom would eventually have minor roles to play as the Koklich mystery unfolded.

Finally, in an unused portion of the northern half of the office structure, Bruce had installed a number of computers, as well as Chris Botosan. This was soon known as the AMOS portion of the building, and was where Chris, using the Macintosh computer he'd been given by the

Union Rescue Mission, and others labored to perfect the software.

Despite its recent gentrification, the Bixby Knolls section of north Long Beach had something of an earlier reputation for street crime. As part of the city of Long Beach's effort to suppress this sort of random violence, and to reassure the merchants along Atlantic Avenue that the local police were on the job, a patrol officer was often assigned to make face-to-face contact with the merchants and to find out whether they'd been having any troubles. In the mid-1990s this task fell to Long Beach police officer Danny Molinar, and over the years he had gotten to know both Bruce and Jana on a social basis, and in fact, had even acquired several pieces of rental property with the Koklichs' assistance.

This, then, was the ambit of Bruce and Jana's lives as the year 2000 turned into 2001—the office people, and the Koklichs' close friends, such as the Bairds, the Endleys, the Ensigns, and Nini Angelini and her boyfriend, John Santitoro, better known as Giani, along with Officer Molinar. The Koklichs spent much of their free time dining in nice restaurants, or attending concerts—they had season tickets to the Pond, the arena in Anaheim—or taking vacations to Mexico, Alaska, and Europe, or going skiing, often accompanied by their friends.

It seemed like a good life—but for Jana, something may have been missing. Indeed, it appears that as 2000 rolled into 2001, Jana began changing—as if Nini's prodding to take more control over her situation began to have a subtle effect. Beginning in April of 2000, Jana began working out three times a week with a friend of Nini's, Dean Costales. The workouts, when combined with dietary restrictions Costales recommended, had a remarkably transformative effect on Jana. From April of 2000 to the summer of 2001, she lost about twenty-five pounds.

She began to take an even stronger interest in her physical appearance, and had extensive dental work done.

As the summer of 2001 unfolded, Jana continued to attend these workouts religiously, even though they usually began in the early morning hours while Bruce was either asleep, or getting ready to go to work. Similarly, she began attending yoga sessions, and continued getting her regular manicure, skin care, massages and hairstyling. In short, she began to look better and better. And the better Jana looked, the more Bruce was likely to put her down with dismissive remarks. Invited by Costales to participate in the workout sessions, Bruce declined. Nini thought that he simply couldn't stand to have another man tell him what to do, especially in front of Jana—he had to be the expert in everything. And while Jana continued to be deferential to Bruce, at least in public, later her closest friends began to wonder if she was finally beginning to realize that Bruce needed her a lot more than she needed him.

Enter NABUCO

In June of 2001, Bruce and Jana went to Hawaii for a vacation, celebrating their eleventh wedding anniversary. Kathy and Neal Ensign accompanied them. Kathy noticed that Jana was down, or at least somewhat preoccupied. "On the trip," Kathy said later, "there just seemed to be something that was bothering her."

Bruce, however, seemed oblivious to Jana's mental state, according to Kathy. He spent much of the vacation on his cellphone, conducting business back in California, including a number of calls to Chris Botosan. The AMOS project was occupying more and more of Bruce's attention.

At a luau both couples attended, Kathy noticed that Bruce seemed to be paying a lot of attention to an attractive woman sitting nearby. After he made some sort of remark to Jana, Kathy and Neal as to the woman's physical attributes, he then struck up a conversation with her. To Kathy, it seemed like he was trying to pick her up and that Jana was making an effort to ignore Bruce's behavior, but she could see that Jana was upset. After all, it was their wedding anniversary.

On the way back to their hotel, Kathy recalled, Jana again seemed withdrawn, not interacting with Bruce. "I guess I'm in trouble," Bruce joked.

Later, according to Kathy, Bruce complained about how much the Hawaii trip cost. "Are you guys," he asked, meaning Neal and Kathy, "going to be as broke as we are when you get home?"

After Bruce and Jana returned to California, others also noticed that he appeared to be keeping a tight rein on her spending; some, in fact, thought that the Koklichs were encountering some rough weather, at least financially speaking. Earlier that spring, in fact, Jana and Bruce had asked to borrow $50,000 from Jana's mother. They told Janie that they'd run into a cash crunch over the costs of developing AMOS, and offered to pay her a higher interest rate than she would get from a bank on her deposit. Janie loaned them $25,000.

Still later, Janie recalled, Jana spent much less than she would have previously while buying gifts for family members; Janie concluded that her daughter and son-in-law were temporarily short of ready money, and formed the impression that the real estate software project was consuming all their uncommitted resources, and then some.

Then, in July, Jana signed over two pieces of real estate that were listed in her name alone to both Jana and Bruce, husband and wife, as community property. These two properties were worth approximately $800,000, combined. For some reason, the transfers were not immediately recorded.

Parsing what was going on with Bruce and Jana at this time, financially speaking, is difficult. Based on their documented assets, it's hard to believe that they were really short of cash, as Bruce's prosecutors later tried to prove. But underlying these observations about a supposed cash shortage, as well as the maneuver with the two properties that were solely in Jana's name, is the possibility that the Koklichs were trying to beef up Bruce's net worth, at least on paper, in order to impress would-be investors in the AMOS project, who were to be recruited by a rather curious outfit calling itself NABUCO.

To hear Chris Botosan tell the tale, it appears that NABUCO—a Las Vegas, Nevada, entity of less than well-documented origins—was willing to broker up to $13.9 million in loans to AMOS, provided that the Koklichs put up some of their *own* money first.

The NABUCO role in Jana Carpenter Koklich's story—whether real or imagined—remains one of the most puzzling aspects of the entire affair. One of the main reasons for this was that the police investigating Jana's disappearance never considered it central to her fate, and so largely ignored it. They believed that Bruce had murdered his wife, plain and simple, and all the ins and outs of AMOS' proposed financing were just so much distraction from the salient facts. As a result, they collected only the most cursory information about NABUCO, and most of that from Chris Botosan himself.

And while Bruce's defense lawyers seemed bent on trying to show that Chris Botosan was the *real* culprit in Jana's disappearance, Bruce's own involvement with NABUCO actually buttressed the notion that he might have had a motive for killing her. In other words, NABUCO cut two ways. Bruce's defense lawyers used the NABUCO deal to cast a lot of sinister shadows, but really weren't all that interested in fully illuminating that part of the story, since the whole truth didn't do very much to get Bruce off the hook.

As a result, what was missing from both the prosecution and defense theories of the case was the effect NABUCO's

funding proposal had on Jana's pre-disappearance demeanor, as well as Bruce's possible motive for wanting his
wife dead.

As best as could later be discerned, it appears that about
the time Bruce hired him, Botosan told Bruce that he
knew people who might be able to find some big money
financiers for the fledgling company. If Bruce wanted to
take the software national, Botosan suggested, he needed
a national marketing plan. That would take a lot of
money. The NABUCO people, Chris said, could find this
capital for AMOS.

Who or what was NABUCO? Aside from appearing
to be a possible acronym for National Business Company, the outfit's origins were obscure. Neither the California Secretary of State nor the federal Securities and
Exchange Commission have any records for it. However, the Nevada Secretary of State does. Those records
show that NABUCO was incorporated in Las Vegas,
Nevada, on April 20, 1990. The firm's president was
listed as Benet Heller, and the secretary was Dennis Piotrowski, both of Las Vegas. Based on information later
provided to investigators by Chris Botosan, there was
also a Joe Heller involved in the corporation, along with
an attorney, Steve Boyers of Pacific Palisades, California.

Of these names, Piotrowski's, at least, would have some
public significance. In the late 1970s, Piotrowski was one
of a number of people indicted by the federal government
in connection with an alleged defrauding of the Teamsters'
Central States Pension Fund–financed purchase of the
Aladdin hotel in Las Vegas. After a trial that lasted for almost a year, all six defendants, along with the Del Webb
Corp. and The Aladdin Corp., were found not guilty by a
jury after only a few hours of deliberation.

The exact point that NABUCO entered the AMOS picture remains unclear, although most of those familiar with the events of the spring and summer of 2001 believe that Chris Botosan brought NABUCO with him when he first joined up with Bruce; in other words, it was Chris who connected Bruce to the Las Vegas people. Chris would later testify that he owned 11 percent of NABUCO's stock.

As described by Chris, the NABUCO types were the highest of rollers. In statements he made to investigators shortly after Jana's disappearance, and again from the witness stand eighteen months later, NABUCO was prepared to obtain up to $13.9 million in "guaranteed" financing for the marketing of the AMOS software. In return, Bruce Koklich agreed to pay NABUCO an "initial retainer" of $10,000 "to cover related cost [sic] for the preparation and application fee of the guarantee."

If more than the initial $10,000 was needed to get the financing, AMOS and Bruce agreed to pay that, too: "Any dollars required above the initial cost [of $10,000] that are required by the guarantor [NABUCO],[8] lender, public agencies, attorneys or accountants shall be paid by the CLIENT [Koklich]."

Once the financing was delivered, Bruce was also obligated to pay NABUCO still more money, according to the agreement: "Contingent upon obtaining your request, the total fee due NABUCO shall be One Point One Percent (.011%) [sic] of the gross value obtained ($1,100,000)." But, said the "schedule of compensation" NABUCO induced Bruce to sign, the $1.1 million could be financed as part of the $13.9 million loan.

Indeed, all of the NABUCO paperwork—later filed with the court as an exhibit in the trials of Bruce Koklich

[8] Bracketed clarifications added.

for Jana's murder—is larded with impressive, big business-sounding phrases, often with serious-looking capitalization, but the economics of the transaction remained murky on the surface.

"NABUCO understands and issues this Letter [sic] to confirm that we talked with the Investment Banking Firm [sic] and they are prepared to underwrite your project and Centre Group as wholly owned by Zurich Financial Services Group [sic] shall enhance your project as per the terms and conditions outlined in our Letter of Agreement [sic] ... We are unable to control the total timing and issuance of the underwriting it self [sic] at this time but we do know that the enhancement from the Insurance Company [sic] will be Irrevocable and has Committed to have the necessary Credit available on the anticipated date above."

In this sort of situation, in which Bruce was essentially agreeing to pay NABUCO $10,000 up front, and committing to pay still more sums "required by the guarantor [NABUCO]," as well as "lender, public agencies, attorneys or accountants," Bruce and Jana were in a position to shell out significant cash while waiting for financing that might never come. Yet there is no evidence that either Bruce or Jana ever consulted any legal representatives about the proposed deal; it seems readily apparent that any lawyer worth his fee would have told them to investigate this deal very, very carefully.

The concern is that Bruce Koklich agreed to pay money up front to "guarantee" financing that might or might not ever become available.

Just why Bruce would agree to such a proposition is peculiar to say the least—certainly he was smart enough to sniff this out, according to almost everyone who knew him.

The missing part of this equation is what Jana knew about the details of this proposed deal, and whether she was opposed to it, and whether this opposition led to her disappearance and murder; it does not appear that those assigned to investigate her disappearance spent very much time trying to ascertain this critical information.

Certainly Jana's entire professional career had been built on her ability to manage complex transactions, and it seems almost inconceivable that she wouldn't have had concerns about the venture that was being proposed by NABUCO. (It may be significant that the documents officially binding AMOS to NABUCO were signed by Bruce alone on September 12, 2001, three weeks after Jana's disappearance.) As for Paul Carpenter, there's no question that he had the ability to distinguish an opportunity from a potential black hole.

But here again was the similarity between Bruce and Paul: Both were gamblers, people who thought they had the angles covered. It may well have been that Bruce wanted to believe in NABUCO's proposed loan, wanted to believe so badly that, under Botosan's encouragement, he willed himself to ignore any red flags that the proposal may have raised.

"He wanted to be a wheeler-dealer in the worst way," said one of his closest acquaintances afterward. "He was a gambler, a plunger. He enjoyed taking big risks."

It is therefore possible that the way Botosan explained the deal, Bruce may have believed that he was being cut in on some kind of big-time financial action; that's usually one of the hooks in any deal of this kind—giving the investor the idea that he's in with the in crowd, the big boys.

The way Botosan later tried to explain the ins and outs of the NABUCO deal to police and prosecutors, NABUCO was to loan AMOS between $8 million and $15 million—the actual figures kept fluctuating when the story was recounted. AMOS was to pay 8 percent annual interest on the loan. The money, Botosan first told police, was to come from NABUCO's own assets, which Botosan said were "tied up in Treasury bills." Then AMOS would take the loan from NABUCO and deposit it in a brokerage account, which would pay interest at 5.5 percent a month. Bruce's software company would therefore receive a "guaranteed" $431,750 a month [in interest at 5.5 percent a month] against expenses of $67,000 a month to pay the interest demanded by NABUCO.

As anyone can plainly see, this arrangement seems strikingly optimistic. What brokerage house can pay interest of 5.5 percent a month—in other words, 66 percent a year? Not even high-risk credit cards charge that much. And even if there *were* such a brokerage firm, why wouldn't NABUCO deposit the money itself and get the interest for its own account, rather than splitting it with AMOS and Bruce? If NABUCO could get 5.5 percent on its money, why bother with AMOS at all? But surprisingly, the police and prosecutors took the deal at face value.

"The deal works for NABUCO," wrote Los Angeles County Assistant District Attorney Greg Dohi later, "because NABUCO needs to get Treasury bills in small quantities but can't buy them directly. [The brokerage firm] uses client accounts to buy Treasury bills in convenient quantities. NABUCO was to get everything above the 5.5 percent."

Just how Treasury bills paying three percent a year could generate 5.5 percent a month (or "above") in income wasn't made clear. Dohi said later that while he didn't exactly understand how the whole thing worked, "it seemed to make sense in a crazy sort of way."

Here again, however, is the notion that there's some secret way to get ahead of the game, perhaps by methods not available to the ordinary investor: "but [NABUCO] can't buy them directly." The obvious question is: why not? Why *can't* NABUCO buy them directly? The proposition recounted to the authorities and later from the witness stand by Chris Botosan was cloaked by financial arcana that make it sound impressive to the unsophisticated person, who is too embarrassed to admit that he doesn't really understand it, and so never questions it.

The Treasury note shuffle was only one version of the NABUCO proposal advanced by Botosan. Later, as a witness at Bruce's trials, he testified that NABUCO was going to obtain the proceeds of a $100 million bond issue sold by a major Denver bank, and place portions of it with AMOS, which would pay NABUCO back from all the business the software would generate, once the software was sold to the banks.

Here Botosan sketched for police the largest imaginable atmospheric pastry: the plan was to sell the AMOS software to banks, who would each sign two successive three-year contracts for real estate management services by AMOS. "The business was going to make $10 million a year," Dohi summarized from Chris' statement to police, "or $60 to $70 million over six years. The costs of running this business would be low, and 65 percent of its earnings would be profit. Botosan calculated the cash value of the venture at $600 million."

The Mystery Caller

Six hundred million dollars! Was this the Big Bonanza, or what? And all Bruce and Jana had to do to get this financial cornucopia to start spilling was put up a paltry $10,000. The financing was guaranteed!

Or maybe not. By the middle of July 2001, there is evidence that Bruce and Jana were in dispute over the wisdom of Chris Botosan's proposal. In mid-July, they drove to Sonora to attend the wedding of Bruce's step-brother, Dave Titchenal. Two decades earlier, Bruce's father John had married Dawn Titchenal, who had two sons from a prior marriage, Dan and Dave. The John–Dawn marriage in effect merged the Koklich and Titchenal families, and the four sons remained close to one another even after John Koklich died in 1988.

Those who saw Bruce and Jana at Dave's wedding thought Jana was distracted. Although never very demonstrative with Bruce's step-brothers—"she wasn't a hugger," Dave would later recall—Jana seemed even more reticent than usual. Botosan, for his part, thought that Jana seemed upset after the return from Dave's wedding. So did

Nini Angelini. In fact, Nini thought Jana was unusually edgy or jumpy from the time of Dave's wedding until her disappearance.

The wedding was on July 21, 2001. The following weekend, Jana and Bruce took separate planes to San Antonio to see Paul Carpenter, and to conduct some business with associates there. The day they arrived, July 27, 2001, they met with real estate associate Linda Vargas. After pitching the AMOS software, they had dinner with her and one of her friends at a San Antonio restaurant.

During the dinner, Bruce seemed rapt in animated conversation with Linda Vargas' friend. That was when Linda casually asked Jana how things were between her and Bruce.

"She kind of looked at me," Linda said later, "and said, 'Well, we've fallen in and out of love for the last fourteen years.'" Linda was taken aback that Jana would be so forthcoming about something that clearly made her unhappy. It simply wasn't Jana's usual way to make such self-revelatory remarks.

"It surprised me so much," Linda said, "that I didn't say anything further about it. Because I've never known anyone with that depth of privacy, and for her to say something like that just shocked me. So I didn't say anything further on that except to ask her, 'Well, are you going to have a baby?'" She and Jana had talked about this in the past.

Almost as soon as the word "baby" was out of her mouth, Bruce stopped talking to Linda's friend and shot a look at Jana. Jana didn't say anything, and Linda formed the impression that Jana thought this subject was a sore one between the two Koklichs. They dropped the topic, Linda said. Instead the conversation turned to AMOS. Bruce was excited about the software company's prospects. Linda thought Jana was far less enthusiastic.

Bruce and Jana spent that Friday night and Saturday with Paul Carpenter and Doris Morrow. Then Bruce flew back to southern California early Sunday morning, leaving Jana behind. Doris would later remember that Jana spent much of the day Sunday and Monday apparently weeping about something. "She would go upstairs, and she would come back down, and her eyes would be red," Doris said later. This was classic Jana, who didn't like anyone to know how she really felt.

At one point on Sunday or Monday, "Her father asked her if she'd heard from Bruce about the financing for the new business," Doris later recounted. "They said Bruce hasn't called, and she [Jana] said, 'I called him.'"

This is one of the most cryptic remarks in the entire Koklich affair. What did Doris Morrow mean—that Paul was aware of the proposal from Chris Botosan and NABUCO by remarks made to him by Jana, and wanted to know if Bruce had told his own wife if the deal was going to go through?

If so, this seems to indicate that Bruce was keeping the progress of the NABUCO proposal secret from Jana. And then there is the "they" referred to by Doris, quoting Paul—"They said Bruce hasn't called"—which could mean Jana and Paul noting that Bruce hadn't called them, after going back to southern California, and that Jana had in response called Bruce to see if he'd heard anything from NABUCO.

Alternatively, the remark might mean that Paul Carpenter had himself been in contact with the NABUCO people—"They"—who had told him that Bruce hadn't gotten back to them on the proposal, which in turn makes it sound as though it was *Paul* who had first referred Bruce to NABUCO, not Chris Botosan. And if that were the case, what did Jana mean when she told her father, "I called him." Who did Jana call, if it wasn't Bruce?

At this point, with Paul dead and Jana missing and presumed dead, it's no longer possible to discern the meaning of these remarks, which, after all, were only the recollection of Doris Morrow, who presumably knew little of the details of the NABUCO maneuvering, and wasn't necessarily in the best position to understand what she was overhearing. Unfortunately, the significance of these puzzling statements was never unraveled by those assigned to investigate Jana Koklich's disappearance; it wasn't considered relevant.

That these remarks might still have been very significant was apparent in another remark Jana made to her father immediately afterward, according to Doris: "She said, 'I think he's trying to ease me out of the decision-making process for the new company.'"

It was later believed logical to assume that the "he" referred to by Jana was none other than her husband, Bruce. On the other hand, if "he" wasn't Bruce, but someone else entirely, the whole picture changes. In that case, one has to try to find out who "he" was.[9]

Whatever was troubling the marriage of Jana and Bruce, it still seemed to be going on the following week, when Bruce, Jana and Janie attended the Festival of Arts' Pageant of the Masters in Laguna Beach, California. That world-famous production, featuring costumed human models reenacting famous paintings, always draws a huge crowd for its evening presentation. After the show, Jana and her mother wanted to use the restroom, but Bruce told them no. He wanted them to stand in a place where he

[9] Doris Morrow, contacted by the author in San Antonio in 2004, declined to elaborate on these remarks. She said that she had been asked by Paul's attorney, Jeff Baird, to refrain from comment pending Bruce's appeal of his conviction in Jana's presumed murder.

could pick them up in the car, parked some distance away. "I thought that was rather ungentlemanly of him," Janie said later. Bruce made Jana carry all their coats and other belongings, too, as if she were some sort of beast of burden. But Jana didn't complain, seeming to be as deferential to her husband as always.

At some point around the time of this incident at the pageant, Jana had returned home to find a strange message on the Koklich telephone answering machine. The caller, who never identified himself, unnerved her, at least according to Bruce.

"Hey, hiya, Jan," said the mystery caller, laughing. "How you doin', Jana? Give me a ring back, you know who it is, bye-bye."

When he got home, "she brought me over," Bruce said, "and played this, and said, 'Bruce, do you know who this is?' You know, 'Does this voice sound familiar to you? I don't know the son of a bitch,' okay?"

There are several interesting things about this mystery message, which would eventually become a focal point of the investigation into Jana's disappearance. The first was that it was still on the Koklich answering machine two to three weeks later, after Jana vanished, rather than having been erased. The fact that the message was retained on the machine supports the notion that it was kept by Bruce to cast suspicion on the unknown caller even before Jana's disappearance, which in turn suggests premeditation, if indeed Bruce was responsible for whatever happened to Jana. Bruce's recapitulation of Jana's supposed reaction, "I don't know the son of a bitch," was almost certainly a case of Bruce putting words in Jana's mouth, since she wasn't known to use off-color language, and certainly not that phrase, which is almost always the speech of a man trying to sound macho with other men—in this case, the two Los

Angeles County Sheriff's Department detectives who were interviewing Bruce at the time.

A second interesting thing about the message is that it initially refers to Jana as "Jan," a common mistake made by people who didn't know her. This in turn suggests that the caller was a stranger—yet the context of the message seems to indicate that Jana *should* know who the caller was.

According to Bruce, he and Jana asked Officer Danny Molinar to come to their office to listen to the mystery call. Molinar didn't think the message was particularly threatening. He said that if the calls continued, the Koklichs should document them by writing down the dates and times.

That there *was* a mystery caller seems established, however. Nini Angelini, for one, told police later that Jana had told her that there had actually been two or three such calls. "I told her to report [them] to the police or change her phone number," Nini recalled. But, she said, Jana wasn't particularly scared by the calls, just puzzled and mildly irritated. She told Nini she had no idea who the caller was, or why he would think she should know him. "I think it's some idiot," she told Nini.

Whatever the origin or purpose of the calls, they would later help form the basis of Bruce's alibi.

On Saturday, August 11, 2001, Bruce and his associate Jim Rivas left early in the morning to drive to Las Vegas, where Bruce and Jana were scheduled to attend a conference of the California Mortgage Bankers Association. Bruce hoped to peddle his software to the mortgage people, since they were among his best customers, and the source of many of the Koklichs' listings. Later that same day, Chris Botosan came to the Koklich house in Lakewood, and that afternoon, he and Jana headed for Las Vegas, too, with Jana driving her white 1996 Nissan Pathfinder SUV.

At the conference, which was held at the Bellagio hotel on the Las Vegas strip, Bruce and Rivas set up a sales booth in an effort to attract customers for the AMOS software; Bruce also helped install the software for a client in Las Vegas. Bruce, Jana, Chris and Jim Rivas spent most of Sunday, Monday and Tuesday morning staffing the booth.

According to Bruce, the conference was fatiguing. "You know," he said later, "on your feet all the time, clients coming by, demonstrating the software to brokers, trying to keep yourself organized, talking with other software vendors. Very busy schedule."

While preparing for the conference, Bruce renewed his acquaintance with a Chicago real estate man, Jeffrey Tumbarello. Tumbarello was about to take over his mother Connie's real estate business in Chicago, and Bruce convinced him that the AMOS software was a good way to organize the inventory of properties listed by her firm. Connie briefly met with both Bruce and Jana; she later had no recollection of seeing Botosan, the software maven. The Tumbarellos decided to buy the AMOS software, and Connie wrote a check for $500 to the Koklichs. Later, she would say that she had only the vaguest recollection of meeting Bruce and his blonde wife that day. But because of the transaction, police would eventually trail Bruce to Chicago—where he would go to repair the software nearly nine months later. Until then, "It didn't work," Connie would tell police.

It isn't clear whether Bruce met any of the principals in NABUCO while he and Jana were in Las Vegas, but it seems possible that he did. According to Botosan, the NABUCO types often conducted their meetings in various coffee shops.

On Tuesday afternoon, August 14, the Koklich contingent returned to southern California. While they had been gone, the Koklich maid, Consuelo Lopez, had cleaned the Lakewood house, and put clean sheets on the Koklichs' king-sized bed. The sheets—Jana's favorite, Consuelo would later recall—were distinctive: white, black and red, with printed designs and letters on them. They would later become critical to the question of what happened to Jana.

The following day, Bruce and Jana returned to the office. According to Bruce, a lot of work had piled up in their brief absence. "When you're out of town," he said, "things build up. With both Jana and I out of town . . . when both of us are gone, you get back, you have stacks, you have contracts to do. You have new properties that need to be inspected. You have clients calling. Very stressful."

Despite all the work, Jana kept all her appointments that week, including a session with her long-time manicurist, Robina Olson. On Wednesday, August 15, Jana seemed "joyful and happy," according to Olson, and talked about the Eric Clapton concert she would be going to with Nini on the forthcoming Friday night. It thus appears that whatever had been beclouding the Koklich marriage in the weeks before that, it had at least temporarily dissipated.

"Did she ever indicate to you she was having problems in her marriage?" Olson was asked later.

"No."

"Did she ever say that she was not in love with her husband?"

"No."

"Did she ever say her husband was treating her badly, beat her up, or treated her horribly?"

"No."

"Appeared to be happy?"

"Yes."

But then, Olson also said, Jana wouldn't discuss those sorts of things with her—it just wasn't Jana's way.

Distracted

On Friday, August 17, 2001, Jana began her day with her usual early morning workout with trainer Dean Costales. Her friend Nini, who had originally introduced Jana to him, was also there. Together, with several others in Costales' 6 A.M. group, Jana and Nini puffed their way through the exercises, which included a "beach workout" on the sand for one hour, and another ninety minutes of circuit training. Over the previous year, Jana had never missed a single workout, even though most were in the early morning hours. Altogether, she had lost almost twenty-five pounds over this time, and, as Nini put it later, at 5 feet, 7 inches, and 130 pounds, Jana looked "fabulous." Nini also thought that as Jana looked better and better, and became healthier, this change was a threat to Bruce, who relied upon Jana's previous lack of self-confidence to keep her deferential.

For years, Nini had been encouraging Jana to stand up for herself against Bruce. Nini thought it was ridiculous the way he bossed his wife around. And while Jana wouldn't be forthcoming about her relationship with her husband, Nini had an idea that Jana was, for the first time, thinking seriously about leaving the marriage.

"I think there was just an accumulation of things," Nini said later. "The change of heart about the adoption was a heavy blow. He wanted her in the office, because she was essential to the business, and he wanted money more than anything. He had made her sign over her property to him, but he kept his property separate. And she knew that he had a roving eye. As she improved her looks, she was beginning to get more self-confident. She had made some unbelievable changes over the prior year. And I just think she'd decided she wasn't going to put up with Bruce's behavior anymore."

Although Bruce continually chided Jana for spending money, Jana began to ignore his strictures, according to Nini. When she showed Nini some new clothes she'd just bought, Nini asked her what Bruce had said about the spending. "He doesn't know," Jana said, which was certainly an indication that she was starting to develop her own mind.

And there was also Jana's father Paul: After his years of being driven, controlled to a fault, Paul was dying in Texas, and the approach of death had made him far more human, philosophical and even mellow. Why shouldn't his daughter have her happiness? Although Paul's break-up with Janie had been especially bitter—one reason, probably, that Jana had stuck by Bruce despite his often abusive nature—Paul made Jana see that dissolving a marriage wasn't the end of the world, not if staying in it was making her miserable.

But all or most of these thoughts Jana kept to herself. Even Nini, probably her closest friend at this time, had no real clue as to what was going on inside Jana. As the two women religiously followed the workout regimen laid down by Dean Costales, and as Jana's health and appearance got better and better, Nini kidded her: "Now that we're jocks," she said, "we can pat each other on the butt."

But even this kidding talk, with its suggestion of intimacy, caused Jana to draw back. Like Paul, Jana was one who held her cards close.

That same Friday, Consuelo Lopez returned to the Koklich house to clean, and on this day she prepared a meal for the Koklichs, putting the finished dish of chile rellenos, rice and beans in the refrigerator. Jana, as was her habit, came home during the day, and picked up a dessert that Consuelo had also prepared, sharing some of it with Consuelo. Then she returned to the office with the rest of the dessert to give some of it to Bruce. And in this, there seems to be a possible discrepancy in the events, because while Consuelo later said she was sure Jana had come home for lunch, Jana's handwritten calendar for the same day indicates that she actually had lunch with Bruce and Chris Botosan.

Later, no one asked either Chris or Bruce what had been discussed that day at lunch, although, if Chris was present, it almost certainly had something to do with AMOS.

By this time, Chris was something of a fixture at the Koklich real estate office, working on the AMOS program on the Wells Fargo side of the building with the Macintosh computer the Union Rescue Mission had provided for him. According to Chris, he was then still working part-time for the Mission.

By that summer, Bruce was spending probably 60 percent of his time on AMOS, which left more work for Jana, at least from the normal real estate operation. That was one reason, people said later, that Bruce had lost interest in adoption: having a child would mean that Jana wouldn't be able to spend as much time at work, which would in turn mean that Bruce would have to cut back on his own efforts in support of AMOS.

When Bruce and Chris Botosan grew closer that summer, the Koklichs invited him into their small social circle, occasionally asking him to accompany them to dinners with Nini, her boyfriend, Giani, the Endleys, or others. At one point, in fact, Jana asked Nini if there wasn't someone she knew who might be interested in dating Chris. Nini thought of a friend of hers, Melinda McBride, and gave her telephone number to Jana. Jana then called Melinda, told her that she was also a friend of Nini's, and asked if Melinda might be interested in meeting Chris. Melinda agreed, and in July, went to dinner with Jana, Bruce and Chris. It seemed to Melinda that Bruce and Chris spent most of their time talking about the AMOS project, or wheeling and dealing on their cellphones. Melinda soon began dating Chris, and on the evening of August 17, in fact, she came to visit him at his Downey apartment. Chris, she said later, cooked dinner for both of them, and they stayed at his apartment that entire night.

Sometime between 4 and 5 that afternoon, Jana left work. Everyone in the office knew that she was treating Nini to the Clapton concert. Jana had been looking forward to the evening for weeks. Nini had always said that before she died she wanted to attend concerts by Clapton, Bob Seger and Van Morrison. Now her friend Jana was going to make one of these must-see events happen. Before leaving for home, where Nini was to pick her up, Jana told several people in the office that she would not be in to work on Saturday; ordinarily, both Koklichs habitually spent at least part of the weekend in the office.

Just where Bruce was when Jana was getting ready to leave work wasn't later completely clear; investigating officers did little to establish Bruce's movements on Friday evening. But at one point, Jim Rivas took a telephone call from Bruce. He, too, said he didn't intend to come into work the following day.

Just before 5 P.M., Nini drove up to the Koklich house in

Lakewood. She rang the doorbell, and Jana opened the door, wearing black pants, black shoes and a sheer blouse with a teddy beneath. "I knew you'd be on time for this," she told Nini, and together they left for a Long Beach restaurant where the two had planned to have dinner before the concert. Bruce was still at work, Jana said.

At dinner, Nini and Jana split some chicken and a steak, as well as a glass of wine. Dean Costales' training and dietary regimen decreed that workout participants consume significant protein the night before a workout, and very little alcohol. After dinner, Nini began driving to Staples Center for the concert, with Jana, who had been there before, giving directions.

Up to this point, everything seemed to be going well. The Koklich employees and others who had seen Jana that day said she seemed to be upbeat, happy, glad to be attending the concert with Nini that night. But Nini said that on the way to the concert, Jana suddenly seemed to become distracted. They soon became lost.

"What's wrong?" Nini asked.

"I'm okay," Jana said.

Nini was convinced that there was something bothering Jana, but Jana, as was her wont, refused to let it out. They eventually found their way to the Staples Center, and whatever mood had seemed to possess Jana in the car soon went away.

At the concert, Nini and Jana joked about Dean Costales' restrictions, with Jana noting that if it weren't for Dean, they could have had more wine and really enjoyed themselves. But Jana was committed to getting up early the next morning and attending her regular workout, so they'd desisted.

By the time the concert was over, it was near midnight. Nini and Jana drove back to Lakewood. As they turned down Jana's street, they could both see that all the lights were off at the Koklich house. It was clear that Bruce wasn't giving them a very warm welcome.

"Where the hell is Bruce?" Nini asked.

"I have absolutely no idea," Jana said. And Nini realized that Jana was making a rather emphatic statement about her husband, for all practical purposes saying that not only did she have no idea, she didn't care.

"Why don't you go in, check the alarm, look around, turn some lights on and open and close the door to let me know everything's okay?" Nini said.

"All right," Jana said, and she got out of the car and approached the front door. Nini could see Jana extract the door key from her purse, then open the door. After a few seconds, the interior lights blinked on and off three or four times, and the door opened and closed several times.

Nini assumed that everything was as it should be, and drove away.

No Calls

Just after 7 A.M. the following morning, August 18, 2001, Dean Costales assembled his Saturday morning workout group. Jana was not present. Sometime around 7:25 or so, he called the Koklich house.

"Hi, this is Jana," said the recorded answer. "Please leave your name and number and we'll get back to you."

"Jana," Dean said, "where are you? It's Dean. Give me a call." Costales thought it was very unusual that Jana hadn't shown up. Over the previous year and a half, she had never, ever missed a scheduled workout. But Jana didn't call him back, and neither did Bruce.

Jana had previously scheduled a massage at Nini's shop for 2 P.M. that same day, but when the appointment time came, she didn't show up. When the masseuse told Nini that Jana had missed her appointment, Nini called the Koklich office shortly after 2 P.M., but no one answered. She decided to call Jana at home.

"Hi, this is Jana. Please leave your name and number and we'll get back to you." Nini listened to the recorded greeting. "Jana? It's Nini. Where are you?" she asked, leaving a message. She then called Jana's cellphone, but this call also went unanswered.

About 2:30 P.M., Nini called Bruce's cellphone. His recorded greeting came on, and she left a message for him to call her.

An hour later, Nini was growing worried. She called Cynthia Correa, the Koklich buyer's agent, who also worked out with Dean Costales, and asked her what was going on. She told Cynthia that she'd called the office, but no one was there. Nini knew that Cynthia usually screened Bruce's calls, and that Bruce would always take a call from Cynthia. Cynthia was on her way to get her own manicure at the time.

"Is there some sort of meeting going on, that they aren't answering the phones?" Nini asked Cynthia. "Did something happen? Did it burn down? Did something happen at their house?"

Cynthia told Nini that she would call Bruce and try to get him to call her. A few minutes later she called Nini back, and told her that she'd left a message on Bruce's cellphone. Later Cynthia would tell the police that she'd called what she thought was Bruce's cellphone number twice, but then realized she wasn't actually sure of the number.

That same evening, Janie Carpenter sat down at her computer to check her email. Throughout the previous week, she and Jana had communicated in this fashion, discussing plans to get together on Sunday afternoon to see a movie. Janie wanted to see *Legally Blonde*. She'd looked up theaters in the Koklichs' neighborhood and found several that were showing the movie. She wanted to firm up the date with Jana. Jana had said in her last reply email that she'd call her mother with the times for the movie on Saturday.

But by Saturday night, she hadn't called. Now Janie,

checking her email, realized that Jana hadn't responded to her last message, sent Friday afternoon. Janie didn't think about calling the Koklich house. It never occurred to her that anything might be wrong.

The next morning though, Janie realized that she and her daughter had never firmed up a time for the movie. Shortly after 9:45, Janie called Jana. The answering machine picked up on the first ring. That was unusual; ordinarily it rang several times before picking up.

"Hi, this is Jana. Please leave your name and number and we'll get back to you."

Janie left a message. "Are we still on for the movie this afternoon? Please call me."

Just past 11:15 A.M., Janie called again. "I hung up when I got the answering machine," she said later.

Now somewhat miffed as well as perplexed, Janie dialed Jana's cellphone number. No one answered, so she dialed Bruce's cellphone. Again, no one answered.

Altogether, Janie made nine different calls to Bruce and Jana's various telephone numbers that Sunday, occasionally leaving messages. No one ever called her back. By the late afternoon, she'd gotten very worried.

"I wish somebody would call me back and let me know what's going on," Janie said in her last message on the machine. And in a message she also left on Bruce's cellphone, she said, "I've been trying all day to reach Jana. Can you give me any clue to what's going on?"

By that night, Janie was thoroughly concerned—"very scared," as she put it later. She considered driving the ninety minutes or so it would take her to get to Lakewood to see what she could find out. Her imagination constructed all sorts of dire scenarios. "I had this theory that maybe there was a home invasion, that they were tied up, gagged and bound and tied up in their home," Janie said. "I very much wanted to go and see about it, but I was afraid if I got over there, and they weren't there, that I wouldn't be able to get in." She didn't think her key to the house still worked.

It was very unlike Jana and Bruce not to call back, Janie thought. She wondered again what was going on.

MISSING

The Setup

The following Monday, August 20, 2001, Bruce arose around 5:45 A.M. He took a shower and dressed for work in his habitual conservative suit. As he later put it to police, he liked to dress in a coat and tie—when he inspected "distressed" properties, he wanted people in the neighborhood to think he was a cop. That way they wouldn't give him any trouble.

According to Bruce, he left the house about 6:15 A.M., but not before kissing Jana goodbye. "See you at the office," he said he told Jana as she lay in their king-sized bed, still dozing.

The office in Bixby Knolls was about five minutes from the Koklich house. All Bruce had to do was get out of the neighborhood, then turn right on Carson Street, head west to Atlantic Avenue, and then pull into the asphalt parking lot behind the office.

"I got in," Bruce said later. "I checked my email. I reviewed some property information about new listings, kind of got my day organized. I did call a couple of clients back east on a couple of different properties." No one else was in the office when he arrived.

About 7 A.M., Barbara Hauxhurst came in. The escrow coordinator greeted Bruce, who was sitting at his desk inside a small interior cubicle. At about the same time, Wells Fargo's Larry Garcia, one of Bruce's close friends, arrived at the bank's side of the office building. He, too, saw Bruce, but at one of the computers in the AMOS part of the office. Garcia also greeted Bruce. Briefly they discussed their plans to attend the funeral of a mutual friend later that morning.

About fifteen minutes later, Bruce left the office to inspect some new properties. He would be gone for about an hour.

About the same time, on the same morning, a woman named Theresa Thornton left her small apartment in the nearby community of Signal Hill, sandwiched between Lakewood and Long Beach, about ten minutes south of the Koklich offices, to pick up her newspaper. There, parked at the curb of Lewis Avenue, in front of her apartment, Theresa saw a white SUV. The odd thing about the car—aside from its sudden appearance in what Bruce Koklich would have called a "distressed" area—was the fact that all its windows appeared to be rolled down. Theresa picked up her newspaper, marveled at the stupidity of its driver to leave his car so vulnerable in a place like her neighborhood, and went back inside her apartment.

On returning to the office about 8:30 A.M., Bruce found that several other employees had arrived. One was Rosa Canedo, who worked as the office's administrative assistant. Bruce gave his list of newly inspected properties, and asked her to prepare a list of his notes on what needed to be done to each to make them resalable. Bruce then went back to his desk and called Nini Angelini at her skin care studio, leaving a recorded message on her answering machine.

"Got your message," Bruce told Nini, referring to her calls from Saturday. "Finally found your number. On my way to a funeral. You can get Jana at home."

When she came in to her studio and heard this message a little later, Nini was taken aback. Why was Bruce saying he'd "finally" found her number? Bruce had been going to Nini's masseuse for years, and he still didn't know the right number? But then Nini realized that in the past, all of Bruce's appointments had been made by Jana. This was the very first time in all the years they had known each other that Bruce had called her personally. Nini thought it was odd that Bruce would call her to tell her to call Jana at home. She called the Koklich house, but again the answering machine picked up.

Around 9:15 A.M., Bruce and Larry Garcia went out to the parking lot to get in their cars for the drive to the funeral service, which was supposed to begin at 10. Bruce followed Garcia in his own car, since Garcia had decided to attend the interment afterward, and Bruce had not.

But about the same time that Bruce and Garcia arrived at the funeral service, Theresa Thornton's next-door neighbor in Signal Hill, a 14-year-old named Raesean Hollie, woke up. After first turning on the television to watch a children's show on Fox TV, Raesean looked out his front window and saw the white SUV parked at the curb. He, too, noticed that the windows were rolled down. He decided to investigate. After looking at the strange car for a few minutes, he was joined by Michael Freeman, who lived across the street.

Freeman, who was 18 years old, and a bit more experienced in the ways of the world, had seen the SUV about twenty minutes earlier when he was on his front porch, smoking a cigarette. Like Theresa and Raesean, Freeman realized that the car didn't belong to the neighborhood. He decided to do a little reconnaissance. He walked around the block, looking for possible undercover police cars. He didn't see any. He went back inside his apartment, and kept watch through the front window. He soon saw Raesean, known as Rayray to his friends, looking at the SUV. He decided to join him.

"It was parked pretty far from the curb," Freeman recalled. "The windows was rolled down." Like Rayray, Freeman noticed the keys in the ignition. "Stepped back," Freeman said.

"Why?" Freeman was asked.

"It looked like a setup."

"Why?"

"It was too good to be true."

This had to be some sort of entrapment by the cops, Freeman and Rayray decided. There it was, ready for the taking: a car with the keys in the ignition, windows rolled down, expensive leather purse on the seat. They guessed that all they had to do was reach inside, and the cops would be all over them. Probably they were watching them look the car over right then.

But Freeman, having already cased the neighborhood for the law, decided it was worth the risk. He reached into the car and quickly snatched the purse. Nothing happened: no sirens, no squealing tires of cop cars. All was quiet. He and Rayray went across the street, went inside Freeman's apartment, shut the door and opened the purse. Freeman found $105 in cash in the wallet inside, along with a cellphone, a checkbook, credit cards and a driver's license. Freeman split the money with Rayray, and gave him the cellphone. Then they left the apartment with the looted purse. They walked a short distance down the block, and then Freeman gave a mighty heave, sending the purse up onto the roof of another apartment building. Freeman remembered the name on the credit cards and driver's license. It was Jana Carpenter Koklich.

. . .

Just about the time that Freeman was pitching Jana's purse onto the rooftop, Bruce was sitting in church, attending the funeral service with Larry Garcia. By about 11 A.M., he was driving back to the office, Garcia having gone on to the interment. Meanwhile, Janie Carpenter was calling the Koklich office to see if Jana was at work. Rosa Canedo told her that Jana hadn't come in yet. Janie now called Bruce on his cellphone, and this time Bruce answered. He told Janie that he'd left Jana at home that morning about 6:15, and that she was probably driving to the office right then.

Bruce got back to the office about 11:20. By that time, Chris Botosan had also arrived, and in fact, the entire complement of Koklich employees was now present. Almost as soon as he was through the door, Bruce asked if anyone had seen Jana. No one had. Bruce went into his office. It appeared to the employees that he was on the telephone, although no one could later say for sure that he actually made any calls. He came out again and encountered Chris Botosan. Botosan told him that he'd asked about Jana shortly after he'd arrived at 9:30 or so, and everyone in the office agreed that Jana hadn't come in yet.

"I saw her this morning while I was getting ready to go to work," Bruce told Chris. He and Chris discussed Jana's workout schedule, but both knew that no workout was scheduled for Monday morning. They looked at Jana's appointment calendar, and saw that she had no appointments listed.

At that point, Bruce began to talk about going over to the house to check up on her. Chris decided to go with him. Bruce called Janie.

"I can't find Jana," he told her. "She's not at home or at the office. I'm going out and look for her."

"Call me back when you've found out anything," Janie told Bruce.

Bruce went to the backdoor of the office, Chris following. They went out to the parking lot. Barbara Hauxhurst happened to be outside smoking a cigarette when they emerged.

"I saw Bruce head toward his car, and I saw Chris come out after him," she said later. "I saw him put his arm around Bruce. And they left together."

Hauxhurst thought Chris was behaving oddly, she said later. "He seemed to be much more agitated, concerned," she said. "His face had an expression that was sort of like impending disaster—that's the only way I can describe it."

Using Bruce's car, a white Nissan coupe, Bruce and Chris drove to the Lakewood house, getting there just before noon. Bruce pulled into the driveway, and both men got out of the car. The door to the double garage was closed. Chris went up to the small glass windows set at eye level in the garage door and peered inside.

"Her car isn't here," Chris told Bruce. Bruce didn't look for himself, Chris said, but went immediately to the front door and opened it. Once inside, Bruce looked at the alarm, and called out, "Jana?" The alarm appeared to be set. Bruce deactivated it, and headed upstairs to the bedrooms. Chris stayed downstairs. A few seconds later, Bruce returned. Jana wasn't upstairs, Bruce indicated to Chris. Chris now suggested that she might have had an accident on the way to work.

"We can ask Danny Molinar," Bruce told Chris. Just then Nini called the house again, and this time Bruce picked up the telephone. Nini told Bruce that she'd just had a call from Cynthia Correa, looking for Jana. When Nini asked Cynthia what she meant, Cynthia told her that Jana was missing, and that Bruce had gone home to look for her. That was why she'd called the Koklich house yet again.

"What's going on?" Nini asked Bruce.

"What do you mean, 'What's going on?'" Bruce asked Nini.

"What do you mean, 'What do you mean?'" Nini demanded. "Cynthia tells me that Jana is missing."

Bruce now said that that appeared to be the case. He said that her car was gone, her purse was gone, and the house alarm was activated. Nini told Bruce to call the alarm company to find out what time the alarm had been set, but Bruce said the alarm wouldn't show that. This was the beginning of Nini's suspicions of Bruce—"He knew instantly that they didn't have that kind of alarm," she recalled. It was almost as if Bruce didn't want to find Jana, Nini thought. She gave him a number of other suggestions for how to look for Jana, and Bruce seemed less than enthusiastic about carrying them out.

After the call from Nini, Bruce and Chris left the house, Bruce setting the alarm and locking the door behind them. They drove back to the office. When they arrived, Bruce told Barbara Hauxhurst, as he had just told Nini, that Jana appeared to be missing, that her car and her purse were gone, and that the house alarm had been set. That seemed to suggest that whatever had happened had taken place after Jana had left for work, not in the house itself.

Bruce now called Long Beach police officer Danny Molinar. It was Molinar's day off. He agreed to make some telephone calls to see if Jana had been in an accident, or if she'd been the victim of a crime. Although Lakewood wasn't in the Long Beach Police Department's jurisdiction—it was in the policing territory of the Los Angeles County Sheriff's Department—Molinar thought he should do what he could to help out, since he was friends with both of the Koklichs.

Bruce sounded "a little panicky" over the telephone, Molinar said later. He called the California Highway Patrol, his own department, and the county sheriff. None had any reports of accidents or crimes involving Jana Carpenter Koklich. A few minutes later, Molinar called Dean Costales, the trainer. Like Jana, Nini and Cynthia Correa, Molinar also worked out with Costales. Costales told Molinar he hadn't seen Jana that day. Molinar said that Jana appeared to be missing. Costales told him that Jana had missed her regular Saturday morning workout. Molinar next called Jana's cellphone provider, identified himself as a police officer, and learned that there had been no calls made on Jana's cellphone since the previous Friday.

That same afternoon, a number of people who lived in the Lewis Avenue neighborhood of Signal Hill—less than five minutes from Dean Costales' exercise studio, as it happened—came by to look at the apparently abandoned SUV, the one with the keys in it. It turned out there were still more goodies inside: a gun, in fact, a semiautomatic SIG Sauer .380 pistol. That sort of top-of-the-line armament was worth real money on the street.

By 3 P.M., a group of young African-American boys—most between 13 and 17—had been in and out of the car several times. The gun was far too much of a temptation to be left alone. It could be clearly seen inside the driver's-side door pocket, and by 3 P.M., had disappeared.

Late that afternoon, one of the boys got into the car, turned the key, and drove it away.

Everything's Here

By the middle of the same afternoon, Bruce and Chris had been back and forth to the Koklich house several times. Bruce began calling the Koklichs' friends to tell them Jana was missing and to ask if they had any idea of where she might be. He called Patti Endley and Harry Parrell and Kathy Ensign and Jan Baird. All said they had no idea of where Jana might be, and were immediately concerned that something bad might have happened to her.

– "Did you guys have an argument?" Kathy Ensign asked. No, no, Bruce said.

Bruce's friend Larry Garcia returned from the funeral and in the bank side of the Koklich office building, heard that Jana was missing. He told Sandy Baressi, one of the people who worked for him, that no one could find Jana. Sandy asked Garcia if Bruce and Jana had had a fight. "God damn it, Sandy," Garcia told her, "don't go there."

At the office, Chris Botosan and others used the office computers to create a flyer to circulate in the community. The flyer noted that Jana was missing, and asked people to call the office if they had any information about her. Then, while some of the office staff fanned out to circulate the flyers along Atlantic Avenue, Chris and Bruce returned to the house in Lakewood.

There Bruce played the mystery caller tape for Chris:

"Hey, hiya, Jan. How you doin', Jana? Give me a ring back, you know who it is, bye-bye."

This would be the first time that Chris had heard about the unknown "idiot" who had been calling, and the first of many times that he, Bruce and others would listen to the voice that day. About this time, apparently on the advice of Danny Molinar, Bruce and Chris decided that someone needed to notify the Los Angeles County Sheriff's Department that Jana was missing. They called the local sheriff's station, and were told that a uniformed officer would be sent out to take a report.

Botosan later tried to explain his feelings at the time:

"I was confused," he said, "wondering what was happening. I really didn't know. And concerned about her and what—getting the word out really quickly, because I know that when someone is missing or someone disappears, that the quicker the police could get on the case, I knew that they could— they would have a better chance of possibly finding the person . . . so I felt a sense of urgency, anyway."

With the uniformed deputy apparently on his way, Chris decided that the Koklich residence was ill-equipped to deal with what was happening. It was possible, he thought, that Jana had been kidnaped, and that someone might soon call to demand a ransom. He drove to a nearby electronics store and bought a caller i.d. system for the Koklich home telephone line. On the way back to the Koklichs', he stopped at his own apartment and picked up one of his pillows; he had decided to spend the night with Bruce.

About the same time that Botosan was picking up the caller i.d. and his pillow, Danny Molinar was arriving at the Koklich house. After making his initial calls, he had gone to the office, where he learned that Bruce and Chris had returned to Lakewood. When he got to the house, Molinar made a cursory search, looking for evidence of a break-in. He couldn't find any, he said later.

While they were considering what to do next, Janie called the house. Bruce answered the telephone. "Did you find Jana?" Janie asked.

"No," Bruce said. "We've called the police. They're coming over to take the report."

"Shall I come over?" Janie asked.

"If you want to," Bruce said.

"I'll be right there," Janie said.

Late that afternoon, a number of Koklich friends began arriving at the Lakewood house. The gathering had an odd atmosphere—a curious aura of anxiety mixed with, well, mourning. It was as if Jana were already dead, even though she'd only been missing a few hours.

Janie got to the house about 5 P.M. Bruce played the mystery tape for her. He told her that he'd played the tape for Molinar, and that he and Chris Botosan were worried about the possibility of kidnaping.

"I have loved your daughter since the day I met her," Bruce told Janie.

By about 6 P.M., others began arriving. The first among the Koklich friends to get to the house were John and Patti Endley, who had been friends with Bruce and Jana for nearly two decades.

"Well, first I gave him a big hug," John said, referring to Bruce, "and then we settled down. He sat on the couch." Bruce said he had no idea what could have happened to Jana. Then he asked the Endleys to go upstairs to the bedroom, where the answering machine was, at the head-board of the king-sized bed. Bruce played the mystery caller's taped voice once again.

"There were a lot of voices on there," John recalled. "The very first one was a male, the start of the recording." Bruce told him that there were nineteen different messages still on the tape.

Endley couldn't help noticing the bed. "I could see that somebody had slept in it. There was the imprint [of a sleeper]—on the right side." He saw that the top covers were thrown back toward the left side. It did not look to Endley as if that side, the left, had been slept in.

By about 7, still others had arrived at the house: Harry Parrell, Larry Garcia, Lee Higgins—an escrow officer friendly with the Koklichs—Rosa Canedo and her son Albert all arrived. Bruce played the mystery tape again and again. No one recognized the voice, or knew what to make of it. It didn't sound threatening, but now that Jana was missing, who knew?

Nini got to the house about 7:15. Everyone was sitting around, she recalled, "as if nothing is going on."

Nini decided people had to get busy. She began asking if Bruce or anyone had done some obvious things to look for Jana.

"I wanted to know if they'd gone to talk to the neigh-bors, if Bruce had called her dad in Texas, if they had— I asked if they had an Auto Club card, maybe there had been some service." Nini continued making suggestions to Bruce and the others.

It was Nini's idea that no woman should be without $5,000 she can put her hands on quickly, in case she needs to get away. If the "stash" was gone, Nini said, that suggested that Jana might have gone away voluntarily.

"Do you know if Jana has some money put away?" she asked Bruce. "A stash?"

"Well," Bruce said, "we have a stash that's in the bedroom, but I don't think anything's missing there. But let's go look."

Everyone trooped up to the bedroom. Bruce went to a dresser and removed a small box. Inside he found cash and credit cards. He counted the money.

"No," he said when he was finished, "everything's here."

At some point that evening, whether under prodding from Nini, or Larry Garcia, or Chris Botosan—all of them later claimed credit for the idea—it was decided that Bruce should visit each of the neighbors' houses to see if anyone had seen Jana that day. According to both Chris and Larry Garcia, Bruce was a bit reluctant to do this. He told Garcia he was a bit embarrassed to make any inquiries because he didn't really know the neighbors that well.

"We talked about the fact that when something like this comes up, all of a sudden, you realize that you don't know who your neighbors are, and you wouldn't know them by name," Garcia said later. "You'd know them by sight, you know, who they are. I told him the same thing. In my neighborhood I don't know—I didn't know—ten percent of the people who lived on my street. I wouldn't even know their name."

Nevertheless, it seemed to be a good idea, so shortly after 8 P.M., Bruce and Chris Botosan began to visit the houses of the neighbors. No one was in immediately next door, at the home of Marguerite Grinder, who probably knew more about Bruce and Jana than anyone else in the neighborhood. She and her husband had left to attend a baseball game earlier in the afternoon.

At one house, Bruce and Chris encountered a man and his children viewing stars with a telescope. The man said he hadn't seen Jana, and in fact, wasn't even sure what she looked like. Chris later said that Bruce seemed more interested in talking about the telescope than Jana.

Next Bruce and Chris rang the doorbell of the neighbor across the street, Donna Baker. Ms. Baker was a school principal; she'd moved into the neighborhood only two years before. She had never talked to Jana, although she had waved at her from time to time as Jana was leaving for work. She did not recognize Bruce at all.

"He was basically looking for his wife," she said of Bruce's unexpected visit. Donna said she told Chris and Bruce that she thought she might have seen Jana's white SUV in the open garage that morning. "Or," she said, "it might have been yesterday." She just wasn't sure.

After thanking Donna Baker, Chris and Bruce crossed the street once more, and rang the bell at the house of a dentist, Dr. David Romberg. Bruce at least knew Romberg by face and name; they'd had occasional contact over the years. But Romberg knew very little about Bruce and Jana's personal lives.

"Our neighborhood is one of those neighborhoods where it's quite affluent," Romberg said later. "Everybody drives in, opens their automatic garage door, shuts the door, and they're not seen from since."

As it happened, the Romberg family was hosting a church group that night. Bruce and Chris rang the bell about 8:45 or so, and Helen Romberg answered it. She recognized Bruce. Bruce asked whether she or her husband had seen Jana that day, and explained that she was missing. No, Helen Romberg said. But one of their guests was an off-duty deputy sheriff, Howard Cooper. Maybe Cooper could help, she suggested.

Howard Cooper now left the church meeting and accompanied Bruce and Chris back to the Koklich house. Inside they found Janie Carpenter, the Endleys, Larry Garcia, Rosa Canedo, her son Albert, Danny Molinar and Nini.

"Have you reported this?" Cooper asked. Bruce, Chris and Danny Molinar assured him that they had called the sheriff's department to file a missing persons report. At this point, Cooper learned that Molinar was an off-duty Long Beach police officer. Still, Cooper decided to telephone the Lakewood sheriff's station to make sure a report had been taken. He discovered that there was, in fact, a report in the system, and that, as per the normal procedure, it had been copied to the sheriff's homicide bureau as a precaution.

Cooper asked Molinar to fill him in on what had been done so far. Molinar told Cooper about his fruitless calls to the California Highway Patrol, to his own department, to the sheriff's department, and to various hospitals. At Chris' suggestion, Molinar explained, contacts had also been made with various credit card companies and banks used by the Koklichs to see if there had been any activity that day in the accounts. There had been none.

Patiently, Cooper tried to sort through the bits and pieces of information available. Janie explained that she and Jana had planned to see a movie together, and told him of her repeated, unanswered calls on Sunday; Nini recounted the missed appointments with Dean Costales and the masseuse. Bruce explained that he and Jana had decided to spend a quiet weekend together, resting after the trip to Las Vegas, and so hadn't bothered to answer any of the telephone calls. Janie kept saying she didn't understand this, that it wasn't at all like Jana not to call her back. And Nini thought Bruce's explanation was very lame.

While listening to all this, Cooper was also surreptitiously observing all the people who were present, most particularly Bruce. Cooper had no idea what was going on, other than what he had been told, so all of his senses were acute, particularly when it came to people's behavior.

"He was pretty cool," Cooper later recalled, referring to Bruce. "There wasn't much emotion present. Pretty calm, as a matter of fact. These are always touchy situations—"

Cooper meant that he was hardly in an environment where he could press Bruce for information "—a missing person, and family and friends present, and there was the mom, Jana's mother, present, and she was a bit more emotional . . . but I didn't sense any emotion from Bruce. He was kind of very matter-of-fact. I was very concerned about different answers I was getting from different people in the residence, so I was trying, without being too assertive, to get information delicately from various people there," Cooper said later.

Cooper now asked if the house had been thoroughly searched. Although Molinar told him that he'd inspected the place for signs of a break-in, Cooper now decided that a new search had to be made. He asked everyone to split into small groups and look through the house—closets, cupboards, storage bins—anywhere they could think of. There was no sign of Jana; or rather, there were all sorts of signs of Jana, but not a single clue as to where she might be right then. Cooper now suggested that they look under the house's crawl space. Chris Botosan found a flashlight, and wormed his way under the house to look, finding nothing but dirt and spiderwebs.

Cooper went up the stairs to the master bedroom with its king-sized bed. The mystery caller tape was played once more, and Cooper looked in the closets. Nini was with him. She noticed that Jana's overnight bag was still in the closet, along with her sneakers and workout clothes. In the adjoining bathroom, she saw Jana's cosmetics case. On the carpeted floor, midway between the bed and the doorway, she noticed a number of small dark spots, tiny drips, she thought. She didn't say anything, at least right then.

Next Cooper decided to look over the back yard. On the other side of the rear fence, Cooper could see the darkened expanse of the Lakewood Country Club golf course. It was always possible that someone had come over the fence during the day to get into the house, but it wasn't very likely that someone could have gone out that way with a kidnaped Jana; surely someone else would have seen them.

As Cooper made his way along the fence, shining his flashlight into the underbrush, Nini caught up with him. "Do you know if there are any marital troubles here?" he asked Nini, when they were out of everyone else's earshot. "Any problems financially?"

Nini told Cooper that as far as she knew, there were no money problems, and Bruce and Jana's marriage was fine. Not that she approved of it, but that there seemed to be no real difficulties. Cooper asked what Nini meant. Nini said she thought that Bruce was far too controlling of Jana, but it didn't seem to bother Jana that much. She told Cooper that she and Jana had attended the Eric Clapton concert together on the previous Friday night.

"Oh?" Cooper asked. "Did the husband go with you?"

"No," Nini said, "and you know, that's the first time I've ever gone anywhere with her that he has not been with her. They're usually inseparable."

Back in the house, people were leaving. Janie decided to drive back to her own house in Orange County. There didn't seem to be anything more that anyone could do, except hope that Jana had, for some reason, simply decided to be alone for a while. It was certainly behavior that was out of character for Jana, who was usually so responsible as to be nearly compulsive about letting people know where she was, but who knew what had been in her mind? It was possible, someone suggested, that Jana had decided to go to Texas to see her father; perhaps she had decided to drive all the way there, and just hadn't arrived yet.

Cooper buttonholed Molinar on the way out to the street. He told his fellow officer that there were some "red flags" with the disappearance—things that didn't add up.

Molinar agreed. They got into Cooper's car, and Cooper asked Molinar to show him the way Jana would have taken to get to work that morning. They followed the route, looking for Jana's white Pathfinder SUV, but didn't see it. Later, Cooper drove back to the Koklich house and let Molinar off to get his own car. Molinar drove away.

Cooper, meanwhile, decided to call the sheriff's homicide bureau to make sure someone there knew that there might be a problem with the mysterious disappearance of a wealthy, once politically well-connected, 41-year-old real estate lady.

Eating With Spoons

That night, after everyone had left, Chris Botosan made his way to one of the Koklichs' spare bedrooms. Because he had neck troubles, Chris said later, he'd gone home to get his own special pillow. This was a down-filled sleeping accessory that was about three feet in length, and about four inches thick at its center. "It's just a feather pillow. It's nothing out of the ordinary," Chris said later. The pillow was from Scandia Down, he said, and he'd had two of them for a number of years. But the strangest thing about Chris' pillow was that it was virtually identical to one that Jana had.

Here we are venturing into the area of odds and coincidence. What were the chances that two different people connected by a potentially sinister circumstance would each have the same sort of unusual pillow? While it seemed weird—even suspicious to some people—the fact that both Chris and Jana had identical pillows from the same manufacturer was entirely plausible, if remarkable. Still, the fact that Jana's pillow would later turn up missing made the coincidence seem significant.

Chris was later questioned about his decision to spend the night with Bruce.

"I was concerned about him, [the] possibility of phone calls coming, the possibility of ransom," he said. "There were all sorts of possibilities. There was someone missing."

At one point that night, Chris went to the open door of the master bedroom. Bruce was about to get into bed. Chris noticed that the sheets didn't seem to fit the bed. In fact, it appeared to Chris that there was only one sheet, a bottom sheet, and that it wasn't a fitted sheet, but a flat sheet. "It was as if a bachelor had made the bed," Chris said later—someone who was so clueless about bed-making he'd failed to find the appropriate fitted sheet, and instead had just put down a flat sheet, then casually covered it with a comforter.

He and Bruce talked for a few minutes, then Chris went to the spare bedroom, where he spent the rest of an edgy night.

By 8 A.M. the next morning, Bruce and Chris were up, getting ready to go to the office. As usual, Bruce dressed in his coat and tie. Bruce's decision to go to work this day of all days was later cited as a suspicious circumstance. Why else would he have taken the chance of not being home when a possible ransom call came in, if it weren't because he knew for a fact that there wouldn't be one?

At about the same time, Sheriff's Deputy Howard Cooper drove up to the Koklich house. He wanted to get a few minor details for his report. He saw Bruce standing at the trunk of his white coupe, putting a large cardboard box into the trunk. Cooper thought that Bruce was taking Jana's disappearance far too calmly. As he put it later, this was another "red flag" that had caught his attention.

After Bruce drove off to his office, Cooper went to the Lakewood station operated by the sheriff. There he finalized his report, and again called the sheriff's homicide bureau to make doubly sure they knew what was going on.

Not long after Bruce and Cooper left the house, Consuelo Lopez arrived for her regular Tuesday cleaning day. Consuelo opened the front door with the key the Koklichs had given her, and began her work.

Consuelo had worked for the Koklichs for nine years, and had become quite familiar with Bruce and Jana's routine. Because the Koklichs frequently ate meals in their bedroom, it was one of Consuelo's first tasks each day she cleaned to go up to the master bedroom and pick up all the dirty dishes. On this morning, Consuelo found no plates or other dishes—"just a few glasses," she said later.

Picking up the glasses, Consuelo descended to the kitchen. There she found things were out of order. "In the kitchen, there was bread and toast and salsa that was old. It was unusual to find it like this," she said later.

When she thought about it, she realized that the sheets she had put on the king-sized bed the prior Tuesday had been removed. In their place was an old flat sheet—one that Jana had relegated to the linen closet located halfway up the staircase, and used only on one of the spare beds from time to time.

"I noticed that the sheets that were there were not the ones I had placed," Consuelo said. "It was from another bed." Even more peculiar, the sheet was the wrong size. As long as she had worked for the Koklichs, Consuelo had never known them to change their own sheets. That was *her* job. And whoever had done it had botched it, putting the wrong kind and the wrong size sheet on the bed, as if having no idea where to find the good sheets—the ones located in a cabinet in the master bathroom.

Then there was Jana's pink nightgown: that was on

the floor near the bed. Jana never left her nightgown on the floor like that, Consuelo thought. A towel was also missing from the master bath. And in one of the spare bedrooms, Consuelo noticed that a pair of black pants, a sheer blouse, and teddy had been thrown casually onto the bed. A pair of Jana's black shoes were on the floor. Consuelo didn't know it, but this was the same clothing that Jana had worn to the Eric Clapton concert on Friday night. But Consuelo did know that Jana never left her clothes strewn about that way. Consuelo didn't immediately notice what appeared to be a tee-shirt from the concert, still wrapped in its plastic package.

While Consuelo was mulling over these anomalies, Janie Carpenter arrived. Janie now informed Consuelo that Jana was missing, and Consuelo responded by telling Janie about the odd situation with the sheets. Consuelo asked Janie if she had changed the sheets the previous day. No, Janie said. What did Consuelo mean? Consuelo explained that the sheets now on the bed didn't fit—and that she hadn't put them on.

Janie immediately recognized that this information might be important, although not at that point its full significance. She told Consuelo not to touch anything else in the house. She called Bruce at the office to tell him what Consuelo had said.

Bruce had just finished talking to Linda Vargas, the Texas real estate person, who'd said she hadn't heard from Jana. He'd already talked to Paul Carpenter and Doris Morrow, learning that they hadn't seen Jana either. Paul, sick as he was, immediately began making plans to fly to southern California.

After hearing about the sheets from Janie, Bruce left the office and drove back to the house, accompanied by Chris Botosan. Meanwhile, Janie and Consuelo searched the house for the missing sheets, looking in the closets, in the laundry hamper, in the trash, anywhere they might reasonably be found. By the time Bruce got home, Janie was convinced that the sheets were missing, just as her daughter was. That seemed very ominous to Janie, who could easily visualize what might have happened: that Jana was killed in her bed, and that her body had been taken away from the house wrapped in the missing sheets.

Bruce now called the sheriff's department to report this latest information.

By that point on the morning of August 21, 2001, the routine report taken the previous day by the uniformed deputy had made its way through the sheriff's department to the homicide bureau, which had a special section to deal with suspicious missing persons cases. The report included a description of the clothing Jana had been wearing when she was last seen. Bruce had given this as a skirt and blouse, even though the last time he had seen Jana she was still in bed. He also indicated that Jana would have been carrying her purse—a large brown leather bag—and that he was certain that she'd left the house that morning because the alarm had been set, and the SUV was gone. The only way to close the garage door, Bruce had said, was by pushing a button inside the SUV, and that, he added, required the user to know the correct code. These were all indications that Jana had arisen, dressed for work, and had left the house for the office before someone, or something, had inexplicably interrupted her.

By 11 A.M. or so, this bare-bones report and Cooper's supplemental, with its noting of "red flags," had made its way to the missing persons section of the homicide unit. Next had come the information from Bruce about the missing sheets and towel. At the missing persons unit, detectives Delores Scott and Mary Bice evaluated these facts. While the sheriff's department received as many as 1,800 missing persons reports each year, most did not receive immediate attention. This one was different, however. After reading Cooper's supplemental "red flags" report, they called him and received his subjective impression of the previous night: there was something seriously wrong about Jana's disappearance, Cooper said. And now the missing sheets—that seemed to prove it.

Shortly after noon, Scott and Bice arrived at the Koklichs'. By this time, several other people were also there. The first thing the detectives did was ask everyone to assemble on the patio in the rear. Scott and Bice looked through the house, but didn't notice anything that jumped out at them as obvious evidence of foul play, apart from the single unfitted sheet on the bed. Then they interviewed Bruce and Consuelo privately, one at a time, while Chris, Janie and the others waited on the patio outside.

Bruce was interviewed first, starting just after 1 P.M.

"There's too many hands in the pot," Detective Bice began, referring to Molinar, Cooper, the earlier written report taken by the uniformed deputy, and now the new information about the missing sheets, "so we'll just have to start from the beginning."

She took Bruce through the preliminaries for the tape—names and background. Bice asked what Bruce and Jana did for a living, and Bruce explained about selling foreclosures.

"You know," he said, "real estate is a lot like law enforcement—you have specialists who do certain things. We represent major banks, all over the country."

Bice asked about the canvass of the neighborhood that Bruce and Chris had made the previous evening. "The only one who saw anything was the neighbor directly across the street [Donna Baker], who indicated that she did see her [Jana's] truck [SUV] in the garage. She didn't think she saw her, but she did see the truck, so—"

"Who was canvassing with you?"

"Chris Botosan."

"He's your good friend?"

"He's a business partner. I haven't known him that long, actually. I think I've known him for about eight months, but he's become a friend."

"Hmm," said Bice. She and Scott were surreptitiously measuring Bruce, trying to get a fix on his emotional state. Both thought he was being altogether too blasé, considering the circumstances. Bruce smiled at them brightly, and Scott, at least, formed the impression that he was actually trying to flirt with them.

Bice asked Bruce to go over the events, beginning with when he'd last seen Jana.

"That was about six in the morning?"

"Correct," Bruce said.

Bice drew on the information she had so far to ask about the Long Beach police officer who had come to the house the previous day.

"Danny Molinar," Bruce supplied. "He's the same officer that we actually reported the phone calls to, as well." Bruce had already played the mystery caller tape for Bice and Scott.

"You're gonna ask me how our relationship is," Bruce said, laughing. "You know, were we fooling around and all that stuff . . . I understand. And I want you to do your job, so that's fine." Bruce indicated that neither he nor Jana had outside love affairs.

Bice returned to Danny Molinar, trying to figure out where he fit into the picture. She was puzzled as to why Bruce would make his first report of Jana's disappearance to a Long Beach police officer, when that department had no authority to investigate.

"Well," Bruce said, "if it wasn't for Danny, I don't think we would have got a report out of the Lakewood sheriff's

station, to be quite honest with you." Bruce said Molinar
was insistent that the sheriff's department come and take
the report, even though the sheriff normally didn't take
missing reports until at least twenty-four hours had passed.

Bice tried to find out what the Koklichs' ususal work-
day routine was. Why had Bruce gone to work so early?

"I usually get in between six and seven," he said. "The
reason is, we work with banks back east."

"By three P.M., then, you're pretty much wrapped up?"

"Not really," Bruce said. "Because we have property
inspections to do. We work twelve-hour days, usually.
But—it's not really work to us, we enjoy real estate."

"I mean, you don't go to work together?" Bice asked.

"Correct," Bruce said.

"Okay, but you *do* work Monday to Friday?"

"We don't work at all," Bruce said, laughing again.
Now Bice and Scott were sure—Bruce *was* flirting with
them. Bruce's wife might be missing, but he certainly
seemed to be enjoying himself.

"Okay," Bice said, mentally making note of Bruce's
seemingly lighthearted attitude.

"I don't classify real estate as work," Bruce explained.
"We enjoy it, and we—we—we perform our business on
weekends and Sundays and—You know, it's real estate."
There were no set hours, Bruce continued, but both Bice
and Scott noticed his stammer when he mentioned the
weekend. Had something happened over the weekend
that Bruce wasn't telling them about? Cooper's report had
mentioned Nini's remark the previous night that Jana
had inexplicably missed her Saturday morning workout,
and her later appointment with the masseuse.

"I mean," Bruce continued, "we try to take Sunday off,
but a lot of time we'll take a day off during the week and
work Saturday and Sunday . . . but I don't really classify
it as work. I mean, it's my profession, I enjoy it."

But, Bruce added, they hadn't gone into the office on the weekend just past. After coming back from Las Vegas and working hard to catch up in the office on Wednesday, Thursday and Friday, "we had a very busy work schedule, and we had a relaxing weekend doing nothing, okay?"

"Uh-huh," Bice said. She wondered if Bruce was trying to convince her with his "okay."

"Well, I shouldn't say, 'doing nothing,' but we stayed home," Bruce amended. "She—She went to a concert Friday night, uh, slept in late. Uh—We kinda hung out the weekend together, okay? So she was rested, uh—uh, Sunday morning."

Experts who have studied the mannerisms of people undergoing interrogation have long noted that when people are being deceptive, or trying to be deceptive, they will often stammer or hesitate just before delivering a falsehood. Adding the "okay?" to the end of the statement only adds to the notion that the speaker is attempting to convince the listener of something that might not be true. That's why so few people are able to lie convincingly to experienced interrogators, although many think they can get away with it, which is why so many try it. Having been trained to observe these hesitations, Bice and Scott picked them up immediately in Bruce's case.

Bice started closing in on him.

"Now," she said, "this is just information that I have. She was supposed to go to some meetings, like she had appointments with a trainer, and she was supposed to go to the movies with her mom, and—"

"Correct. Correct," Bruce said.

"She didn't?"

"That's—correct. No. She basically, the trainer appointment, she didn't get back to the . . . the . . . from the concert until late."

Bice wanted to know what time Jana had returned from

the concert early Saturday morning. Bruce apparently didn't want to commit himself to a time.

"Early morning," he said. "Early morning hours . . . I mean, I basically had my glasses off. I couldn't tell. Nini said it was eleven-thirty [P.M.]. I thought it was later. But I just remember snuggling her and saying, 'How was the concert?' and that was when I saw her Friday night."

"Saturday morning," Bice said.

"Saturday, early morning, correct."

Bruce again explained that he wasn't sure of the actual time because he couldn't see the clock with his glasses off.

Bice asked Bruce to explain again about Jana's missed appointments.

"Don't ask me why she didn't call," Bruce said. "I mean—we were pretty—We were, you know, she was reading. I was sleeping, you know. It was pretty relaxed. I don't really have the answer to that question. That's what her mom keeps asking. 'It's not like her to not call.' No, it's not like her—wasn't like her."

Both Bice and Scott noticed the slip into the past tense.

"One of the interesting things that Nini said," Bruce lumbered on, "was that she could tell she was—what was the word she used? 'Distracted,' I guess, when she went to the concert with her. Figured that has something to do with why she didn't call. Conjecture at this point."

Bice wanted to know why Bruce had first called Jana "Jan at the beginning of the interview." Bruce apologized, saying his mouth was dry, he probably wasn't enunciating clearly. It was Jana, J-A-N-A, he said.

But, said Bice, Jana was not distracted on the weekend?

"No, we were fine," Bruce said, not recognizing that he'd just contradicted his own conjecture for why Jana didn't accept any calls over the weekend.

Bruce said that on Sunday, he and Jana had gone bicycle riding in the neighborhood. But, he said, he couldn't think of anyone they had seen who might remember seeing them.

"I don't remember talking to any of the neighbors on Sunday," Bruce said.

Bice and Scott now went over all the events that had taken place since Monday morning—Bruce going to work, to the funeral, discovering that Jana hadn't come into the office, the search of the house with Botosan, contacting Molinar, checking the hospitals and the law enforcement agencies.

The conversation gradually segued into the mystery calls. The strange voice, Bruce said, bothered Jana a lot.

"There was one call that really shook her up, like another week before that [one that was kept on the answering machine]—so, three weeks back. I mean, she was to the point where she wasn't answering the phones, she wasn't listening to the voice mail at home, because she didn't want to get these calls. I mean, that's how upset she was."

Now, at last, Bruce had an explanation for why Jana hadn't returned any of the calls from over the weekend: she hadn't known about them, because she was 1) afraid to answer the phone for fear it would be the mystery caller; and 2) afraid to listen to recorded voice-mail messages in case the mystery caller was one of them.

"And she had no idea who they were from?"

"She said, 'Bruce, listen to this. Who is this? I don't know this person. Do you know who this is?' And it's like, 'No, I don't,' you know? And that's when she said, 'Well, we should report this.' I said, 'Yeah, we should.' So we— That's when Danny told us to do it with a report, which we didn't do. I mean— We reported it to him." Danny had told them to make notes on the dates and times of the calls, Bruce added.

Bice asked if there might have been other calls that Jana could have erased. Bruce said it was possible.

"She was very clear to tell me how upset she was when she got these calls," Bruce said. "It's just the sound of this one that scared her. And you know, it scares me . . . It's a little bit sinister-sounding. It depends on your frame of mind, I guess, but to me, it's not too fun. For a woman, anyway."

Bice maneuvered the subject away from the mystery caller and onto Bruce himself. She asked how Bruce and Jana got along with each other, by asking if Jana had ever disappeared like this before.

"She's dependable," Bruce said. "I work for her. Let me explain it to you this way. I'm the relationships guy and she's the organization. I mean, she runs the systems. I basically—bring in the business and she closes it, okay? That's pretty much how our business works. I mean, we're together. We live together. We're very close. We've been in a loving relationship for twenty years."

"Do you argue?"

"I can't remember the last time we had a fight. I mean, we argue at work over business stuff. But it's a difference of opinion on a specific point, which to me is not an argument, we're talking about business strategy."

"Well," Bice said, "there's never been other interests then, in your life, with other women or other men?"

"Definitely not with other men, no with other women."

After this assertion, Bice asked a few more background questions. Then Scott turned to the pressing issue of the changed sheets.

"That just happened," Bruce said. "I got a call from Jana's mom at the office. I have no clue about—sheets—I mean, I was so bent out of shape yesterday. I mean, they could've been nails on that bed and I probably wouldn't have noticed, to be quite honest with you."

"Well," Scott said, "you slept in the bed last night?"

"Correct."

Scott wanted to know how Bruce usually made the bed.

"Consuelo does it," Bruce said. "I just kinda sleep here." He laughed. "You know, if you ask me what color sheet it was, it would be tough for me to tell you . . . I don't really pay that much attention to it. I don't know if that's the male in me or, you know. I just didn't notice."

It was Consuelo's job to take care of the bed, Bruce said again. "I mean, basically, one of my anniversary gifts was, to Jana, was, you know, the housekeeper. She [Jana] doesn't get to do dishes. She doesn't get to clean bathrooms. She doesn't vacuum, she doesn't do laundry. She doesn't do any of that stuff, okay? It's all done by our housekeeper on Tuesdays and Fridays."

Scott asked about Bruce and Chris' inspection of the house the day before.

"At that time did you notice anything weird, other than her car not being here?"

"No," Bruce said.

"I mean, you went upstairs—?" Scott prompted.

"Yeah, we looked. We looked for notes that say where she might go. You know, I looked for her purse. Her purse was gone. She has a nice one that she takes to work and uses on weekends."

Scott asked whether Jana's SUV had a theft reporting system installed. Bruce said no. Scott said it didn't matter, because the car had to be reported stolen for the system to work, and Bruce couldn't report it as stolen until they had more evidence that a crime had actually been committed.

"So I can't even report the car stolen?" Bruce asked.

"Well, no," Scott said.

"I didn't think so," Bruce said.

"Unless there's more information that leads us to believe—"

"Well, hopefully they'll find her and the car," Bruce said.

"So there's nothing— I know she's reliable and everything," Scott continued, "but there's nothing that you can think of that might have been bothering her, that she could have just gone away, to get away? And if so, where would she go?"

"Well," Bruce said, "I was talking to her dad, and one of the things we want to do is, do a press release, because he's an ex–state senator. And he said, 'Bruce, what you need to do is say, "This is the West Coast Chandra Levy," and make sure they'll take it and run it.' And I said, 'Paul, I know, her mom knows, she's not having an affair with anybody.' I mean, she's not that type of lady."

"Like your father-in-law said," Scott told him, "unfortunately, when it comes to the media, we get fifty to one hundred missings a week, that's a rough count."

"God," said Bruce.

"And I can honestly say, for the most part, ninety-nine point nine percent of the time it's people who just want to get away. You do have that small percentage that, something is suspicious, that something has happened to the person."

Scott said the sheriff's department put five to ten missing reports a week out to the media, which mostly ignored them. "You know," she said, "anything that we think is newsworthy, we put it on the news wire, and then the media bites if they want to bite. If they don't, they don't. And for the most part, they don't."

"Yeah," Bruce said. "Well, we think we can get a bite pretty easy."

"You have to make it—you know."

"Fluff it," Bruce said.

"Fluff it. And you don't want to fluff it too much."

"Well, the bottom line is, whatever it takes to get it out there," Bruce said.

"Yeah, right."

"I mean," Bruce continued, "I don't give a shit. I mean, if it gets her back I'll do whatever fluff I have to fluff."

Bruce said he was sure the media would pay attention to Jana's disappearance.

"I mean, him being a senator. I mean, he's a convicted senator of Sacramento. There was an Abscam-type sting operation."

"Oh," Scott said.

"Yeah. He's very prominent—for anybody who's been around politics for a while, so he's not just a senator, he's a convicted-and-served-time senator."

"Yeah," said Scott, "the media should bite."

"Oh yeah," Bruce said, "they'll eat it up with a spoon."

The Sheets

After finishing with Bruce's statement, Bice and Scott invited Consuelo into the house to hear her story. This interview was initially conducted in Spanish by Scott, who was bilingual. Then Scott conducted the interview again, this time in English, and on tape. To Consuelo, 37 years old, her employer was "Mr. Bruce."

"So you got here today," Scott began, "and what happened?"

"When I get in, I noticed that the kitchen was a mess, and she never do that," Consuelo said, using her second language. "And I said, 'Well, something is wrong here' . . . and when I went upstairs, the first thing I saw was the bed. And I noticed that the sheets were not the same sheets, because I change the sheets every Tuesday . . . and I thought, 'Well, maybe they changed the sheets,' because I thought somebody was sick. But I leave it there and I bring the dishes down. I start doing the kitchen. I was mopping the kitchen when her mother came in and asked me, 'Do you talk to Bruce?' And I said, 'No, why?' 'Do you know that Jana is missing?' "

That was when she'd told Janie about the sheets, Consuelo said. After that, she and Janie had looked throughout the house for the missing sheets, the good sheets with red and black and white, with writing on them, but couldn't find them.

Scott now went upstairs and looked at the bed. There was no doubt about it: there was only one sheet on the bed, and it was a flat sheet, not a fitted sheet. Nor did it have any writing on it. In fact, it was the wrong size for the bed.

At that point Bice and Scott decided to call in the rest of the murder squad. It was beginning to look and sound as if something very bad had happened to Jana Carpenter Koklich.

As the afternoon wore on, friends of Bruce and Jana once more began to arrive at the Koklich house. Among the first to arrive was Kathy Ensign, who had known Jana since they'd been in the fourth grade together, and had been with the Koklichs on the recent Hawaii vacation. Jana had called her the previous week to wish her a happy birthday. But only three days later, on Monday, Bruce had called to tell her that Jana was missing.

"I was very shook up," she said later, about her arrival at the Koklich house. As soon as she got to the house and saw Bruce, she started weeping. They hugged each other. Bruce played the mystery caller tape for her, and led her to the patio, where Chris and Janie were waiting, since the police had asked them to stay out of the house. It was the first time that Kathy had met Chris, she said.

A bit later Jan Baird arrived. Janie, Consuelo, Kathy Ensign and Chris Botosan met her at the front door and escorted her around the house to the patio. Bruce was still inside, being interviewed by Scott and Bice. When he came out and Consuelo went in, Bruce again played the mystery caller tape. The police had taken possession of the original, so Bruce had re-recorded it.

"How you doin', Jana? . . ." with the laugh. The voice, deep and resonant, was not known to anyone on the patio.

After he played the tape, Bruce seemed to grapple with finding the appropriate emotion to display. Kathy Ensign thought he was acting a bit strange, but put this down to the strained circumstances. "I don't know how I'm going to live without her," Bruce told the others. He put his hand in front of his face, apparently overcome with grief.

Meanwhile, Scott and Bice had briefed Sheriff's Lieutenant Ray Peavy, who supervised one of the department's "tables" of homicide detectives, back at Homicide Bureau headquarters in Commerce, California, just east of East Los Angeles.

"My partner and I discussed our concerns," Scott said later. The interview with Bruce had raised still more "red flags," Scott said, echoing Cooper's phrase from the night before. Apart from the puzzle of the sheets, the main red flag was Bruce's demeanor—the laughing and flirting.

Just before 4 P.M., two teams of detectives from the sheriff's homicide bureau arrived, dispatched by Peavy. The first to arrive were Joe Sheehy and his partner, Steve Davis. Under the sheriff's rotation system, they were the first up to catch any new murder case.

Sheehy was from Boston. With his massive weightlifter's upper body, he looked as though he might have played noseguard or linebacker for a college football team. In actuality, his favorite sport in Massachusetts had been ice hockey. Taciturn, he had a way of just looking at people that could be intimidating. He'd moved west from Massachusetts in the late 1970s, and joined the sheriff's department in 1981. He'd been in the homicide bureau for about three years, and had already had experience investigating nearly fifty murders.

Davis was taller and slightly older than Sheehy, and somewhat more talkative. He also had a biting sense of humor. It would be Davis who would take most of the two detectives' notes during interviews.

At almost the same time, two other homicide detectives, Sergeant Richard Longshore and Detective Karen Shonka, arrived to assist Sheehy and Davis. Longshore had been assigned to homicide for more than two decades, and was a veteran of hundreds of murder investigations. He was generally regarded as one of the sheriff's department's most gifted investigators, a man with an ear sharply attuned to the nuances of human behavior. As Longshore put it later, the Koklich case got a full-court press by the sheriff's department in part because of Paul Carpenter. The fact that Paul was a former state senator, and perhaps more significantly, a man with some powerful enemies, influenced this decision.

Because Sheehy and Davis were designated as the primaries, Longshore and Shonka were assigned the task of inspecting and documenting the prospective crime scene—that is, the house, the garage, and Bruce's own sport coupe. Sheehy and Davis, meanwhile, familiarized themselves with the interior layout of the house, met the people on the patio, and conducted brief interviews with Consuelo and Kathy Ensign. They decided to interview Bruce and Janie at the nearby Lakewood station, where they would be shielded from distractions.

And distractions there soon were: shortly after the four detectives drove up, so too did several television trucks—the same Lakewood station had put out a press release announcing Jana's disappearance, and the fact that an investigation was under way. Bruce had been right—Jana's relationship to her controversial father had sparked the intense interest of the newspeople. Overhead, at least one news helicopter circled, drenching the neighborhood with its noise, so that people came out of their houses to see what was going on.

Standing in front of the house, Bruce gave a quick press conference. Sheehy and Davis watched this quietly, while Longshore and Shonka continued their inspections. Bruce was wearing a tee-shirt with a real estate logo on the front. He passed out a business card with his and Jana's photograph on it. "We're a husband-and-wife real estate team," Bruce told the newspeople. "One of the leading teams in the nation, actually." He smiled brightly, as if he were making a presentation to a roomful of potential investors.

Bruce sketched in the circumstances of Jana's apparent disappearance—the house empty, the SUV gone, Jana's purse gone, no notes. He said he and Jana's family were very concerned about her, and hoping that she would soon be located. He did not come across as someone who was worried sick about his missing wife.

For some reason, Chris Botosan was sitting in his car when Bruce conducted this first press conference. Just why he would have gotten into his car about the time the police arrived wasn't clear. But it did appear that the police didn't want him to leave, and soon Chris was being asked to make himself available for an interview.

As Molinar and Cooper before them, Longshore and Shonka found no evidence to indicate forced entry—no broken glass, no pry marks. They noted the nightgown on the floor, and the fact of the single flat sheet on the bed in the master bedroom. Under the mattress, on each side of the bed, they discovered two loaded Smith & Wesson .38 caliber handguns. Beneath the bed, they found a sawed-off shotgun. They also learned that the front doormat was apparently missing, along with one of the towels, and the original bed sheets.

Just after 5 P.M., as a team of criminalists—forensic

technicians—arrived at the house to photograph the various rooms and search for possible bloodstains and fingerprints, Longshore and Shonka looked through Bruce's
sports coupe. In the glove compartment, Longshore discovered yet another handgun, this one a SIG Sauer .380
semiautomatic, and an official Los Angeles County
deputy sheriff's badge, brightly shined, still in its original
leather holder.

About 7 P.M. that night, Sheehy and Davis escorted
Bruce, Janie and Chris Botosan to the Lakewood station
for a new round of interviews. Janie, as usual, held her
own emotions tightly. She was still mystified by Jana's
disappearance. After first thinking that perhaps Paul had
taken a turn for the worse, and that Jana had gone to
Texas to be with her father, those hopes had been dashed
by Paul himself, who said he hadn't heard from Jana.
Now Paul was getting ready to fly to southern California
instead.

At the station, in a separate interview room, Janie
quickly perceived that Sheehy and Davis were suspicious
of Bruce. To Janie, the idea that her son-in-law could
have done something to his wife, her daughter, her only
child, was simply inconceivable. Bruce was so much a
part of their lives, traveling with them, helping to take
care of her after her hip replacement operation earlier in
the year, that she just couldn't imagine that he could have
done anything to harm Jana.

Well, said Sheehy and Davis, if it wasn't Bruce, who
else might have done it? What other explanation could
Janie suggest for her daughter's abrupt disappearance?
Had Jana ever done anything like this before? Never, Janie
said. Jana was utterly reliable, never missing appointments,
and especially about providing telephone numbers where

she could be reached. And with Paul's medical condition so perilous, it was doubly important to Jana to be where she could be reached at a moment's notice.

But Janie also said that she and Jana had had less frequent contact over the preceding months. Her daughter and Bruce were both busy, she said. It was her impression that as the summer unfolded, Jana was spending very long hours at the office, picking up some of the slack as Bruce spent more and more time on the AMOS project. Janie thought Jana had been under a lot of pressure at work; maybe that was one reason she'd taken off. Janie still hoped that Jana might turn up, that perhaps she'd just decided to get away from everyone and everything for a few days.

Next, Sheehy and Davis turned to other possibilities. At first blush, they thought, if it wasn't Bruce, what about Botosan? After the husband comes the business partner in the hierarchy of possible culprits, they knew.

Chris told the detectives that he'd known Bruce since around the first of the year. Bruce was paying him $1,000 a month to serve as a consultant for the AMOS project. He wasn't asked about and made no mention of NABUCO, or the stock he was supposed to receive in AMOS for every bank he signed up to buy the program. He certainly didn't tell the detectives about Dennis Piotrowski's past with the Central States Pension Fund of the Teamsters, the Aladdin hotel and the kickback trial twenty years earlier that ended in acquittals all around.

Sheehy and Davis asked Chris about his own movements on Friday, and here it appears that he did not tell the truth, or at least the whole truth. Chris said that on Friday, about 5:30 P.M., he'd met a woman in a sushi bar in Los Angeles. He'd left the sushi bar sometime between 7 and 8 P.M., and gone directly home. He did not tell the detectives about Melinda McBride, but said he went to a video store and rented a movie.

What about Monday morning, when Jana was first reported missing? Chris said he got up about 6:30, and did some work for the Union Rescue Mission. He arrived at the Koklich office about 8:30, he said, and Bruce was not at work when he arrived.

Sheehy and Davis asked Chris about his going to the house with Bruce to look for Jana. They also wanted to know if he'd seen Bruce make any telephone calls to search for his wife. Chris said he had not seen Bruce make any calls, at least not before they'd gone to the house to look for her. Of course, that came to the question of Jana's cellphone. If Molinar was right, there'd been no calls to Jana's cell since Friday afternoon. Wouldn't Bruce have called the cellphone as soon as he heard that Jana hadn't come to work? That was the most likely way to reach her, and there should therefore be a record of Bruce's call to Jana's cell, if Bruce was telling the truth about calling her. But Chris said he hadn't seen Bruce make any calls.

The drift of the detectives' questions convinced Chris that they had in fact targeted Bruce as the most likely suspect—if indeed Jana was dead, as seemed increasingly possible. As Sheehy and Davis now prepared to question Bruce himself, Chris did an interesting thing: he called Bruce's lawyer friend, Gary Mitchell—the same attorney who had drawn up the pre-nuptial agreement eleven years earlier—and told Mitchell that Bruce was in trouble, and that he needed a lawyer. Mitchell asked Botosan what the trouble was, and when Chris told him that Jana was missing, and that police suspected that Bruce was responsible, Mitchell referred Botosan to another lawyer friend of his, Clive Martin.

Unlike Mitchell, Martin was an experienced criminal defense attorney. After getting the barest facts from Chris, Martin began driving to the Lakewood station. He wanted to get there before Bruce talked his way into even more serious trouble.

There's No Issues

Sheehy and Davis began their encounter with Bruce at 7:35 P.M., even as Martin was fighting the traffic.

At this juncture, Sheehy, at least, already believed that Bruce was the most likely culprit, if indeed, something bad had happened to Jana. Scott and Bice had told him about the sheet problem, and Sheehy had seen for himself that the sheet didn't belong to that particular bed. Sheehy believed that if Bruce had killed Jana, he had used the printed sheets to drag her body down the stairs and out to the missing SUV while it was still parked in the garage. Then he would have put the wrong sheet on the bed, in part because the domestically ignorant Bruce didn't know where the good sheets were kept. What was it that he had told Scott and Bice—that making the bed was Consuelo's job? That indicated that he had no idea of where the good bedsheets were kept, and possibly explained why the wrong sheet wound up on the bed—Bruce had grabbed the wrong sheet from the closet.

Sheehy further believed that Bruce thought Consuelo was too stupid to notice such a thing, or at least to recognize the significance of it.

Like any other homicide detective, at this point Sheehy wanted Bruce to start talking. Once he put forth a story, and began to flesh it out with details under Sheehy's prodding, Bruce would be locked in to a version of the events; and then Sheehy could go to work finding contradictions, evidence that would show Bruce was lying. Once he could demonstrate that, Sheehy thought, he'd have 90 percent of the case solved. That was how confessions were made—by confronting suspects with their lies.

Probably the hardest thing for any person under interrogation in a criminal case to realize is that the police questioners are usually very, very good at this game—far better than the subject of the interrogation, no matter how intelligent, may realize. A detective may come across as genial, sometimes bumbling, or even a bit mentally slow, and a guilty suspect may therefore conclude that it is safe to lie. But while a detective may cultivate an air of seeming to be not too bright, or at least non-judgmental, inside his own mind he is noting every statement, every motor reaction, every facial tic, every hesitation, on the part of the subject. And at the same time, the detective is sifting these behavioral clues for the slightest sign of deception, and storing them for later comparison.

In fact, there probably isn't a more efficient lie detector in existence than the average homicide cop. And why not? Most have had years of experience of dealing with people *in extremis*, at the heights and depths of some of the strongest emotions a human being can experience. They've seen just about every form of human behavior there is. And if there is the least bit of falseness about an interrogation subject's behavior, the homicide cop will notice it. When there are two or more homicide cops present, the effect is not only doubled but significantly magnified. A subject might be able, on the rarest of occasions, to fool one detective, but pulling the wool over the eyes of a group of them is just not humanly possible. It's that simple.

That's why lawyers like Clive Martin tell their clients to shut up, and conversely, why the cops will do whatever they can to make a suspect disregard that advice.

A good interrogation will also begin at the outermost edges of the problem, usually with an invitation to the subject to describe his or her ordinary life, almost as if they were in a job interview. Where were you born? When? Where did you go to school? What kind of work do you do? Who's your boss? All of these and similar background questions are put in the most easy-going of conversational tones, much like casual conversation between friends.

As the interrogation subject becomes more relaxed, and more likely to believe that the people who are asking the questions are really harmless, he or she begins to feel that these detectives are not such bad fellows. As the police are reasonable people, what could be more reasonable in response than to establish one's innocence by answering all their questions?

In the Koklich case, there was another factor at work as well: Because Jana was a missing person—not necessarily a crime victim—that meant Bruce felt compelled to answer the detectives' questions. How would it look if, when the detectives were asking for his assistance to find his missing wife, he refused to provide that help? If he said, "Sorry, I can't answer any questions, upon the advice of my lawyer," that would be tantamount to standing at the corner of First and Main and yelling *I did it!* And if Bruce understood he was the logical focus of the detectives' investigation at that point, he could also well imagine how much more convinced the detectives would be of his guilt if he refused to cooperate with them in looking for Jana.

Sheehy's two decades as a cop gave him yet another advantage over Bruce. He had a good working grasp of psychology, and it took him only a few minutes to realize that Bruce believed he was the smarter one. "Bruce was a very arrogant type of person," Sheehy said later. Sheehy's game plan was to give Bruce plenty of rope to boast about himself, then pull the noose tight with the most pointed of questions.

Under Sheehy's questioning, Bruce sketched in the dimensions of the Koklichs' business, and the hopes for the AMOS software company. "There's other stockholders," Bruce said, "but I'm the president and Jana's the secretary, and we're the majority stockholders in the corporation. So there's other shareholders, but just the minimum percentage of ownership . . . But we're the majority, we're the controlling."

Giving Bruce a chance to expound on his brainchild maneuvered him onto ground where he felt ascendant, to lecture Sheehy and Davis on the arcana of the real estate business. He dealt with all the clients—banks, mostly— while Jana bossed the employees in the Atlantic Avenue office. He made Jana sound as if she were merely technical help, easily replaced. Giving an interrogation subject the idea that he was on top of things, that he was in control of the interview, also helped elicit more details.

Sheehy steered the conversation to Friday, August 17—an indication that even at that early point in their investigation, neither he nor Davis were buying the notion that Jana's disappearance had actually taken place on Monday, rather than days before. Bruce said the last time he saw Jana on Friday was about 4 P.M., at the office. She was headed home to change clothes for the concert she was going to attend with Nini, he said.

"And she got home about what time?" Davis asked.

"I didn't have my glasses on," Bruce said. This was the second time he'd avoided this somewhat crucial question, and with the same explanation. "I'm assuming," he continued, "it's between one and twelve [sic]—uh . . . but I have a hard time without my glasses on. I can't see the clock real good. It's kind of a blur unless I stick my face up to it."

"Were you awake when she got home?" Sheehy asked.

"She snuggled me," Bruce said. This was potentially significant, at least psychologically. In the interview with Scott and Bice, Bruce had said that he had "snuggled" Jana. But six hours later, it was Jana who had "snuggled" Bruce.

Davis asked what had happened when Jana came in. This sort of open question was useful, in that it gave Bruce a chance to provide detail that might be contradicted later with additional evidence. Davis gave Bruce a suggestion: had Jana gotten into the bed?

"Yeah," Bruce said. "She jumped into the sack with me as usual."

Here, the phraseology may be significant: "as usual" indicates that Bruce was suggesting to the detectives that he was a sex object for Jana. Yet, the discovery of Jana's concert-going clothes in the spare bedroom suggests that Jana was avoiding intimate contact with Bruce immediately following the concert. This was an example of a statement by Bruce that revealed something of the state of his ego, one that might be contradicted later by additional facts. In other words, it was a possible lie.

"What time did you get up in the morning?" Sheehy asked.

"What time did I get up in the morning?" Bruce's repetition of the question, rather than his immediate answer, was also an indication of deception to Sheehy. As a general rule, innocent people quickly answered such questions with facts: "Six o'clock," or "About seven." Bouncing the question back at Sheehy gave Bruce extra time to consider the viability of a possible fabrication.

"I kinda slept in," Bruce now said. "'Cause she was sleeping in. I think—I didn't really get up. I kinda awoke around ten A.M. Saw that she was still sleeping. Yeah."

Bruce said they'd worked hard the week before, especially in Las Vegas. "So . . . we talked about relaxing and having . . . a weekend to do nothing."

Sheehy knew about the plans that Jana had made to see *Legally Blonde* with Janie. "Didn't [she] mention any plans about going to the movies with her mother?"

"No, she didn't," Bruce said.

Sheehy pressed Bruce on this point, but Bruce insisted that Jana had kept her own schedule. "I just come and go with the flow," Bruce said.

After Jana awakened around noon on Saturday, Bruce continued, they went for a walk. This happened about 2 P.M., in the neighborhood, he said. Davis asked how he and Jana were dressed. He wanted to establish this, in case witnesses could verify this, or alternatively, repudiate it. Bruce said he and Jana were both wearing shorts.

After walking for about half an hour, Bruce said, they'd returned to the house, where they resumed reading. At one point in the afternoon, he said, Jana had made him a sandwich and brought it upstairs to him in the master bedroom.

Davis said that Consuelo had told them they often ate in the master bedroom, usually leaving dirty dishes there.

"We do," Bruce said. "We have a habit of doing that. She [Jana] also has a habit of bringing stuff down and cleaning dishes, which I have to jump her ass for, because she's not supposed to do it. Because that maid is my anniversary gift to her, so I have to jump her ass because I find her on weekend doing dishes . . ." They spent so many hours at work, Bruce added, that he didn't want Jana doing housework, too.

"Right," Sheehy said.

"So, I jump her butt for that."

Both Sheehy and Davis thought it was odd that Bruce three times in less than a minute had told them that he'd "jumped" on Jana. It was as if he wanted to impress them that he was some sort of macho man, the one in control. Yet the fact that there had been no dirty dishes in the bedroom other than a few glasses, according to Consuelo, seemed to suggest that either Jana had ignored Bruce's "butt jumping" or that Jana hadn't been around to eat anything that night.

Sheehy got Bruce back on to the topic of what he and Jana had done on Saturday. Bruce said that after eating dinner, Jana had watched television: *Who Wants to Be a Millionaire?* Bruce said he didn't pay much attention to the show, because he was still reading.

Sheehy asked if they'd received any telephone calls on Saturday. He already knew that both Dean Costales and Nini had called, leaving messages. Bruce said the phone had rung once or twice, but they'd let the answering machine pick up. The mystery calls had made Jana reluctant to answer, he said.

Bruce said he was asleep when the first call had come in. He didn't check the machine until the following day. Jana did not check them at all, he added.

Sheehy asked who the calls had been for. Bruce said he wasn't sure.

On Sunday, Bruce continued, he and Jana had gotten up in the morning, and gone on another walk around the neighborhood. This one lasted for about an hour and a half. After coming home for lunch, he said, they'd gone on a bike ride past the local community college. On the way they'd passed a soccer game at a local park. Bruce added that the players weren't wearing jerseys. Sheehy was thinking the fact they had no uniforms would make it difficult to track down the team members, who might otherwise have been asked if they had seen Bruce and Jana.

After they'd returned home, Bruce said, they ate and Jana watched more television—*60 Minutes,* he thought.

Sheehy asked if any more telephone calls had come in on Sunday. Bruce sighed. He said he thought there had been more calls, but they didn't answer these either.

"Any reason you weren't answering the phone?"

"Basically the same—she didn't want me to answer it, because of these—"

The mystery caller, Bruce explained; it was Jana's idea to ignore the telephone.

"What did she say?"

"Basically—you need to talk to Danny Molinar. Long Beach PD." Bruce said once more that they'd reported the mystery calls to Molinar. To Sheehy and Davis, it seemed as if Bruce was trying to interpose Molinar between himself and the detectives' questions on the unanswered weekend calls. Jana had been bothered by the calls more than he had, Bruce added, "because she talked to this guy personally and I did not. But I mean, she's like, emotionally upset. You know: 'Hey, Bruce, who is this son of a bitch?' "

Bruce and the detectives spent the next ten minutes or so talking about the mystery calls. Bruce said he had never been home when the caller rang.

Davis wanted to know if Bruce had told Jana about the calls from her mother—nine of them, in fact.

"No, I didn't."

"Why?"

"I should've," Bruce said. "I didn't. I just spaced on it."

He was upstairs when Janie's last call had come in, and he'd heard Janie leave her last message. Jana was downstairs watching television.

"You didn't just call down to [Jana] and tell her about it?"

"Nope."

"You have no explanation for that?" Sheehy's incredulity was obvious.

"I was reading and not paying attention," Bruce said. "I mean—no, I don't have an explanation for that."

Sheehy and Davis now asked Bruce to account for his movements the following day, Monday. He'd last seen Jana early that morning, Bruce said. "She was just getting out of bed as I was leaving. I'm assuming she was getting in the shower."

"Did you talk to her?"

"Yeah, I said, 'I'll see you at the office, sweetie.' Gave her a kiss. But—that was the last time I ever spoke to her."

After getting to the office, Bruce continued, he'd gone out to inspect properties.

"Did you speak with anybody when you were out there?"

"No, I don't think I did."

He came back to the office, Bruce continued, and then headed for the funeral, following Larry Garcia in his own car. On the way back from the funeral, he'd received a voice message on his cellphone from Janie. He'd called Janie back, Bruce said, and told her to call Jana at the office. Janie asked him why they hadn't returned her nine calls on Sunday, and Bruce explained to her that he had "spaced."

But when he returned to the office, he continued, and discovered that Jana hadn't arrived yet, "I called her cellphone and I called home. No response."

But hadn't Molinar checked, and discovered that there'd been no calls to or from Jana's cellphone since the previous Friday? If Bruce had called Jana on her cell Monday morning, there should have been some record of that call. Neither detective asked this question, possibly because they weren't completely sure that Molinar's check had actually been done.

"And you've got those phone records?" Sheehy asked.

Well, it wasn't very likely that Bruce would already have the records from cellphone calls made only the day before. But Sheehy, sensing that Bruce was on shaky ground, decided to press him.

Bruce first said he had the records, then amended this to say he could get them. Then he said he and Molinar had tried to do a trace on calls made to and from Jana's cellphone, but that the cellular company wouldn't do it without a court order. "Which I'm hoping to get from you guys," Bruce added. "But the longer it takes—either somebody's been using it, or she's been using it."

Bruce now described going to the house with Chris Botosan to look for Jana. The house was locked, the alarm was set, and Jana's purse was gone, he said, the clear implication being that she had left for work, and that whatever happened to her, had happened on her way to the office, not in the house.

The detectives asked what Jana kept in the purse.

"The normal stuff she keeps," Bruce said. "She's got her i.d. Her wallet's got credit cards, her checkbook, her i.d." The detectives noted the types of credit cards.

"Have you reported them stolen yet?"

"No, I haven't," Bruce said. "Because basically one of the officers told me not to. He said, in case somebody uses them, we can track them."

"Anything else in that purse? Is her cellphone missing, too?"

"Cellphone's obviously in the purse," Bruce said. "'Cause she leaves it in the charging rack on the windowsill." The charging rack was clearly empty.

"Her car is obviously missing," Davis said.

"No word on that, I—"

Bruce seemed to be interested in finding out whether the police had recovered the SUV.

"Was the garage down? The garage door was down?"

"The door was down, correct."

"In order to do that, you have to use the garage door opener?"

"Correct."

"So, whoever left or had her car, they shut the door when they left."

"Correct."

"And locked the house."

"Yeah," Bruce said. "And it would almost have to be her, because it's not one of those button-clickers. I've got it programmed into the visor [of the SUV] . . . you have to know the correct button on the visor to get it down."

This seemed to indicate that only Jana could have lowered the garage door, not some intruder. Except that Bruce also knew the code.

"I need to ask you about something," Davis said. "Your maid has told us about the bedsheets."

"Yeah," Bruce said. "I just learned about that today. That was pretty wild."

"What's up with that?"

"Sh— I mean, I— You know, I slept on them last night. I mean—"

"Well, she said she changed them last Tuesday."

"Yeah."

"So at what point did they get changed again?"

"To be quite honest with you, I'm oblivious. I mean, I don't remember my wife changing them. I didn't change them."

"Any idea where [the missing printed sheets] are?"

"No clue. Doesn't make sense."

"Any explanation as to why or how that could happen?"

"I am— I— I am, like, at a loss totally on that one."

"Okay, were they like that in the morning when you left?"

"She was in bed when I left."

"Well, I know, but you slept in the bed, didn't you?"

"Yeah, but I can't tell you what sheets were on it when I left. I really can't. I— I didn't— I'd tell— I—couldn't tell you."

Sheehy and Davis pointed out that the sheet that was on the bed was a flat sheet, and that it was the wrong size. They asked if it was possible that Jana had changed the sheets herself for some reason that morning. Given a lifeline, Bruce said it was possible. But the detectives noted that it was odd that if Jana had changed the sheets, she'd put the wrong kind and size on, and only one at that.

"That's a little disturbing, frankly," said Sheehy.

"I agree," Bruce said. "I'm very disturbed by it."

"So am I," Sheehy said.

"Yeah," Bruce said.

"I'm disturbed because you don't have an answer for that question."

Bruce sighed again. "I don't know what to tell you. I just didn't pay attention to what type of sheets were on the bed."

Having put Bruce firmly on the hook with the last exchange, Sheehy and Davis decided to take a short break. This would give Bruce a chance to mull things over. Sometimes, when a suspect thinks matters through, he may realize he's made a mistake in lying. When questioning resumes, he may try to extricate himself with a new fabrication. Or, sometimes, he may decide to backtrack, which can lead to a confession. Giving the subject a chance to think things over after putting the barb in can be very effective.

When they resumed, Sheehy brought up the missing SUV.

"Anyway," he said, "everyone in the world is looking for your wife's car right now." He asked Bruce for the license plate number, but before Bruce could give it, Davis interrupted, saying they'd had to take care of a few things during the break.

"Okay," Bruce said.

"Okay," Davis said. "I wanted to just mention something to you, so you know. We're not trying to hide anything here. There was a lawyer who called."

"By the name of Clive Martin," Sheehy said. "He said he was your attorney. Okay, he said he was on his way down here. Do you know who Clive Martin is?"

"No clue," Bruce said.

"We'd like to continue the interview," Davis said.

Here was Bruce's chance, if he took it, to halt the interrogation. With a lawyer on the way, Bruce could say he didn't want to say anything more for the time being. Of course, that would tend to reinforce the suspicions that the detectives had already let Bruce know they had. "The choice is yours," said Davis.

"Well," Bruce said, "you guys haven't Mirandized me."

"No."

"This is just an interview," Bruce said.

"No—"

"I have no problem continuing—"

"No, you are obviously not in custody."

"Right," Bruce said.

"You are free to leave any time you want."

"Yeah."

"You can walk right out that door."

If they chose to give him a Miranda warning advising him of his right not to speak, or to consult with an attorney, Bruce said, he would probably ask to see a lawyer. But since this was just an interview, he was willing to continue.

"Okay," said Sheehy.

"I don't know who Clive Martin is," Bruce added. "I know zero criminal attorneys."

After telling Bruce again that he was free to leave at any time, Sheehy said, "the only thing we're trying to do here is find your wife."

"And that's why I'm sitting here," Bruce said. "I'll sit here all night."

Bruce had obviously been thinking about the missing sheets while the detectives were out of the room. It appears that he realized that he had to give the detectives something better than "no clue." He suggested that maybe Jana had removed the sheets. "Screwed up her sheets, put them in the car, wanted to throw them away," he said. "I'm grasping at straws . . . I apologize that I don't pay attention to what sheets are on my bed." If they asked him about his computer magazines, Bruce added, he'd know exactly what happened to them. But not sheets.

"All right," Sheehy said. "Well, since we're into speculation at this point, can you give us some sort of an idea in your own mind of what happened here? Can you give us some direction to go? Who we need to speak with, other than you? I mean—what do we need to do to solve this thing? In your opinion."

"You need to get some kind of lead," Bruce told them. "Some kind of—something on the vehicle, you know." The fact that he and Jana dealt in foreclosed property was one possibility, he said; someone may have wanted to get even. Or there were places that Jana habitually went, such as the dry cleaners, or her workouts, or her yoga class. Maybe someone had been stalking her.

"Well," Sheehy said, "I was just gonna ask you. Have you had any problems with your wife?"

"Zero problems with her," Bruce said.

"Have any reason to kill her?"

This was putting the ball squarely in play—if Bruce didn't understand with this that Sheehy and Davis considered him the prime suspect, he had to be dreaming.

"Uh—She's like the love—Hell, no. She's the love of my life. I mean, you know, she runs our business—I mean, she's great in bed. She's cute. She works out. She—I mean, there's no issues."

Anyone listening with the psychologist's proverbial "third ear" would find much to interpret with this ode to Bruce's love for Jana. *She's the love of my life . . . she runs our business* . . . then, hearing himself, he switches gears abruptly: *I mean, she's great in bed. She's cute . . .* ((let's see, what else?)) . . . *She works out . . . there's no issues. . . .*

"Did you have anything to do with her disappearance?" Sheehy asked.

"Definitely not," Bruce said.

I Was a Victim

Now Sheehy and Davis asked about Chris Botosan, who was still in the lobby of the sheriff's station, apparently waiting for Bruce.

"The gentleman that's in the lobby? Chris, I believe his name is?"

"Chris Botosan," Bruce said.

"He's your—your partner?"

"Partner," Bruee said. "He's kinda like an employee, but he's more of a partner."

"In the computer software business."

"The computer software," Bruce agreed, "not the real estate side."

Bruce sketched in some of the background of his relationship with Chris: how they'd worked together for the previous eight months on AMOS, and how they'd actually met the first time more than ten years earlier, in connection with Berkeley Federal Savings in West Palm Beach, before the S & L had gone bankrupt.

At that point Sergeant Longshore came into the interview room, and was reintroduced to Bruce. They'd met briefly before Longshore had begun his search of Bruce's house and car earlier that afternoon.

Davis now took up the questioning. He produced the sheriff's badge Longshore had found in Bruce's glove compartment, along with the SIG Sauer pistol.

"Apparently they found this in your car," Davis said, holding the badge out to Bruce.

Bruce took it. "Okay," he said.

"Where'd that come from?" Longshore asked.

"I found this in a house in Signal Hill, back in— should've turned it in—back in 1989 or so. I have one of these, too." Bruce fished his honorary Long Beach Police Department badge out of his pocket, and passed it to the detectives.

"What's this?" Longshore asked.

"I'm a member of the Long Beach Police Officers Association," Bruce said. "I'm an honorary member."

Bruce now tossed the sheriff's badge, still in its leather holder, onto the floor at the detectives' feet. If he'd spit on it, he couldn't have offended the deputies more, with his cavalier treatment of their badge. Bruce seemed oblivious to the effect of his action, however. Longshore picked up the badge.

"Any reason why you didn't turn it in?" Longshore asked.

"Uh—neglect," Bruce said.

"Well, you should have turned it in," Longshore said, still doing a slow burn.

"Yeah, I should've, definitely . . . I didn't even know it was in my car."

"Have you ever used that illegally in any way?" Longshore asked.

"Never," Bruce said. "Never."

"You have not gone out and buzzed your way? You know what I mean by buzzing your way?"

"No, I—"

"Showing that badge to somebody and—"

"I don't—I don't want to be put in jail," Bruce said.

"Okay," Longshore said.

"I don't want to be put in jail," Bruce said again, apparently meaning that he had never used the badge to misrepresent himself as a police officer.

"Have you ever been arrested, by the way?"

"I was arrested when I was, uh, under eighteen," Bruce admitted.

"For what?"

"For burglary." But Bruce went on to laugh. "But I was a victim." He started to explain what had happened, but Longshore cut him off.

"Since you were an adult?"

"No. My buddy narked me off for something I didn't do," Bruce said, still trying to explain what happened when he had been arrested as a juvenile.

"Why do you have all the guns?"

Bruce explained that his father had collected guns, and that he did, too. As for the sawed-off shotgun under the bed, he'd found that one in a foreclosed house.

"What about the two SIG Sauers that were in the . . ." Longshore meant the .38 pistols under the mattress, but got momentarily confused by the SIG Sauer .380 he'd found in the car.

"Those are both registered," Bruce offered.

Remembering that the mattress guns were Smith & Wessons, while the gun in the car was a SIG Sauer, Longshore now realized that Bruce was talking about two *more* SIG Sauer pistols. That meant Bruce had access to at least five handguns—one in his car, two under the mattress, and now, it appeared, two others as well.

"Where are they?" Longshore asked. "I didn't find those."

"The two?"

"No."

"Well," Bruce said, "didn't you get the one out of the other seat of my car?"

"Okay," Longshore said. "There's that one."

"There's that one, and there's one at the office," Bruce said.

"Oh, okay."

"And there's one in Jana's car."

"Okay," Longshore said. "There's one in *her* car."

"So," Davis interjected, "there's a gun missing, too?" This was the first that anyone from the police had been told that not only Jana and her car were missing, so was a gun.

"Why does she carry a gun in the car with her?"

"Most of our business right now is in Compton," Bruce said, implying that they both needed pistols to travel safely in economically distressed areas south of Los Angeles.

Longshore asked him if he wasn't afraid of getting arrested for carrying an unlicensed gun. But Bruce said he'd told the sheriff's department station in Compton that he was carrying the gun, and that a deputy there had told him he'd be approved if he only applied. He just hadn't done it yet, he said.

This was a perfect lead-in to something else Longshore wanted to know.

"If something were to happen to you or your wife, who would benefit financially?"

"Well, we have a million-dollar life insurance policy for both of us. The beneficiary is the company."

"What happens if somebody disappears?"

"If somebody dies—I mean, I don't know," Bruce said. "I have no clue."

When Bruce, still trying to make sense of the sheets, finally offered the theory that perhaps someone had gotten

into the house after he left in the morning, had knocked
Jana out, wrapped her in the sheets, and put her in the
back of the Pathfinder, he could see that's exactly what
the detectives also thought had happened. Except they
thought it hadn't happened on Monday, but early Saturday morning, and that it wasn't "someone" who had done
it, but Bruce himself.

By the end of this interview, both sides knew that the
other was the enemy. Sheehy and Davis were certain that
Bruce had murdered his wife, and Bruce was certain that
the sheriff's detectives were going to blame him for whatever had happened. From this point forward, the battle was
joined: the detectives trying to find the evidence, and Bruce
trying to hold his believers, like Janie and Paul, together,
despite the onslaught of evidence, and the waiting, waiting
for the other shoe to drop—his inevitable arrest.

While Bruce, now joined by Clive Martin, and Janie
drove back to the Koklich house, and Botosan returned to
his own apartment in Downey, the detectives sat down to
consider what they had, and where they needed to go next.

One thing was clear: Bruce was the obvious suspect.
He'd had the best opportunity, at home alone with Jana
after she'd returned from the concert with Nini, a point
seemingly buttressed by all the telephone calls that had
gone unanswered by either of the Koklichs on Saturday
and Sunday. He had an apparent financial motive: the life
insurance policy, not to mention complete control over
the business. And he'd had some apparent means: the
man was armed as if World War III were about to break
out. And after all, a gun was missing.

And that was another matter: the car. While Bruce
hadn't seemed to press them very hard on the point, it
seemed to all three detectives that he was quite eager for
them to look for the car. It was almost as if he wanted
them to find the car so they would . . . what?

If they found the car, and Jana wasn't in it . . . What? What would Bruce think? What would Bruce *want* them to think? At first he'd taken great pains to impress on them that Jana had to have left the house voluntarily on Monday morning. The house had been locked, the car was gone, the purse was gone—Bruce had come back to that point about the purse again and again—the cellphone was gone, and the garage door had been closed by someone who knew the visor code. QED: Jana had left under her own power, and something had happened to her on the way to work, like a carjacking. It could have happened that way, but it seemed too pat. And there were all the unanswered calls over the weekend, and the mystery of the sheets.

No, the way it was playing out, it was more logical to theorize that Bruce had almost told the truth, but had put someone else in place of himself. That *he'd* been the one who killed Jana, not on Monday, but early Saturday morning, that he had been the one who had used the sheets to remove the body to Jana's car, that he'd hidden the car and the body someplace, had come back to the house, had ignored all the telephone calls on Saturday and Sunday, and had gone to work on Monday morning. And had only then reported Jana "missing."

But Bruce was right about one thing: they needed to find the car. If they could only find the car, they could begin to unravel some of this confusion.

"Everybody in the world is looking for your wife's car," Sheehy had told Bruce. But so far, no one had been able to find it.

Pillow Talk

The next day was Wednesday, August 22, 2001. Jana had officially been missing for two days, and as Bruce had predicted to Detective Scott, the news media was unlimbering its spoons. EX-LAWMAKER'S DAUGHTER MISSING headlined the Long Beach *Press-Telegram*. Bruce made all the local television news broadcasts, standing in front of the Lakewood house, wearing his National Association of Realtors tee-shirt. Every single station had him saying that he and Jana were among the leading real estate salespeople in the country, and grinning.

Chris Botosan had watched Bruce's standup on the news and was appalled. He thought it looked like a commercial for the real estate business. He wasn't alone in that assessment; the cops thought so, too. Longshore, watching the replay on the news, was convinced there was something that didn't ring true about Bruce.

"You know, you always look at these things with a jaundiced eye," Longshore said later. "The husband's always the first person you look at, for obvious reasons. And just the totality of the thing—the fact that the sheets didn't match, according to Consuelo, the way the thing went down, his—the fact that he never called us initially, he called Long Beach PD. There were just a lot of things didn't ring true. It was very artificial, very contrived. It became obvious that he was a very controlled person. There was no emotion at all, I mean none. People grieve differently, but when your wife is missing and you allegedly love her with all your heart, we do need to see more emotions than that. And there was just nothing. He was just very cold."

But, Bruce said later, it wasn't that he was cold—he was scared.

"It appeared to me that they were looking very strongly at me as a suspect, and it frightened me," Bruce said later. "I mean, very much so. I was grieving for Jana. I was trying to figure out where she is, and these guys are, are talking to me about the weekend we spent together, when I'm trying to figure out how I can get her back and what I can do."

When they'd returned to the house that night, after the interviews at the Lakewood sheriff's station, Janie decided to spend the night. She used the same bed that Chris Botosan had used the night before. On this bed she found a long, flat pillow.

"There was a pillow, a very nice, soft pillow in that bed, and I liked it, so I slept on it," Janie said later. She assumed that the pillow belonged on the bed, that it was one of Jana and Bruce's pillows.

The next day, however, Chris told Janie that this was *his* pillow. He told her he wanted to take it home with him, so Janie reluctantly surrendered it.

But here was one of those mysteries that would later seem to be significant, at least to Bruce's partisans. It was only later that Janie learned that Jana had owned a pillow

exactly like the one that Chris claimed was his; and when
Jana's pillow subsequently turned up missing, Janie could
not help but wonder whether the pillow Chris had taken
from her that day had actually been the one that belonged
to Jana. This was one reason Janie later developed suspicions about Chris Botosan. It seemed very odd that Jana's
pillow would go missing, just like Jana, and that Chris at
almost the same time would claim that an identical pillow
actually belonged to him.

Chris's own later statements on this pillow confusion
hardly helped matters. He said that he'd brought the pillow to the Koklich house on Monday afternoon, slept on
it in the spare bedroom Monday night, left it there Tuesday morning and asked the detectives "after they had
come and photographed the house and done their search"
if it was all right to remove it.

"I asked them if I could take the matching pillow. I
have two of them," he said. "So I wanted to bring it back
to my house."

The seeming problem with this, of course, is that if
Chris took the pillow home on Tuesday *after* the detectives had made their search, Janie couldn't possibly
have slept on it Tuesday night. And if the pillow figured
somehow in whatever happened to Jana—if it was used,
say, to smother her early on Saturday morning—its later
removal to Chris's house would have some important
evidentiary significance. Bruce's supporters would eventually suggest that Chris had absconded with this pillow
in order to conceal evidence. But it's equally possible that
the pillow slept on by Janie was in fact Jana's—and that
that pillow was later removed by some other person, possibly even Bruce, after Chris had taken his *own* pillow
home.

The lack of investigative coherency about the pillows

would later foment the establishment of a number of conspiracy theories about Jana's fate.

Nevertheless, the mystery is somewhat clarified if one assumes that Chris was imprecise in his description of when he reclaimed the pillow. Detective Sheehy, for one, believed that Chris had asked to take his pillow home on Wednesday, not Tuesday after the search. That would explain how Janie had come to use Chris's pillow Tuesday night. Later, unfortunately, the detectives never asked Chris to produce his, an omission that only fueled speculation that there was something ominous about this dance of the pillows, especially when, only a few days later, Jana's pillow, a potentially crucial piece of evidence, would be reported as missing by the observant Consuelo.

Janie wasn't at all sure what to make of Chris. Like almost everyone else, she was struck by his nervous, almost antic demeanor. She especially noticed that Chris seemed to talk as if he were some sort of software genius, someone who was indispensable to the big deal Bruce envisioned. Nor was Janie alone in this perception of Chris. Others in the Koklich office thought he was snooty, condescending.

"He was always talking big," Barbara Hauxhurst later recalled.

And by Wednesday morning, the night after the interviews at the Lakewood station, Chris appeared to be moving to take charge of the entire business, not just the AMOS project. According to some working in the office, he told them that any decisions would now be made by him—that Bruce was not to be bothered. Chris later said he didn't recall saying any such thing, but others—admittedly, all Bruce partisans—said he seemed intent on screening all contact with Bruce, and giving orders himself. They thought Chris was taking over, moving in.

"He said that Bruce wasn't handling things very well, and that we shouldn't bother him," Barbara Hauxhurst said later.

As for Nini, who after all had set Chris up with her girlfriend Melinda McBride, she thought that the real Chris was "a wanna-be," someone long on talk but short on performance. She thought that Jana's disappearance had seriously unnerved him. In fact, Nini said, she thought the whole situation "scared the crap out of him."

At some point, either that day or the night before, Chris had spoken with Bruce about his television performance.

"I had a discussion with him," Chris recalled, "just saying that maybe he was in shock or maybe that he just didn't understand what was occurring, but he didn't seem to be showing any emotions . . ."

Bruce took this observation impassively, Chris said. "He said, 'Okay.'"

But as the morning of August 22 unfolded, Bruce decided to do an audit of sorts. He called Kathy Ensign, wanting to find out what she had told the police the day before, when Sheehy and Davis had first come to the Koklich house.

"I asked him how he was doing," Kathy said later, "and he said he was frightened and lonely." It was the first time Bruce had ever called her. After filling him in on what she'd said to the detectives the previous day—essentially an innocuous statement that as far as she could tell, Bruce and Jana seemed happily married—Bruce thanked her and said goodbye. Replacing the telephone, Kathy thought the entire call seemed strange. Why was Bruce asking her what she had told the police—unless Bruce was worried that she might have said unflattering things? She decided to begin keeping notes on her contacts with Bruce, as well as the police.

Even while Bruce was talking to Kathy Ensign, Long-shore was interviewing Nini Angelini; if anyone knew what was going on with Jana shortly before she disap-peared, it was probably Nini, who had said she'd last seen Jana going inside the Koklich house early Saturday morn-ing. Nini now filled Longshore in on the night she and Jana had spent at the Clapton concert, and how she'd left Jana at the front door about 12:30 in the morning. Jana had turned the lights on and off, Nini said.

Then, she said, when Jana had missed the appointment on Saturday afternoon, she'd called the house and Jana's cellphone, but no one had answered. After Bruce had told her Monday that Jana had vanished, Nini had come to the Koklich house that night, as had the others.

"Chris seemed to be running the show," Nini told Longshore. When she'd asked about the "stash," Bruce had led them upstairs to show them that the cache was un-touched. When she'd left that night, she'd asked Bruce, in a whisper, whether he'd told Deputy Cooper about the gun Jana had in her car. When Bruce said he hadn't, Nini had urged him to tell everything to the police, and he had told her he would. Longshore, of course, knew that the fact that there had been a gun in Jana's car had only come out the next night when he was questioning Bruce.

Nini also told Longshore that Jana had told her about the mystery caller.

"Nini insisted that Jana let her hear the tape," Long-shore reported later, "and after having done so, she and Jana agreed that the caller did not sound threatening. Jana told her that she had reported the calls to the telephone company, and had been advised to change her telephone number. Jana told Nini that she was unwilling to do that."

This certainly didn't sound as if Jana had been all that

worried about the mystery caller, Longshore thought. And
Nini was someone who looked as if she could take care of
herself, and who therefore probably knew what a threatening voice sounded like. A runner, Nini was in excellent
physical condition, and she was under no illusions about a
woman's vulnerability to attack, and the need to be vigi-
lant. Jana would hardly be an "easy victim," Nini told
Longshore. Jana, too, was in excellent shape from all of
her workouts over the previous year. Besides that, Jana
had her gun; she'd assured Nini that she knew how to use
it, and would, without hesitation, if she had to. This bolstered Longshore in his belief that Bruce had to be the
culprit—no one else could get close enough to Jana to do
her in, he thought.

Bruce was the controlling person in the marriage, Nini
continued. "The only thing he cares about is money," she
said. Bruce was highly intelligent; when he focused his attention on something, he had the ability to tune almost
everything else out while he thought matters through. "She
went on to say," Longshore reported later, "that if [Bruce]
had decided to kill Jana, there is no doubt in her mind that
his plan would be well-thought-out and executed."

Some help was on the way for Bruce. Barbara Hauxhurst
routinely had her hair done at Arrita LePire's hair salon
two doors down from the Koklich office. In the course of
her appointment that same morning, she'd told Arrita that
Jana was missing.

Arrita, who knew Jana and Bruce both by sight, told
Barbara that she'd been cleaning out the salon on Sunday
morning. Her husband, Allen Radcliffe, had just emptied
the trash in the back when he'd seen a young blonde
woman walk across the lot and get into an SUV. Radcliffe
went into the salon and told Arrita that he hadn't known
the people in the real estate office worked on Sundays.

Oh, Arrita said, that was probably Jana. She and Radcliffe then left the salon, and Arrita saw a blonde woman driving northbound in the alley behind the building that housed the Koklich office as well as the salon. All Arrita saw of the woman was the rear of her blonde head. But she was pretty sure it was Jana, just as she was sure that the SUV they'd seen driving away was also Jana's white Pathfinder.

Then, on Wednesday, August 22, Arrita recounted to Barbara Hauxhurst what she and Allen had seen three days earlier.

That afternoon, Bruce had come to the office and met with Clive Martin. Somehow Martin had learned of Arrita's account to Barbara Hauxhurst about seeing Jana on Sunday morning. Martin later recalled standing in the parking lot behind the Koklich office and telling Bruce about Arrita's information.

"I was excited," Martin recalled. "I thought this was the break we were looking for."

They went into the office, into Bruce's cubicle. Martin explained to Bruce that they had to find people who would establish that Jana had been alive and well the preceding weekend. Martin decided to call in a private investigator, Jay Hoffman, and put him to work running down the leads they *did* have: school principal Donna Baker's observation of Jana's white SUV in the Koklich garage on either Sunday or Monday morning, and Arrita LePire's supposed Sunday sighting of Jana in the office parking lot.

Later that afternoon, Bruce held another press conference, this one on the sidewalk in front of the office. With Janie standing stoically by his side, Bruce pleaded for anyone with information to come forward. At one point he appeared to choke up with emotion, his hand covering his face. Janie moved closer to him and appeared to be comforting him. During this event, Bruce offered a $100,000 reward for Jana's safe return. Later he told Janie that while he didn't have that amount of money readily on hand, "I could get it."

That caused Janie to eventually wonder whether Bruce and Jana had been having money problems when Jana had vanished.

After the media people had left, Bruce, at least according to Chris Botosan, later approached him.

"There," Chris later said Bruce told him, "I cried for you on national television." Bruce would later say he never said any such thing, that Botosan was lying in order to make Bruce look bad.

About the same time that Bruce was talking to the news media, Detectives Sheehy and Davis arrived at the Koklich offices to talk to the employees. They wanted to piece together Jana's last hours at work on Friday, and find out how husband and wife had been getting along in recent days. They also wanted to see if there were any other problems related to the business that might account for Jana's sudden disappearance. Among other things, they collected two calendars—one from the office computer that everyone had access to, showing business appointments and various employees' whereabouts on any given day, and the other a large desk-blotter calendar that Jana habitually used to note the minutiae of her life: "went to circus with Bruce and Marguerite," "dinner with Bruce & Mike & Chris," "ran circuit," "go to bed early—tired," that sort of thing.

On this calendar, Jana had noted that she'd had lunch with both Bruce and Chris on the Friday before her disappearance. It does not appear that the detectives noticed this or put much significance to it. That may have been an important oversight, however.

Given that Jana habitually went home for lunch—indeed, Consuelo later said that Jana had come home around 2 P.M. that day, shared a dessert with Consuelo, and then returned to the office for a few hours—the fact that Jana had noted this lunch with both men seems possibly meaningful.

What was talked about during this lunch? It appears that no one ever asked either Bruce or Chris. But it seems almost certain that the subject of AMOS had to have come up, and possibly the NABUCO proposal. It was entirely possible that at this lunch, Jana had told Bruce that she would not go along with the NABUCO deal. It's also possible that Bruce had told Chris not to worry—he could convince Jana to go ahead anyway.

Then, the following Monday, when Chris heard from Bruce that Jana had disappeared, it might have seemed, to Chris, to be far too much of a coincidence: Friday Jana was balking at the deal; Monday she'd vanished. And there was Barbara Hauxhurst's parking lot observation of Chris on Monday morning: "His face had an expression that was sort of like impending disaster—that's the only way I can describe it."

The lack of probing of this critical lunch meeting, with its potential to uncover Bruce's possible motive, was one of the largest flaws of the sheriff's investigation, it now seems clear.

The detectives had their chance to ask about this critical lunch between Jana, Bruce and Chris after they picked up these calendars. They then met with Bruce and Martin. Following Bruce's press briefing, Martin told the detectives that he would be representing Bruce, and that he'd hired a private investigator to help look for Jana. Sheehy and Davis arranged to meet with Bruce at the Koklich house the next day. The detectives wanted Bruce to show them exactly where he and Jana had gone walking over the weekend. Bruce said he would be waiting for them at the house at 9 A.M. He still seemed willing to assist the detectives, at least to some extent.

"I'd told him to cooperate, but not to answer any questions. He had a hard time with that," Martin said later. Martin meant that Bruce couldn't help himself—he had to talk to the detectives, it was just part of his nature as a salesman.

By this time, Paul Carpenter had arrived from San Antonio. At the Koklich house that night, Bruce, Janie and Paul tried to figure out what might have happened to Jana. As Janie put it later, the detectives had asked her who else it could have been if it wasn't Bruce. The three decided to make a list of other possibilities. Neither Paul nor Janie at this point were prepared to believe that Bruce was involved in any way with Jana's disappearance. They both knew, however, that the police were very suspicious of their son-in-law. They put this down to standard police operating procedure.

Because neither Paul nor Janie knew many names of people who knew Bruce and Jana, the list was general in nature. There were about a dozen possibilities other than Bruce, they thought.

"One of them we put down was 'meltdown,'" Janie said later. By "meltdown," Janie and Paul meant that their daughter might have had some sort of mental breakdown. "There had been an incident with a film star shortly before this," Janie said, referring to actress Anne Heche's temporary vacation from reality, which had been in the news, "in which she [Heche] had gone into a fugue state. We didn't really think it could possibly have happened [to Jana], but we put it on the list."

Still thinking, the trio listed the grandson of a neighbor, because the neighbor had a spare key to the house;

possibly some acquaintance of Consuelo, someone from Jana's yoga or beach workout classes who had followed her home; someone who had seen her at the supermarket; possibly some other household employees who had keys to the gate. Number nine on the list was a secret lover. But no one believed that was possible. Jana just wasn't the type, they agreed. In fact, none of the explanations or suspects on the list seemed very likely. That brought them back to the mystery caller—and Bruce.

Sneak Preview

That same evening, just as Sheehy and Davis were finishing their interviews with the Koklich employees—Barbara Hauxhurst told them what Arrita LePire had told her, about seeing Jana on Sunday—and at about the same time that Bruce, Janie and Paul were making up their possibilities list, Sergeant Longshore was paged by the homicide bureau. Would Longshore call someone who wanted to speak to a detective in connection with the Jana Koklich disappearance? The intense news media coverage was generating some reaction from the public.

The caller was a young woman named Rosie Ritchie, and when Longshore called her back, he learned that Rosie had first met Bruce in the early 1990s, shortly after he'd married Jana. Later the same day, Sheehy and Davis also interviewed Rosie.

At the time, Rosie told the detectives, she'd worked in the real estate business herself, in the title insurance field. One day Bruce had asked her to meet him at an apartment building in Long Beach, Rosie said. When she'd arrived at the place, Bruce invited her into a vacant apartment and shut the door. He told her that he was trying to buy a large block of foreclosures, and that he had some clients coming in. He wanted her help. Could she assist him in setting up some entertainment?

Rosie said she didn't quite understand, at least in the beginning.

"I thought, 'Dinner, great,' " she said later. " 'Where do you want to go? What restaurant? You want to set them up, take them here, take them there? Not a problem.' And my boss at the time was also aware of it. I was letting her know, 'Gosh, this would really be good for us to get this business. Bruce and Jana do an incredible amount of business within the city.' "

But then Rosie discovered what Bruce really meant by "entertainment."

"It took some time," Rosie admitted later. "We were talking. The house was empty. There was a chair. And I said, you know, 'Whatever you want to do.' And he said, 'Why don't you show me?' And I didn't really know what he was talking about. He said, 'We need to entertain the gentlemen. Why don't you give me a sneak preview?' and he sat on the chair, and I was blown away."

Rosie realized that Bruce wanted her to give him oral sex as a "preview." Bruce told her that his marriage to Jana was "for business purposes," and that they had no sexual relationship. If Rosie could demonstrate her ability to "entertain," Bruce said, he could make sure that her firm got a lot of business from the Koklich enterprise.

"I just thought, 'No. I don't— No, I *do not* do this,' so I—said no. He was very quiet, very melancholy, and he said, 'Okay. All right. See you later.' So I left, ran downstairs and called my boss, and I was panicked. I'm like, 'Oh God, this is what he wanted me to do! What am I supposed to do? I can't do that.' She said, 'Rosie, let's get the business. I mean, if he wants—Should we hire entertainment for him?' I mean, it was very clear that it wasn't going to be anything *I* had anything to do with. She suggested, 'Gosh, if he needs call girls, do it. Let's get the business.' I did call him back later that day, and I said, 'If you would like us to hire entertainment for you, we will do that. We have no problem doing that.' He said that was not what he had in mind."

Rosie said she soon learned that Bruce was infamous in Long Beach real estate circles for propositioning women. In fact, Rosie told Longshore, she could provide him with the name of another woman who'd had a similar distasteful experience with Bruce.

What was it Bruce had told Bice and Scott: that there were no other women in his life? Here was a story that seemed to contradict that, and one that took place only a short time after Bruce and Jana were married. More to the point, it seemed to show that if Bruce was hardly averse to using his clout in the real estate business to try extorting sex from people, some in the business wanted his patronage so much they were willing to accede to it.

And there was a third facet of this: Jana worked in the real estate business herself. Was it possible—was it even realistic?—that she hadn't known that Bruce was fooling around? That he was using his business influence to solicit sex? It hardly seemed likely. Maybe that was why she'd taken off, finally leaving Bruce. On the other hand, maybe that was why Bruce had killed her.

Longshore, Sheehy and Davis knew they had to find the car.

Over the next several days, both sides redoubled their efforts. The sheriff's detectives tried whatever they could think of to get a lead on Jana or the SUV, while Clive Martin's detective Jay Hoffman kept looking for witnesses who could credibly say they'd seen Jana Koklich alive and well as late as Monday morning.

Whether Bruce's tears were real or faked, the media continued using their feeding utensils. After the coverage on Wednesday night, the detectives the following morning received a telephone tip that Jana had been seen on a Wal-Mart security tape in Cathedral City, California, way out in the desert near Palm Springs. This was one of the disadvantages of media attention, Sheehy and Davis knew: false sightings. If they followed up every single one, they'd never get anything accomplished, yet they still had to be checked out. They asked the Cathedral City police to look at the woman on the tape.

After determining that the Wal-Mart woman wasn't Jana, the detectives went to the Koklich house to walk the agreed-upon walk with Bruce. The detectives wanted to prove one way or another: Had Jana actually been there, or was Bruce making up the story? Taking him over the route was one way to check his veracity—they could later canvass the neighborhood to see if anyone had seen Bruce and Jana as they were on their stroll. At the same time, they decided to pick up Jana's pink nightgown, which had been left by the side of the bed despite the search of the night before. Sheehy later acknowledged that the failure to pick up the nightgown when they'd first come to the house had been a mistake. Had it been laundered—it did not appear that it had—valuable trace evidence, such as blood, hair or fibers, could have been lost. Bruce was later to point to this oversight as an example of what he and his lawyers would call sloppiness in the police investigation of Jana's disappearance.

While Bruce was walking with Sheehy and Davis, detective Jay Hoffman telephoned the Koklichs' neighbor, school principal Donna Baker, who said she was sure— well, pretty sure—that she'd seen Jana's SUV in the Koklich garage about 8 A.M. on either Sunday or Monday, August 19 or 20. This was exactly the same story that

Baker had told to Karen Shonka on Tuesday evening
when Shonka was canvassing the neighborhood, and to
Bruce and Chris the night before that.

On one level, this information seemed to help Bruce—
except for the fact that Donna Baker hadn't actually seen
Jana herself. But if the SUV was in the garage on Monday
morning at 8 A.M., Bruce was off the hook—that was
when he'd been inspecting properties. Maybe.

Of course, there wasn't any proof that Bruce had actually been inspecting properties that morning. Just because he'd provided a list to Rosa Canedo didn't mean
he'd really inspected them. Was it possible that Bruce had
arrived at the office, told his employees he was going out
to inspect, instead driven home, killed his wife, put her in
the back of the SUV, driven it to some still-undiscovered
location, left it there and managed somehow to get home
in time to return to the office by 9 A.M.?

The only way that could work is if Bruce had left the
SUV someplace close to home—close enough so he
could walk or jog back to the house, pick up his own car,
and get back to the office in time to be seen about 9. But
in that case, why hadn't they found the car?

Finding the car still seemed to be the key, for both
sides, and to that end, Bruce rented a helicopter. Sometime that day or the next, he and Paul Carpenter, accompanied by one of Jana's cousins, flew over the area, hoping to
spot the SUV from the air. But if it was out there, they
couldn't see it.

Meanwhile, Sheehy and Davis went to see Arrita LePire
at the hair salon two doors down from the Koklich office.

This was the second time the sheriff's detectives had
talked to Arrita. The day before, Longshore, canvassing
the neighborhood of the office, had encountered her.
Unaccountably, she seems not to have told him about her

supposed sighting of Jana on Sunday, Longshore said later. But in her interview with him, Arrita and Angie Beeks, who operated the party supplies shop next door, were in substantial agreement about one thing: Bruce Koklich was not a nice man.

There was, for example, an ongoing feud over the parking spaces in the rear of the building. Arrita and Angie told Longshore that almost from the day the Koklich business had opened, Bruce had directed his employees to park in their businesses' spaces, instead of his own. "When business owners attempted to talk to him about that practice," Longshore reported, "he became verbally abusive and irate." As a result, the other businesses posted a sign restricting parking to their own customers. Bruce ignored it. Eventually, one of the owners called a tow truck to have Bruce's car towed. Bruce ran out of the office, and after an argument with the tow driver, paid the man $39.50. The tow driver then released the car, and Bruce returned it to the wrong space.

A few hours later, the complainant again called a tow operator. This time, when the car was put on the tow truck, Bruce again emerged, jumped into his car while it was still on the truck, and started the engine. "When he found that the vehicle was secured by chains, he attempted to remove them," Longshore recounted, "but was stopped by the driver, a very large African-American, who warned him that he would use force if Koklich persisted. Koklich again paid the driver thirty-nine dollars and fifty cents to regain custody of his vehicle."

There was another story, even worse: According to LePire and Beeks, an air conditioning repairman was on the roof of the building, and at one point walked across the portion of the roof that belonged to the Koklichs, apparently creating a disturbance. "Bruce came out of the office and began swearing at the repairman," Longshore reported. "As the man descended the ladder, apologizing to Koklich, he fell and sustained head injuries that kept him in a coma for quite some time." A witness later told LePire and Beeks that on his way down, a man had begun shaking the ladder, causing the repairman to fall. No one could identify Bruce as the ladder shaker, however.

This was not a pretty portrait—if one believed Bruce's business neighbors, he was an abusive, violent person with a hair-trigger temper.

Now, the next day, Thursday, August 23, 2001, Sheehy and Davis returned to talk to Arrita about her supposed sighting of Jana on Sunday, having heard this story the day before while they were interviewing Barbara Hauxhurst.

Arrita told the detectives she was pretty sure the woman she'd seen on Sunday *was* Jana. She'd seen Jana many times at the office, and knew that the Koklichs often came to work on Sundays. But when pressed, Arrita admitted that she hadn't seen the woman's face, only her blonde hair—that and the fact that she was driving a white SUV, which had turned out of the parking lot, and headed northbound in the alley. She knew that Jana drove an SUV, so she'd assumed it was Jana. Arrita said that her husband, Allen Radcliffe, had seen the woman before she had.

Arrita now told Sheehy and Davis what she had previously told Longshore—that Bruce was a nasty proposition. She again related the ongoing dispute over the parking spaces, and added that Bruce had once raced through the alley in his car, nearly mowing down Arrita's first husband, Max. After parking his car, Bruce had emerged laughing, Arrita said. On another occasion, she had seen Bruce in the parking lot passionately kissing a woman who was not Jana.

When Sheehy and Davis next talked to Allen Radcliffe, they learned that he wasn't familiar with Jana's face. All he'd seen was a blonde woman, walking across the parking lot, getting into an SUV. The woman he'd seen, Radcliffe said, was between 37 and 40 years old, had medium-length blonde hair, was wearing a short black skirt, a white top, and light-colored heels. The woman also had "muscular legs," Radcliffe recalled. After walking across the parking lot, away from him, the woman had gotten into a "Nissan Pathfinder with gold trim." Then he'd gone back into the salon, idly mentioned what he'd seen to Arrita and, a minute or so later, as they both left the salon, they'd seen an SUV being driven by a blonde woman heading north in the alley.

According to both Allen and Arrita, they'd left their salon about 11 A.M. that Sunday, so this woman had to have been in the parking lot just before that. But according to Bruce, both he and Jana had been in bed at home at about that time. Sheehy and Davis not unreasonably concluded that this must have been a case of mistaken identity.

While this was going on, Martin continued pressing Bruce to identify people who could say they had seen Jana on Sunday afternoon. Bruce told Martin he was sure that their next-door neighbor, Marguerite Grinder, had seen them walking that day. Of all the neighbors, Bruce and Jana probably knew the Grinders best. For one thing, both households employed Consuelo Lopez. Jana had often been in the Grinders' house, and Marguerite occasionally visited the Koklichs in theirs. So Marguerite, unlike Allen Radcliffe, certainly knew what Jana looked like, muscular legs or no.

The trouble was, Marguerite and her husband weren't home. They'd gone to Santa Barbara for several days, leaving just about the time that Bice and Scott had first arrived to investigate on Tuesday.

Now, on Thursday, Bruce somehow managed to track down Marguerite Grinder in Santa Barbara. He left a message for her there, asking her to call him. When Marguerite returned his call, Bruce suggested to her that she had to have seen him and Jana walking on Sunday. Or so Marguerite thought. "You saw me and Jana walk by your house on Saturday or Sunday," Bruce told her. But when Marguerite told Bruce that she hadn't seen them, Bruce didn't insist. "Thank you for your time," he told her, and ended the call.

That evening, Bruce and Paul went to the sheriff's Homicide Bureau offices in Commerce, California. Sheehy and Davis "wanted to get Paul's take on Bruce," Longshore said later, and especially whether Paul thought Bruce was capable of killing Jana. They therefore wanted to interview Paul separately. When Bruce and Paul arrived, Sheehy and Davis escorted Paul into the bureau's coffee room for an informal chat. Bruce stayed in the front portion of the bureau's offices, where Longshore just happened to be manning the telephones.

"It was my turn in the barrel," Longshore said, referring to the telephone duty that all the detectives rotated among themselves. In between calls, Longshore and Bruce conversed casually. Because Clive Martin had already informed the detectives that he was Bruce's lawyer, the discussion had a certain legal dimension. Once a person lawyers up, as Bruce had, detectives aren't supposed to ask questions of potential suspects. But there's nothing that says a detective can't make a record of what a suspect might say voluntarily. This chat between Longshore and Bruce was on the edge of the boundary; Martin said later he had no idea that it had occurred.

By that evening, Longshore had already formed the impression that Bruce was a wanna-be cop. The guns, the badges, the tough talk, all seemed calculated by Bruce to impress the real police. Nothing that came up in the ensuing conversation was to dissuade Longshore from that opinion.

Probing in an off-handed manner, Longshore complimented Bruce on his house, and asked if Bruce wouldn't mind telling him what it might be worth in the real estate market. "It would probably list for about $800,000," Bruce told Longshore.

"It's a nice neighborhood," Longshore said.

"It is a very quiet neighborhood," Bruce agreed. "This thing with Jana is the most excitement they've had in years." Longshore got the idea that this somehow amused Bruce, noting, "he [Bruce] further added, smiling, that he had television cameras outside his residence again that evening."

Longshore said he next told Bruce that, while it was good to hope for the best, with each passing day the chances that Jana had disappeared voluntarily were diminishing. "Without visible emotion," Longshore reported later, "Koklich replied, 'Oh, I know.'"

Longshore turned the subject back to real estate, telling Bruce that, based on his experience, the business was "not without risk to personal safety," especially to female agents who met clients alone. Bruce said he always advised his employees to pre-qualify clients, and never go out by themselves. Longshore asked if Bruce himself had ever had any trouble.

"Oh yeah," Bruce said. "You want to hear about it?" Longshore said he did.

Bruce said he always tried to dress in a suit and tie when he went out into the field, believing that those who saw him might think he was a cop, so they wouldn't try anything with him. A lot of his business, Bruce added, was in "shitty areas," and that meant non-minorities might be a target for crime. Longshore silently inferred that Bruce was a virulent racist.

On one occasion, Bruce continued, he'd been checking a property in Compton, a town heavily populated by minorities. He'd made the mistake of dressing too casually, he said.

"He explained that a black male," Longshore recounted, "apparently deranged, had suddenly appeared and attacked him on the porch. He related that his attacker grabbed him by the front of the shirt and brandished a knife. He added that he 'instinctively' dove off the porch and withdrew a handgun that he habitually carries. He described aiming the weapon at the assailant and commanding, 'Drop the fucking knife, mother-fucker!' The assailant challenged him to shoot him, and Koklich told him he would do just that. He said after several such commands to drop the knife, the assailant fled."

Bruce told Longshore that when he dove off the porch, the attacker still had a grip on his shirt, which was torn almost completely off. Longshore asked what Jana had made of this misadventure, and Bruce told him he hadn't told Jana for several weeks.

He always carried a gun, Bruce continued, even though he didn't have a concealed weapons permit. The sheriff's station in Compton, he said, had told him they'd be willing to issue a permit if he ever asked for one.

Longshore now made a remark about the number of guns Bruce owned. Bruce said he collected guns, and knew how to use them. "He went on to say that he has a friend who is a member of the Long Beach Police Department's Special Weapons and Tactics [SWAT] team. He added that he recently defeated the officer when they engaged in a trap- or skeet-shooting contest armed with shotguns. Koklich said that he had fired a perfect score, adding, 'Can you imagine that? Here's this little real estate agent beating a police officer who trains every day to be a killer.' "

Longshore asked Bruce about the AMOS project. "For several minutes he replied enthusiastically about the millions to be made when the venture becomes operational. He stated that he was very fortunate to have found 'Chris,' who was a computer genius." The foreclosure side of the business was very lucrative, Bruce added, and had the advantage of not having to deal with the homeowners.

As the conversation ended, Longshore realized that Bruce hadn't said anything about Jana's disappearance. In fact, he had asked no questions about the progress of the sheriff's investigation. "He displayed no emotion whatsoever, except for the enthusiasm with which he discussed his encounter with the armed man, the shooting match with the Long Beach police officer, and his business ventures. Koklich's demeanor seemed highly unusual for a man who had reported his wife missing only two days prior to this conversation."

Meanwhile, Sheehy and Davis weren't learning anything very useful from Paul Carpenter. "[We] briefed him on the situation regarding his missing daughter," Sheehy and Davis wrote later in one of their follow-up reports. "Paul said that Bruce and Jana had an ideal marriage and that they got along well together."

Winks

A few hours after Bruce and Paul left, Sheehy and Davis telephoned Bruce at home. Would he mind providing them with a list of properties that he and Jana owned and rented out, as well as properties listed for sale? Not at all, Bruce said. If they stopped by the office on Monday, Bruce said, he'd have a list ready for them.

Later, Chris Botosan would say that Bruce was reluctant to search these properties himself. Chris would say that he'd suggested to Bruce as early as Wednesday, after Jana was reported missing, that they look in each of the listed properties for any sign of Jana. But Bruce didn't want to do this, Chris maintained; he wanted his employees to do it instead, and didn't seem in any great hurry to get it done.

Despite this assertion by Chris, however, it appears that Bruce *did* want a search made of the various properties; in addition to his suggestion that deputies concentrate on finding the car, the detectives' own report of their initial Tuesday night interview says, "He also suggested that investigators check their numerous real estate properties for her whereabouts."

The conflict between Botosan's characterization and the detectives' report was stark.

Despite Bruce's suggestion, going to the properties to look for Jana does not appear to have been a high priority for anyone in the first few days of the investigation, and in retrospect, it seems hard to understand why neither side was in any great rush to check real estate that was under the Koklichs' control, whether rentals or foreclosures listed for sale.

After all, Bruce had already suggested to the detectives that Jana occasionally inspected properties—that was why she was packing a pistol in the missing SUV, to protect her when she was in the "shitty areas." It was entirely possible, at least in theory, that Jana had arisen on the morning of August 20, and driven to one of these properties for some reason, there to have met a fatal end. Although there was no indication on Jana's calendar that any such excursion was planned, that was why the police wanted the property list.

At the same time, if Bruce had killed Jana, what would have prevented him from leaving the body in one of the vacant properties, to be discovered later? The possibility therefore exists that a Bruce who had killed Jana actually *wanted* the deputies to make a search of the properties. A missing Jana did little or nothing to assist Bruce's bottom line: no Jana, no $1 million insurance policy. Besides that, her disappearance had the possible effect of putting a cloud over the legal title to the real estate they jointly owned, worth over $4 million at that point. It was entirely logical that had he killed his wife, Bruce would have left the body in one of these properties to be discovered. He would then gnash his teeth in grief, and blame one of the gangbangers from the "shitty area" for the dirty deed.

Eventually, however, all the properties *were* checked, and no sign of Jana was found. But of course, not all of them were checked for such forensic evidence as blood, fibers, hair and the like—an impossible task without more specific information to go on. It was therefore possible that the body was at one time in one such property, and later moved.

In any event, by Friday morning, August 24, apparently about the time Bruce and Chris were having this conversation about checking the properties at the office, Consuelo Lopez returned to the Koklich house for her regular Friday cleaning day. Both Janie and Paul were at the house. Bruce's mother, Naomi, from Grass Valley, California, had also arrived. Consuelo now asked Janie if she should change the sheets on the king-sized bed in the master bedroom. Janie said she should. That was when Consuelo noticed that one of Jana's pillows was missing—the long, flat one from Scandia Down.

Consuelo descended the stairs to tell Janie and Paul that Jana's pillow was also missing. The Carpenters then called Bruce, and Bruce called the sheriff's department to tell them about Consuelo's latest discovery of a material disappearance. This made Jana, her purse, her cellphone, her car, her gun, the sheets, a towel, the doormat, and her pillow all missing.

The next day, Janie, Chris Botosan, Bruce, his mother, Naomi, his stepbrother Dave Titchenal and Dave's new wife all went out for lunch together. Bruce's family was rallying around him, Dave said later. Still, the gathering was strained.

For one thing, Janie was mystified about the disappearance of Jana's pillow. She knew for a fact that she'd slept on a pillow exactly like the one that was missing on Tuesday night, and that Chris had told her it was his, and had then made off with it. Janie couldn't help but wonder if Chris hadn't actually taken Jana's pillow. And if he had, did that mean that Chris had something to do with Jana's

Jana Carpenter Koklich lived in this Long Beach, CA, house with her husband, Bruce David Koklich, until her disappearance in August 2001. *Photo by Carlton Smith*

Bruce and Jana's house backed up to a golf course. Their neighbor across the street, Donna Baker, told authorities she noticed Jana's SUV parked on the left side of the Koklichs' garage—the side Bruce usually parked on—on the morning of either Sunday, August 19, or Monday, August 20, 2001. *Los Angeles County Sheriff's Department photo*

Bruce and Jana ran a successful real estate business out of this store in Long Beach, CA. Chris Botosan worked out of the office as well, consulting on Bruce's side project to develop AMOS, a software program that would help banks keep track of foreclosed real estate. *Photo by Carlton Smith*

Bruce, Jana, and their employees shared this parking lot with other businesses in the shopping center. *Photo by Carlton Smith*

The Koklichs ran their real estate business out of this shopping center. They did most of their business with banks, including Wells Fargo, which had an office in the same building. An arrow is drawn indicating where the owner of a neighboring beauty salon claims she saw a woman who looked like Jana driving a white SUV out of the back parking lot. *Los Angeles County Sheriff's Department photo*

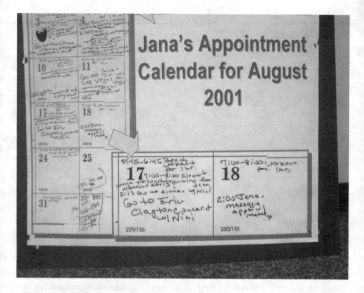

Jana was notoriously organized and lived by her schedule. The schedule indicates she had lunch with Bruce and Chris Botosan on the Friday before her disappearance. However, she did not keep any of her appointments that weekend. Bruce claimed they had both decided to have a quiet weekend at home to recover from a hectic work schedule, but friends and family said such blatant disregard for appointments and phone calls was out of character for Jana. *Los Angeles County Sheriff's Department photo*

Consuelo Lopez, the Koklichs' housekeeper, said sheets and a pillow were missing from the couple's bedroom following Jana's disappearance. *Los Angeles County Sheriff's Department photo*

Authorities searched the area around these oil drills for Jana's body. Bruce was familiar with the location of various oil fields around Long Beach, CA, because he held a series of jobs with Powerine Oil Company, including one in which he maintained pumping derricks. *Photo by Carlton Smith*

MISSING

JANA CARPENTER KOKLICH

California
3SHM565

She was last seen on Monday morning
August 20, 2001

She drives a white 96 Nissan Pathfinder CA. Lic. # 3SHM565
If you have any information that can lead to finding Jana
Please contact the Long Beach Police Dept. at
(562) 570-2500, your local police station
or the following numbers
(562) 818-5007 (562) 427-2718 (562) 424-0333

Friends and family of Jana Carpenter Koklich posted this flyer in the days following her disappearance. Bruce claimed he had seen her on Monday morning, April 20, but Jana did not keep appointments or return phone calls the entire weekend. No one but Bruce saw her after her friend Nini dropped her off at home following an Eric Clapton concert early on the morning of Saturday, August 18, 2001. *Los Angeles County Sheriff's Department photo*

Police found Jana's car in a garage in this alley. Once people in the neighborhood realized it was the same car they had seen parked out on the street a week earlier, they began to worry their children would be accused of involvement in Jana's disappearance. Reverend H. A. Bryant of the Great Deliverance Church of Christ, a respected figure in the neighborhood, acted as intermediary between the neighbors and the media and police. *Los Angeles County Sheriff's Department photo*

Jana's 1996 white Nissan Pathfinder was found abandoned in this garage. The car had been stolen and hidden after someone left it parked in a neighborhood not far from Bruce and Jana's office. Neighborhood kids claimed the windows were rolled down when they found the car, and they stole Jana's purse from the front seat. *Los Angeles County Sheriff's Department photo*

disappearance? Had Chris been worried that the pillow might contain some sort of evidence and walked off with it to protect himself, or someone else?

Dave also picked up a strange vibe from Chris. "He was very, very nervous. Weird. Twitchy," Dave said later. "He couldn't look you in the eye." Chris's conversation was disjointed, Dave recalled. "There were a lot of abrupt non sequiturs." Dave's new bride, who was sitting next to Chris, was repulsed when, for some reason, he kept touching her. "He gave her the creeps," Dave said. Chris seemed oblivious to her discomfort.

By that afternoon, Janie was more suspicious than ever that there was something off about Chris. The salient facts seemed to fit together like a pillow and its case: Chris arrives on the scene, talks Bruce into taking some sort of computer flyer that seemed to be costing a lot of money, then Jana disappears. Chris was in the middle of all these events. Bruce's lawyer Clive Martin was also wondering about Chris. "I got to thinking somewhere along the line that maybe he knew more than he was saying," Martin later recalled.

But by this time, Chris was to say later, he was beginning to wonder, based on Bruce's behavior from Monday forward, whether Bruce was in fact responsible for Jana's disappearance. If that were the case, he worried, the police were going to be all over Bruce—and AMOS. In fact, they already were. That wasn't good for AMOS, it wasn't good for Chris, and it certainly wasn't good for NABUCO and its coffee-shop–meeting, paper-passing people from Las Vegas. That may have been one reason Chris seemed so nervous, unable to look people in the eye.

On the same day, Sergeant Richard Longshore was conducting a rather unusual email correspondence with an East Coast acquaintance named Kellee. He'd known her for several years, and in the course of their friendship, Longshore had discovered that Kellee thought she might be psychic.

"When I first came to Homicide," Longshore said later, "I did some reading, and in the bible on homicide investigations, written by this ex-NYPD guy, there's a section on psychics. It talks about how the FBI's used a couple of them, and why you can't discount them, for a variety of reasons. He says the psychics the FBI use sometimes say they can actually feel the wounds of the victims."

Longshore now decided to try Kellee out. Who knew? Maybe they might get lucky.

"I told her a little about our case, that we had a missing woman, and the husband was very wealthy. That's about it. So she wrote back and she said, 'You're going to find the car in some place dark. It's green. And there'll be kids playing outside.'"

That wasn't as specific as Longshore had been hoping for. He politely thanked Kellee for her contribution, and thought no more of it.

On Monday morning, at 10:15 A.M., Sheehy picked up the list of the Koklich rental properties. At the same time, they talked to Chris, asking him again what he'd done over the previous few days. This time Chris told the detectives that he'd spent most of the weekend at his apartment with Melinda McBride, who had been at his apartment until Monday morning, when he'd left for the Koklich office. It seemed that Chris had a solid alibi for the times Jana might have disappeared, assuming that this could be verified by Melinda, who Chris indicated he'd met through Nini Angelini.

After this, Sheehy and Davis went to interview Nini. This interview with Jana's good friend only increased their suspicion of Bruce.

For one thing, Nini didn't think that Jana had really gone walking with Bruce twice over the previous weekend. Jana had recently been suffering from shin splints, Nini said. The trainer Dean Costales had advised her to stay off hard surfaces like sidewalks for a while. Jana was so dedicated to her exercise regimen, she was unlikely to have ignored Dean's advice, Nini said.

The night she'd gone over to the house, Monday, Nini said, she'd noticed that Jana's overnight bag was still in the closet, along with her workout clothes, cosmetics case and sneakers. If Jana had left voluntarily, she would have taken these things. Nini also told the detectives that she'd seen what she thought were spots on the carpet in the master bedroom that night—maybe blood.

The detectives asked if Jana and Bruce had been arguing over money. Nini recalled that when Jana wanted to buy a Lexus, Bruce had said she didn't need a new car. Nini described Bruce as a tightwad.

What about other women? Nini said that Jana never spoke of these things to her, but suggested that the detectives talk to Patti Endley. Patti, Nini said, had told her that Bruce had once been sued by a former female employee for sexual harassment. Detectives, however, would later determine that Patti's information about a lawsuit was mistaken.

Bruce was extremely controlling of Jana, Nini added, pointing to the Lexus and rafting trip episodes as examples. Bruce also seemed to begrudge the money that Jana spent on her fitness training. He had come once to Dean Costales' workout studio, Nini said, where he'd told Dean that he worked out at home, and explained his own exercise regimen. Dean had mildly corrected him for his technique. After that, Nini said, Bruce had stayed away from Dean's studio. She thought that Bruce didn't want Jana to see another man tell him what to do. She thought Bruce was intimidated by Dean, or at least jealous.

It was clear to Nini that both Sheehy and Davis at this
point believed that Bruce had done something to Jana.
And indeed, according to Davis' interview notes, it appears that the detectives told her they had already ruled
out Dean Costales and Nini's boyfriend, Giani, as possible suspects. That left Bruce, Chris, and the wild card: the
possibility that Jana had been kidnaped, or carjacked.

As it had been for a week now, the key to the mystery
was still in finding the car.

About the same time that Sheehy and Davis were talking
to Nini, a man who owned a block of low-income apartment houses in the Long Beach suburb of Signal Hill
found himself checking the garages of the apartment
block in the rear of the property. This was something he
did periodically, mostly because the garages had doors,
which permitted people to stash stuff in them temporarily, sometimes stolen stuff, much to the owner's annoyance. The property owner had last checked the garages
the previous Thursday, August 23, and the ones that were
supposed to be empty were in fact empty. But on this
early Monday afternoon, the apartment owner raised the
door of one garage and discovered a white Nissan
Pathfinder SUV parked neatly inside.

At that point, he did what he always did: He telephoned the Signal Hill police, and asked them to send a
tow truck over to haul the unauthorized vehicle away.
The apartment owner provided the license plate number
of the SUV. At that point, someone at the Signal Hill Police Department did exactly the right thing and checked
the list of wanted cars, and soon discovered that the
plate, at least, belonged to a 1996 Nissan Pathfinder that
belonged to a reported missing person.

By late that afternoon, a team of sheriff's deputies and
Signal Hill officers were out in force in the alley behind

the apartment, looking for evidence relating to the appearance of Jana's SUV in the garage. A cadaver dog was brought in to look for any corpses in the neighborhood, to no avail. Longshore had just finished talking to Nini's boyfriend, Giani, when he got the word: Jana's long-sought SUV had finally been found—without Jana, her purse or her cellphone.

The gun was missing, too.

Longshore arrived on the scene about 5 P.M. The first thing he noticed was that there were kids playing in the alley. The second thing he saw was that the door to the garage had been down, and it was painted blue-green. And the third was that, with the door down, the garage interior was pitch black; it had no electricity. It seemed to Longshore that Kellee the psychic had been right on the money.

The plan was to remove the SUV as carefully as possible, and take it to a secure garage, where the sheriff's criminalists could go over it in better light, and under controlled conditions. Longshore helped a couple of deputies push the SUV out of the garage, where it was winched up onto the bed of a truck, and driven away. None of the residents present seemed to have any idea when the SUV was put into the garage, or who did it.

Longshore headed over to the Lakewood station, planning to tell Bruce as soon as possible that Jana's car had finally been recovered. He didn't want Bruce to hear about it on the news. But once he was back at the station, Longshore had another call.

This was another woman who said she'd had an unpleasant encounter with Bruce, and as with Rosie Ritchie, the subject was sex. Longshore recognized the name of the caller. It was Michelle McWhirter, whose name had originally been provided to Longshore by Rosie. Now Michelle was calling Longshore before Longshore could call her.

Michelle said that she, too, worked in the real estate field in Long Beach. Some years earlier, she said, she'd received a telephone call from Bruce. Bruce had asked her to meet him at a vacant property in Long Beach. Once she'd arrived, she told Longshore, Bruce had asked her inside the house. At that point, Michelle said, Bruce told her that he had a low sperm count.

"And he wanted to know if I could help him out," Michelle said later. "I didn't understand." Then it was explained. "He just asked if I could give him blow jobs."

Michelle was taken aback by Bruce's crude approach. If Bruce had a problem with his sperm count, maybe he should be talking to Jana, she suggested. "I told him maybe there were things that could be done," to improve it. Bruce didn't seem to understand that Michelle was offended, trying to be polite, but wanting to slap his face. At that point, Bruce offered to pay her $200 for each "blow job."

"I just told him," Michelle recounted, "that, you know, that's not going to happen, and . . . he needed to seek other measures and that I just didn't want to have this conversation anymore. We just kind of ended it." But Bruce asked·her not to say anything to Jana. He didn't want this to get back to her, he told Michelle, "because he loved her very much."

Michelle left the property, and subsequently told her boss about the ugly scene. The boss told her to keep quiet about it—Bruce was a big wheel in real estate, and not someone to offend. Michelle tried to put the episode out of her mind, but the next week, after she attended a breakfast meeting of real estate people, she emerged into the parking lot to find Bruce standing next to her car. He gave her an envelope and asked her not to open it until he was gone. Then she was to read the note inside and check out the contents.

After he drove off, she opened the envelope. Inside was $1,000 in cash and a letter on a medical center letterhead detailing Bruce's sperm count.

"I was kind of freaked out," Michelle said. "Nervous. I called my boyfriend and told him. I told my boyfriend's friend, who also knew Bruce, and then I told the three owners of my company. I wanted them to know that it had happened in case—I don't know—anything ever was brought up. I just wanted them to know for work reasons."

Michelle said she kept the envelope for a few days, trying to figure out how to handle the situation. Two or three days later, Bruce called her, leaving a message.

"He just wanted to know if I had thought about what he had asked any further, and if I could get back to him." Michelle called him back. "I told him that this was not going to happen," she said.

Bruce asked if he could have the money back. Michelle gave it to him.

Days later, she said, when she had to go to the Koklich office, Bruce was still friendly with her. "He just winked at me," she said.

Bumps in the Night

After taking this call from Michelle McWhirter, Longshore drove to the Koklich house. He arrived about 9:30 P.M. Bruce was there, along with Janie and Paul. Longshore didn't know it, but that night at the house, Paul had been meeting with Jeff Baird, his attorney. Feeling that his death might come soon from the cancer, which had spread to his colon, Paul had asked Baird to make some changes to his will. This was a document that left a substantial part of his estate—whatever was left of it, which wasn't much after all the trials of the early nineties—to Jana. Now, since Jana was missing, Paul wanted to make sure that Bruce would be recognized as Jana's heir to anything that Jana had left her father.

By the time Longshore got there, it appears that Baird had already left the house. He sat with Bruce, Janie and Paul in the living room.

"We found the car," Longshore said.

"Oh shit, oh shit, that's great!" Bruce said.

Longshore waited, but Bruce didn't ask. "She's not in it," he finally said. Bruce didn't say anything to this, and didn't ask where the car had been found. Janie asked, though, and Longshore told her.

"Oh, that's a shitty area," Bruce piped up.

Longshore asked Bruce if Jana would have had any reason to be in the area where the car was found—if, for example, the Koklichs had owned property there, or if they'd had listings. Bruce said he could think of no reason why Jana would have been driving in the area.

The rest of the conversation was short and strained. Longshore later remembered that Bruce asked no questions about the investigation—what progress detectives might have made in trying to find Jana. After a few minutes he left.

Outside, Longshore called Nini on his cellphone. "And Nini, of all the people I had spoken to, was the most distraught about Jana's disappearance," Longshore recalled. "I didn't want her to see this on the news, so I called her to let her know." Nini burst into tears, thanked Longshore and hung up.

A few minutes later, Bruce called Nini himself.

"They found the car," he told her. "The cops didn't tell me. I had to see it on the news."

The next day, Tuesday, August 28, the Long Beach *Press-Telegram* put the Koklich story on the second page: KOKLICH'S SUV FOUND. When a newspaper begins referring to a possible crime victim by one name, that's a sure sign that the story is beginning to get legs. The television people were pushing the story hard, as well.

At that same time, Longshore was at the secure towing facility, going over the Pathfinder with criminalists Stephen Schliebe and Christine Pinto, along with fingerprint expert Fred Roberts. The four made a visual inspection of the SUV and noticed some stains on the exterior.

Schliebe tested those stains to see if they were blood; the tests were negative. Under the left-side wheel wells, the inspection discovered some "rice-like" material, as Schliebe put it later, that seemed to have been cast up by the tire. He guessed that this was material that had originally been in the alley or the garage.

Roberts now fingerprinted the exterior and interior of the car, using a sticky silver powder that left streaks of gray across the surfaces. He found only two useable prints, a partial palm print from the passenger-side window, and a fingerprint from an audiocassette, *The Gift of Health*, from the SUV's center console. That was it—whoever had possession of the SUV had either wiped it down, or more likely, simply hadn't left any fingerprints behind.

Inside the car, however, all four noticed a small feather next to the driver's seat, and a second in the rear cargo area. It looked as if the two feathers might have come from a feather pillow. When they looked closer, they could also see what appeared to be an area of discoloration on the cargo area carpet.

Schliebe tested the discolored area, which appeared to be about 14 by 25 inches or so. This time the test for blood was positive.

At about the same time the forensic people were examining the SUV, Chris Botosan was on the telephone to Detective Davis. Chris told Davis that Bruce seemed reluctant to make the search of the properties. According to Chris, Bruce had told him he wanted the Koklich office staff to make this search. "I thought it was a relevant fact," Chris said later. He also told Davis that when they'd gone over to the house to look for Jana on the Monday she'd been reported missing, Bruce hadn't seemed to want him to go along.

This represented a significant development in the case

against Bruce Koklich. With this call, Chris embarked on his eventual role as the detectives' spy on Bruce, inside the Koklich camp. It would take Bruce months to figure out that the man he thought was his close friend, his "partner," was in fact the cops' best source, their most prized informant on what Bruce was doing and thinking. From this point forward, over the ensuing months, Chris made numerous telephone calls to Sheehy and Davis, and responded to calls they made to him. Eventually, in fact, Bruce's lawyers would assert that Chris had effectively become an agent of the police—and if that were so, it would represent an illegal form of contact between the investigators and a suspect that they then knew had legal representation. But the investigators would say that since Bruce hadn't been formally arrested, or even given Miranda warnings, they were entitled to use Botosan, and any others, as potential sources of information on Bruce's behavior. To that point, in fact, Bruce had never invoked his rights under Miranda, which would have limited any questions the police could put to him, even through "an agent," to occasions when Bruce's lawyer was present.

Later that morning, the investigators went back to the Koklich house. Now that they had two partial fingerprints, they wanted to take the fingerprints of those who might have been reasonably in contact with the SUV. Bruce, Janie, Chris and Consuelo were all fingerprinted. None of their prints later matched the ones found by Roberts on the SUV. It was about that time that the detectives also realized they had no fingerprints for Jana. It appears that no one then or later thought to contact the California Department of Real Estate for copies of her fingerprints; state law requires anyone licensed to sell or broker real estate in California to file their prints as part of the licensing process. As a result, the fingerprints from the SUV were never matched with Jana, and in fact, never identified.

Longshore now called the Koklich house from the towing yard. He told Sheehy and Davis about the two feathers recovered from the SUV. He thought the feathers found in the car might match feathers in pillows still at the Koklich house, and wanted Sheehy and Davis to get samples of those feathers. They now asked Bruce to sign a consent-to-search form authorizing them to take feathers from the pillows, and Bruce signed it. Later, all the feathers were sent to a laboratory in Oregon in a fruitless attempt to match the SUV feathers with the ones in the various pillows. Unaccountably, however, neither of Chris's pillows were ever examined.

That day, Sheehy and Davis pressed Bruce to agree to take a polygraph test. Bruce first said he was more than willing to take one. The test was scheduled for the following day, August 29. But when Clive Martin heard about this, he put a stop to it.

"Why?" Janie wanted to know, according to Martin. "I'm a psychologist, and I know they work. Why won't you let him take a test?" By turning the test down, Janie indicated, Bruce was only continuing to fuel the detectives' suspicion of him, whereas, when he took the test and passed it, the detectives could go on to more promising suspects.

But Martin said he never wanted any of his clients taking law enforcement polygraph tests. Bruce called the detectives back and said that Martin wanted to review the questions. The detectives agreed to send them to Martin, and tentatively rescheduled the test for Thursday, August 30.

Meanwhile, Bruce's employees Laura Roman and Albert Canedo had gone to the neighborhood where the SUV had been found, passing out flyers on Jana's disappearance. They'd asked Bruce if it was all right, and he'd told them to go ahead.

While passing out the flyers, Laura and Albert encountered two young boys who told them of seeing the car in the neighborhood the week before. They encountered a woman named Nicole, who told them she'd seen two men holding a woman down in the rear of a Jeep on the previous Friday or Saturday night, and another woman who used the name Star, who told them that she knew of a man who claimed he'd seen a white man in a white shirt drive a white Pathfinder through the alley late one night the week before.

But "Star" and "Nicole" were not the only people in the neighborhood talking about the SUV. The evening of August 28, the recovery of the car was prominently featured on the evening news, along with the mystery of Jana's whereabouts. That was when several neighborhood mothers realized that the car that had been parked on the street the week before—the one all the kids had been talking about—was in fact the same car the cops had been looking for: The car, the TV was saying, might have something to do with a possible kidnaping and murder. All the mothers knew right away this was a potentially big problem. Now that the police had the car, they would be checking it for fingerprints. It was only a matter of time before the police came knocking at their doors, demanding to talk to their kids. And at that point, who knew what would happen? The odds were very good that someone's kid would be arrested, jailed, maybe even charged with carjacking or murder.

And they were right. As Longshore put it later, it was just a matter of pure luck that the car was found alone, in the garage. "Frankly, if a patrol unit had stopped that car, and it came out as belonging to a missing person, gone under suspicious circumstances, and they found her purse, they found a gun, they found blood in the car, that kid would have been charged," he said. "There's no doubt in my mind. And then it would have been up to a jury to decide."

These parents decided they needed to tell the cops what had happened—and in such a way that the police would understand that none of their kids had anything to do with what happened to the missing woman, or even the abrupt appearance of the SUV in the neighborhood the week before. They needed a go-between, someone who had the respect of the authorities, and who could help make sure the kids weren't arrested and framed for the crime.

They decided to call Reverend H. A. Bryant of the Great Deliverance Church of God in Christ. Bryant was well-known in the neighborhood, and highly respected. They told him that if he couldn't get the sheriff's department to grant immunity for any petty crimes, their kids weren't going to say anything to anyone.

On Wednesday, August 29, Bryant found the tip-line number that had been published in the paper, asking for information on Jana's disappearance, and called it. He told the operator that he had information about the missing woman's car.

"At first they didn't want to talk to me," Bryant said later. But when Bryant mentioned the words *purse* and *cellphone* and *gun*, he got the department's immediate attention. "See," he said, "that information hadn't been in the paper."

The deputies on the telephone wanted to know how Bryant knew these facts. But Bryant insisted: The sheriff's department had to agree not to charge the kids with any crimes.

"Most of these youngsters had run-ins with the police before," Bryant said.

Sheehy, Davis and Longshore came to the church. They readily agreed not to investigate or arrest the kids for any petty crimes that might have occurred. The detectives first met with the mothers, Bryant recalled, and when there still seemed to be some reluctance to give details about what had happened with the car, he took them aside.

"Look," he told them, "there's a person missing. The police aren't interested in anything other than finding out where this person might be." Bryant told the mothers the police wanted to find out where the purse, the cellphone and the gun were.

Over a period of hours, shuttling back and forth between groups, the details came out: how Rayray and Freeman had taken the purse and phone, but left the gun, how they had split the cash, and thrown the purse away. "We need the purse," the detectives told Bryant.

"I'll see what I can do," Bryant said. He went back to the mothers and cajoled them some more. It took some time, but by the next day, he learned that the purse had been thrown onto the roof of a three-story building.

"I know where it is," Bryant told the detectives. "I'll take you there." There was actually only one three-story building in the neighborhood. Bryant led the detectives down the street to the building.

Sheehy now called for a fire truck, preferably one with a ladder long enough to reach the roof. The Long Beach Fire Department was glad to assist. "They put a ladder up along the south side of the building," Sheehy said later. "I gave the fire captain a camera to take some photographs of the purse if it was in fact on the roof, which he did, and he retrieved the purse and turned it over to me along with the camera."

There in the purse was Jana's wallet, along with her driver's license, checkbook and numerous credit cards. That seemed to prove that wherever she was, she hadn't gone there willingly. Now they needed to find her cellphone and the gun. They asked Bryant to probe some more; it was clear by now that the only way the deputies

were going to get information from the neighborhood was
by using Bryant as an intermediary.

"I'll see what I can do," Bryant said.

The sheriff's department soon held a press conference,
heralding the recovery of the purse. But none of the news
stories broadcast by the television stations mentioned
Bryant's role in helping make the recovery. Instead, the
prevailing tone was that the detectives, by dint of superior
sleuthing, had managed to find the purse in a high-crime
area.

"The neighborhood was outraged," Bryant recalled.
"People kept asking me, 'How come they didn't say anything about you, Reverend Bryant? What's going on with
the police department?'" People in the neighborhood
were upset that the sheriff's department hadn't given the
neighborhood any credit for coming forward with the
critical information. The fact that the SUV had been
planted on Lewis Avenue, "so that hopefully some person
of color would be blamed for her disappearance," as
Bryant put it, made people wish that the detectives had
given the whole story to the news media—that rather than
carjacking Jana, the kids were helping to solve the crime.

The same day that Jana's purse was reclaimed from the
apartment roof, Longshore contacted his seeming psychic source, Kellee on the East Coast. He told her about
the recovery of the SUV two days before from the darkened blue-green garage near kids playing in an alley.

"So I email her back and say, 'Hey, you did a great job.
What else do you see?'" Longshore recounted later. "And
she says, 'Well, the body is going to be someplace next to
a cemetery. It's smelly, it's dirty, there's strange smells,
and she's under something, but she can see the sky.
There's a road that leads away from it.'"

There was one such area very close to where the SUV

had been found, Longshore, Sheehy and Davis realized: a very large, brush-covered field that was the site of numerous oil pumps, left over from the era decades before when Signal Hill had been one of the most productive oil areas on the West Coast. Hadn't Bruce once worked as a mechanic for an oil company? He had. And was this field on a direct line between where the car had been recovered, and the Koklich house? It was.

Arrangements were made to begin a comprehensive search of the oil field the following morning, August 31.

The detectives sent over proposed lie detector questions: Did you last see your wife in bed? Was this on Monday morning? Did you harm your wife? Do you know where she is now? Do you know what happened to her?

Chris knew that Bruce was scheduled to take a polygraph. That night he called Bruce at home to see how it had gone. "He said he didn't have time to talk about it and hung up," Chris said later. The next morning, Thursday, August 30, just as the purse was being recovered from the roof, Martin had cancelled the sheriff's lie detector test permanently.

Davis now called Chris Botosan, wanting to know how Bruce was acting. Chris told Davis that he'd been thinking about Bruce's behavior since the day they'd reported Jana missing. Chris said that he'd concluded that Bruce wasn't acting the way a person whose beloved wife was missing should act. He told Davis about Bruce's supposed remark, "There, I cried for you on national television," after Chris had confronted him on his demeanor the previous week, and about Bruce's reaction to his question about the cancelled lie detector test.

Davis asked Chris for more. Chris provided it.

Chris told Davis that at first he had thought Bruce was "well-financed," but now he wasn't so sure. He said that some people who knew Bruce told him that Bruce was ruthless as a businessman, that he would "bleed people dry." At night, Chris said, Bruce would sit alone and brood and drink. The disappearance of Jana, Chris added, had severely damaged AMOS's prospects: they had been on the verge of signing GMAC, Household Finance and Bank of America as AMOS clients when Jana had vanished. Now, all these deals were up in the air because of the notoriety.

It seems clear, then, in retrospect, that by August 30, 2001, Chris was definitely trying to put a lot of distance between Bruce and himself, while at the same time making himself essential to the detectives' investigation of Bruce, all without letting on to Bruce that he'd switched sides.

That morning, too, it appears, Sheehy and Davis decided to put more pressure on Bruce. Somehow news reporters learned that Bruce had cancelled two lie detector tests. This was the police equivalent of throwing bloody chum in the water: it was tantamount to saying that the sheriff's detectives were suspicious of him. From this point forward, media coverage of Bruce would turn more and more skeptical.

Apparently as a result of these leaks, reporters descended on the Koklich offices that afternoon. Bruce declined to speak with them, but Janie came out and talked for him.

What about this lie detector test? someone asked. Why had Bruce cancelled two of them?

"He's been given a lot of advice by a lot of friends, some of them . . . in the law field, and even law enforcement," Janie said, in an apparent reference to Danny Molinar of the Long Beach department, "and has heard all kinds of horror stories about how they use tricky questions." That's why he'd decided not to take the test, she said. Asked if she and Paul considered Bruce a suspect in Jana's disappearance, Janie said they did not.

But if Janie and Paul were keeping the faith, Bruce himself was fearing the worst. The next day he told Chris that he expected to be arrested at any moment. He was getting bail money together, Bruce said.

When the news reported that the police even then were searching an oil field in Signal Hill for Jana's body, Bruce was reputed—by Chris, anyway—to have said, "They'll never find her there."

Bruce later said he'd never said anything like this to Chris, and even Detective Davis, to whom Chris was now relaying information, said that Chris had never told him that. But if Bruce actually said this, it certainly made it sound like he had every reason to know.

The afternoon before the oil field search, Sheehy and Davis had located another key eyewitness—actually an "earwitness." This was Catherine Eva Hansen, who happened to be the sister of Marguerite Grinder, Bruce and Jana's next-door neighbor. There at the Comfort Care rest home in Cerritos, California, Sheehy and Davis heard Ms. Hansen, who was 84, describe the noises she and Marguerite had heard next door at the Koklich house late Friday night, two days before Jana's supposed disappearance. Catherine had been visiting her sister in Lakewood at the time.

Marguerite, it appears, had informed the detectives that not only had she not seen Bruce and Jana walking on Sunday, she and her sister had heard strange noises coming from the Koklich house at some point during the evening. She thought it sounded like someone moving furniture.

Now the detectives were trying to verify this information. "She [Catherine] also recalled hearing strange noises coming from the Koklich residence next door,"

Sheehy reported later. "The noises went on for six or seven minutes, and it sounded to her like an argument between a man and a woman. She said it sounded like a man and a woman were quarreling. She said they [Hansen and Grinder] were watching a movie on the western cable channel when they heard this. She did not remember the title of the movie. She said they were in Marguerite's rumpus room watching TV when she heard the noises. She did not accompany Marguerite to Santa Barbara on her trip and had no further information."

But together with Marguerite's story, the detectives thought they now had two witnesses who could say that there had been a possible violent struggle in the Koklich house two days before Bruce had actually reported Jana missing.

Steal Me

The oil field was a very large, hilly patch of brown dirt, scraggly bushes and patches of yellowed, spiky grass that insisted on barbing the searchers with annoying stickers as they scrambled over the ground. Altogether, there were about thirty or forty praying mantis–like pumps scattered over the mile-square area, many of them surrounded by lattice-like fences to keep people out. Just south of the area was a large cemetery.

The search began just after 8 A.M., and involved about forty people, assisted by the cadaver-trained dog, Brindie. The searchers were told to keep an eye out for bedsheets, a towel and a long, flat pillow. The work was hot and dusty. All around them, the long necks of the oil pumps continued their slow, rhythmic rising and falling, silent mechanical witnesses to secrets they could never share. Whatever had happened, if anything, in this scrubby patch of dirt, the squeak of the pump arms was the only audible testimony left behind.

By mid-afternoon, the patch had been thoroughly examined; and if Jana Carpenter Koklich had ever been there, she was certainly gone now.

• • •

The morning had begun unpleasantly for Bruce. The
Long Beach newspaper had clearly turned on him. FIELDS
TO BE SCOURED FOR KOKLICH, the paper headlined. And
in the second paragraph, the paper reported that Bruce
had cancelled the sheriff's polygraph test.

"By virtue of the fact he did not take the test, it does not
assist us in eliminating him as a potential suspect," Lieutenant Peavy of the sheriff's department told the newspaper. The paper noted that Jana had missed her appointments
on the weekend before she was reported missing, and that
she hadn't returned numerous telephone calls made to her
over the same weekend. The paper also reported that Bruce
had claimed that he'd last seen Jana on Monday morning.
The implication was clear: Bruce was lying about when
he'd last seen his wife, for possibly ominous reasons.

Finally, the paper reported that Bruce had refused to
make any statements the day before, leaving Janie to explain why he'd cancelled the lie detector tests.

Given the turn of the paper's coverage, it perhaps
wasn't surprising that Bruce would remark to Chris Botosan that he expected to be arrested at any moment, and
that he was assembling bail money. And in that context,
Bruce's supposed statement about the oil field—"they
aren't going to find her there"—could be interpreted as
an extension of his denial that he had anything to do with
his wife's disappearance, another way of saying that in
looking at him, the police were in the wrong area entirely.

Detective Davis seemed to concede this as a possibility later that afternoon. "We're kind of back to square
one," he told Paul Young, a reporter for the *Press-Telegram*.
"We'll go back to our clues and to the people who called
in and see where we can go from there." When Young
asked why that particular area had been searched, Davis
replied that it was a logical area to look for a body, given

its proximity to where the SUV had been found. Young called both Janie and Bruce, but Janie declined to say anything, and Bruce couldn't be reached.

Meanwhile, Reverend Bryant was still trying to recover the missing gun. He returned to the mothers, who in turn pressed the kids. People were still miffed about the sheriff's department's failure to give any credit to the neighborhood for the recovery of the purse. Eventually, however, Bryant learned that the gun had been sold, and while the buyer was willing to turn it over, he didn't want to be out the $150 he'd paid for the piece.

"Well, I'll put up the money," Bryant said. "I'll leave it in the statue that's in my yard. Whoever has the gun can get the money and leave the gun in its place."

On the evening of September 4, Bryant put the cash in an envelope, and put the envelope inside the statue. The next morning, he came back and discovered the money was gone. Inside the statue, wrapped in a sock, was a SIG Sauer .380 semiautomatic pistol. The ammunition clip had been removed, and emptied of bullets.

Bryant called the detectives. As it happened, Sheehy and Davis were in court, attempting to get approval for a search warrant they wanted to serve on Bruce at home.

"They said, 'We're in court right now, we can't talk.' So I said, fine," Bryant recalled. He decided to call a press conference. He wanted to make sure the neighborhood got the credit this time. "I called all the TV stations," Bryant said. "I called the *Press-Telegram*, the *L.A. Times*. I didn't tell anyone what it was about."

The only media representative to show up was the *Press-Telegram*'s Paul Young.

"Paul, you're going to get an exclusive," Bryant told the reporter. "I have the gun the police are looking for in the Koklich case."

"What?" Young asked.

Now Bryant produced the SIG Sauer, which he had placed in a clear plastic envelope. Young called his desk and told them to send a photographer to the church right away.

The next morning every television station in town was at the church. The detectives were right behind them. This time they were willing to give all the credit to Bryant and the neighborhood. "The gun is a substantial piece of the puzzle," Lieutenant Peavy said.

Finding the gun seemed to have stimulated Bruce to go public again. He began accepting calls from reporters, saying he hoped the recovered gun would help the detectives find Jana. "I'm pretty depressed," he told Paul Young. "I don't know what I'm going to do without my wife. We were very close. I still have some prayer that she's alive."

And as for those who were speculating that he'd had something to do with Jana's disappearance, Bruce was dismissive.

"Obviously, these people don't know anything about our relationship. We did everything together for almost twenty years. Most people describe our relationship as a textbook relationship."

A "textbook relationship"? That made it sound like Bruce had been studying up on how to describe his marriage as if he were about to be given a test.

Which, in a way, he was.

Beginning September 4, in fact, the sheriff's department had put Bruce under covert surveillance. Who knew—if Bruce had killed Jana and hidden the body, was it possible that he might lead a tail to its location? Or— did Bruce have a girlfriend on the side?

These and other considerations now dominated the thinking of the sheriff's detectives. When they stepped back to look at the whole picture, everyone was struck by the way Rayray and the others had discovered the car. The detectives were convinced that Bruce himself had left the car on Lewis Avenue in the expectation that some-one would get into it, drive it off, and soon be arrested as a violent carjacker, and suspect number one in Jana's dis-appearance.

"We know he planted the car," Longshore said later. "He's a racist. He's very anti–African American. So he planted that car, with the gun near the seat, the purse on the seat—all he didn't do was put a flag on it saying 'Steal Me.'"

It was only when someone discovered that the car was hot—red hot—that it wound up in the garage. That, and the fact that Reverend Bryant was around to separate the sheep from the goats, so to speak, were the only things that prevented Bruce from successfully sending the de-tectives off on a wild goose chase after a carjacker who did not exist, at least according to Longshore.

And if it was Bruce who'd left the car on Lewis Av-enue with its virtual "Steal Me" sign, that meant that he had certainly killed his wife.

The evening of the same day that Reverend Bryant turned the pistol over to detectives, the sheriff's depart-ment was back at the Koklich house. This time they had a search warrant.

Blood Drops

The warrant was served about 8:30 P.M. on Wednesday night, September 5. Bruce and Janie were both at the house. Unlike the consent searches that had been made earlier, this one would take place whether Bruce liked it or not.

Ever since the rear of Jana's SUV had tested positive for blood, the detectives had wanted to get back inside the Koklich house. It seemed like a logical thing to do—blood in the back of the SUV indicated that a body had been there in the past. Given that the kids of Lewis Avenue had been cleared, and that the SUV appeared to have been planted in the neighborhood, the next most likely spot to look for blood was in the Koklich bedroom. True, criminalist Christine Pinto had tested the carpet there for blood on the first evening of the investigation two weeks earlier and had found none, but hadn't Nini said she'd noticed some drops on the carpet during the Monday night gathering?

This time, the investigators would use their secret weapon in the search for blood—luminol. A concoction of chemicals designed to flare luminescently under ultra-violet light when certain other chemicals found in blood are present, luminol is usually used to locate bloodstains that would not otherwise be visible to the naked eye. It has to be applied in darkness for the effect to be observed, however, which is one reason the searchers came at night.

Christine Pinto was now joined by Stephen Schliebe. They applied luminol to a variety of surfaces at the Koklich house.

Spraying the luminol in the bedroom, the criminalists found three separate areas in the master bedroom that fluoresced under the influence of the luminol. Photos were taken of the reactive spots. Then, because a luminol reaction could be triggered by a variety of non-blood substances, including fruit juice, the criminalists used a Kastle-Meyer test to check for possible blood. The test, while only presumptive, could indicate whether it was blood that made the luminol shine, or some other substance. They wet a cotton swab with distilled water, and rubbed it on the spot. Then they treated the swab with another chemical.

"If blood is present, you'll get a nice, deep-pink color," Schliebe said later. The swabs still had to be tested to see if the blood was human, and after that—if there was still enough left—they had to be tested for DNA.

This was another problem: not only did the investigators not have Jana's fingerprints, they also had no DNA sample. True, they could have taken samples from Janie and Paul. But neither parent seemed particularly willing to believe their son-in-law was the culprit. It was easier to take Jana's toothbrush and her hairbrush to obtain DNA samples for her.

Pinto and Schliebe luminoled other portions of the carpet, including the hallway and the lower portion of the house, but got no positive reactions for blood.

The amounts of blood found in the Koklich bedroom, however, were very small. It seemed pretty clear that nothing like a bloodbath could have occurred there. It was quite possible, in fact, that the blood could have come from a small cut, or even a nosebleed. And there was no way of knowing how long the blood had been there. For all the investigators knew, it could have been there for years, or even left by the prior occupants of the house, unlikely as that might have been.

The key was the DNA. If the blood in the SUV contained Jana's DNA, and the blood on the bedroom floor contained her DNA, the investigators would have evidence, albeit thin, that Jana had been killed in the house, her body transferred to the rear of the SUV, and then taken someplace as yet unknown to be disposed of. The killer in turn would have left the SUV on Lewis Avenue in the hope that someone would foolishly make off with it, and get himself arrested as the criminal. That that had not happened had led the detectives straight back to the Koklich house.

While at the house, the detectives told Bruce, for the first time, that they had found blood in the rear of the SUV. They wanted to see how he would handle this information. There seemed to be no discernible reaction. But Bruce said later this wasn't the case at all. "Well, you know, I was very distraught," he said. "I mean, it affected my whole thought process. It's just like, you know, I may never see her again, and you know, I'm used to having somebody with me all the time."

The day after the search for blood, the sheriff's department put more pressure on Bruce. Lieutenant Peavy told the *Press-Telegram*'s Tracy Manzer that a search of the Koklich home had turned up blood. In a front page story the next day, headlined BLOOD FOUND AT KOKLICH HOME, Manzer reported that the luminol process had found "trace elements" of blood on the bedroom carpet.

"We have looked at the possibility that she may have been brutally attacked inside her home," Peavy told the paper. "Our crime scene investigators found a small amount of blood . . . that would not be an indication of any massive bloodletting." The spots weren't much larger than a quarter, he added. But Peavy noted that the small amount of blood didn't rule out another possibility: strangulation.

Peavy said the blood taken from the small spots on the carpet would be subjected to a DNA analysis, and in turn compared to DNA that the department hoped to get from Jana's toothbrush and hairbrush. But Peavy did not reveal that the hoped-for DNA would also be compared to the blood found in the rear of Jana's SUV.

Whether as a result of the mounting publicity, or for some other reason, Bruce decided to get away for the weekend. On Friday, September 7, he decided to drive north to his old hometown, Sonora, in the Gold Rush country of central California.

A picturesque town of about 4,800 people nestled in the Sierra foothills, Sonora began as a mining camp in the late 1840s, and was soon known as "the Queen of the Southern Mines." Many of the buildings of the town date back to the mid-1800s, and the place does a lively tourist trade; that was probably one reason why John Koklich opened his jewelry business in the town years earlier. A bit north of Sonora lies the unincorporated hamlet of Columbia, with its small airstrip. Connecting the two was Shaw's Flat Road, and midway between them was the home of Dan Titchenal, Bruce's stepbrother.

Dan was 43, a little less than a year older than his brother Dave. John Koklich had married the two brothers' mother, Dawn, in 1980, after dating her for about a decade. As Dave put it later, once all the boys were grown and out of the house—Bruce, his brother Michael, and Dan and Dave were all about the same age—John had decided that it was time to conclude a formal arrangement with Dave and Dan's mother. So while the four sons were stepbrothers, they hadn't actually grown up in the same house.

Dan had suffered a severe head injury while a teenager, and another one years later during a violent encounter with someone who had broken into his house. As a result, he sometimes lost the thread of conversations, and his sense of time was impaired. As Dave put it to detectives later, Dan's "brainpower" was somewhat diminished. Dave, however, was very bright, a gifted designer who often worked on Internet web pages.

Bruce arrived on the evening of September 7, Dave said later, and spent the first night with Dave and his wife. The following day Bruce went to Dave's houseboat on New Melones Lake, not far away. Just what Bruce did there wasn't later clear to investigators, although some wondered if he might have gone to the lake to dispose of Jana's remains. Just where those remains might have been until then, and how Bruce could have carried them to the lake, three weeks after her disappearance and presumed murder, however, wasn't at all clear. And on Sunday Bruce visited Dan at his house for a family gathering attended by Dave and his wife, as well as Dan's 18-year-old daughter, Jennifer.

By this point, the disappearance of Jana had been a frequent subject of discussion among the Titchenals. Bruce had arrived for the weekend with all the bad publicity from Long Beach trailing along behind him like a dark cloud. Everyone knew that he was the prime suspect in his wife's disappearance, even if they didn't believe that he could actually be responsible. But for Jennifer— "a wild child," as Dave described her later—Bruce came with a certain cachet of dangerousness that added spice to the fact that he was reputedly very wealthy.

Sometime during the weekend in Sonora, Jennifer took a ride with Bruce in his car. Kidding around with her rich "uncle," Jennifer made an off-hand remark: Now that Jana wasn't around any longer, she suggested, maybe she and Bruce could go out and pick up girls together.

She was only kidding, Jennifer said later. "It was a joke to make him feel a little bit more happier [sic] about his situation. It was a complete joke."

But this remark seemed to have fired Bruce's imagination, if not his libido. Before he left that evening to return to southern California, he asked Jennifer if she had any interest in coming to stay with him in Lakewood. "He offered to help me out, to get a car, and get me into school, and work at his office, possibly," she said later.

At that point in her life, Jennifer had troubles of her own. She had been using methamphetamine for quite some time, along with alcohol and pot, she later admitted. "I'm an alternate addict," she said. Partly as a result of her drug use, she had fractious relationships with the rest of her family, particularly with her mother, Jill, Dan's former wife. She kept moving from house to house, as various relatives became exasperated with her, and kicked her out.

According to Jennifer, even before Bruce had given her this invitation, her father, Dan, had suggested that she go to stay with her step-uncle-by-marriage. So when Bruce proposed the idea on his own, Jennifer was more than willing.

But, said Bruce, Jennifer wasn't to tell any of her family where she was going. When Jennifer asked why not, Bruce said, "It's nobody's fucking business."

Jennifer agreed not to tell anyone, and Bruce arranged to return to Sonora to pick her up about a week and a half later.

But first he had another pressing matter to attend to.

In the week after Bruce's return from Sonora, he and Chris took steps to get the AMOS–NABUCO business back on track. Based on Nevada corporate records, both men were involved in creating a new corporation in that state, "AAMOS." Exactly what AAMOS was supposed to do wasn't entirely clear later, but it appears that it was formed in part because of Jana's sudden disappearance.

"AAMOS was really a financial shell, isn't that correct?" Chris was asked later.

"That's correct," Chris said. He signed the Nevada incorporation papers as secretary and director of AAMOS. Bruce was listed as president.

According to Chris, the plan was for NABUCO—when and if it ever found the money it was going to broker as a loan to Bruce—to send the cash to AAMOS. AAMOS, in turn, would send the money on to AMOS.

This Tinker–to Evers–to Fat Chance relay may have had to do with the fact that Jana was no longer around to sign the commitment papers for the advance fees to NABUCO. In the absence of one of the principal stockholders and directors of AMOS, NABUCO needed to have a legally defensible position for the fees it intended to collect for brokering the loan. Thus, AAMOS, under the control of both Bruce and Chris, rather than Bruce and Jana, would serve as an appropriate pass-through vehicle from NABUCO, since Jana wasn't a stockholder in the shell corporation, AAMOS.

It appears that Chris and Bruce both went to Las Vegas to incorporate AAMOS. Chris would later tell detectives that while they were in Las Vegas, Bruce tried to pick someone up. "He was making advances to the waitress," Chris said. "He was making remarks about her coming home with him."

This wasn't the first time that Bruce had attempted to find someone to share his now-empty bed, it appears. Linda Vargas would later recall that within a few weeks of Jana's disappearance, Bruce had called her in Texas,

telling her he was lonely. He invited Linda and her girlfriend to come and stay with him in Lakewood. Linda
simply said that she was too busy to leave right then. She
thought the invitation was weird.

After filing the AAMOS papers, Bruce and Chris apparently met with the NABUCO people in Las Vegas.
Documents later filed in court show that Bruce, as president of AAMOS, signed papers providing the $10,000 fee
to NABUCO on September 12. Signing for NABUCO
was Joe Heller, who identified himself as "Consultant."

This was the same agreement that appeared to give
NABUCO 1.1 percent of the loan proceeds as a broker's
fee, and which also made "any dollars required above the
initial cost . . . paid by the client," meaning Bruce. Once
this was signed, there was nothing to prevent NABUCO
from coming back to Bruce to demand additional money
to facilitate the brokering of a loan.

The timing of this transaction with the NABUCO people may be significant, in part because it appears that it
had been in the offing for some weeks prior to its actual
execution. By September 12, 2001, Chris Botosan had
already become the sheriff's department's prized secret
informant on Bruce; by that time, according to his then-
girlfriend Melinda McBride, he had already confided to
her that he suspected Bruce was responsible for Jana's
disappearance. Yet, here was Chris, helping Bruce obtain
an ethereal loan from unnamed parties through a company in which he held an ownership interest. If Chris really believed that Bruce had done away with his wife,
why in the world was he still attempting to put Bruce together with NABUCO, if not only to maintain his cover
as Bruce's "partner"?

And there is more: The incorporation of AAMOS
three weeks after Jana disappeared, and the apparent payment of $10,000 to NABUCO by Bruce on or about that

date,[10] suggests that this was a transaction that Bruce could go forward with, now that Jana was no longer around to object. Otherwise, why hadn't the deal been done while Jana was still around—before AAMOS had to be incorporated?

The creation of AAMOS to stand in for AMOS suggests that Jana may have refused to go along with the plan put forward by Chris and NABUCO. Thus the possibility exists that Jana was killed in order to free Bruce to consummate the NABUCO transaction.

And if true, this would be motive for murder.

But by the middle of September 2001, no one in the Los Angeles County Sheriff's Department knew any of these details about AAMOS, AMOS, or NABUCO, or Bruce's decision to pay the Las Vegas group ten grand up front. The detectives were still collecting anecdotal information about Bruce, focused particularly on his sexual peccadilloes. As Sheehy and Davis saw the crime, Bruce's motive wasn't financial: After all, Jana's body was missing, so he couldn't collect on the insurance. No, the way the detectives viewed what happened, Bruce had disposed of his wife in order to clear the tracks for another woman.

Who would soon present herself for the detectives' further investigation.

---

[10] Chris Botosan later testified that this $10,000 had actually been paid to NABUCO early in 2001, well before September 12.

THE JENNIFER SITUATION

The Lost Week

Sometime after returning from Las Vegas with Chris Botosan, Bruce met again with his lawyer, Clive Martin. Martin was growing exasperated with his client.

"I said, 'Bruce, I'm working for you,'" Martin recalled. "I've hired an investigator, and I'm on your side. I'm putting myself out for you. Now you've got to feed me." Martin wanted Bruce to pay some of his fees up front, as a retainer.

But Bruce seemed reluctant to do this. Finally, Gary Mitchell, Bruce's old friend, called him.

"Bruce," Mitchell said, "you've got to pay him."

Meeting with Martin again, Bruce apparently paid over some money. But, Bruce told Martin, "I don't think I'm a suspect anymore."

Martin couldn't believe what he was hearing.

"You've got to be kidding," Martin said. "Not only are you still a suspect, you're the *only* suspect. And until you can find someone who's more of a suspect than you are, you're going to continue being the only suspect."

Bruce's momentary belief that the detectives had turned their attention away from him may have stemmed from the fact that Sheehy and Davis didn't seem to be around anymore. Of course, Bruce did not then know that he was under covert surveillance by the sheriff's department, which apparently was still of the belief that Bruce had a mystery girlfriend.

At the same time, however, forensic technicians at the sheriff's crime laboratory were conducting DNA tests on the blood samples recovered from the house and the SUV. Once those were completed, the detectives would have a theory of the case that they could present to the prosecutors in the Los Angeles County District Attorney's Office.

In the meantime, the detectives continued their covert conversations with Chris Botosan.

Early on the morning of Tuesday, September 18, Bruce again drove north to Sonora. He'd made arrangements to pick up 18-year-old Jennifer Titchenal at a church not far from her father Dan's house, but apparently Bruce decided to alter these plans without telling her. As Jennifer left her father's property, she spotted Bruce in his white coupe atop a nearby hill, obviously waiting for her.

As she got into the car, Bruce asked her if she'd told anyone where she was going. "I told him that I told my family I was going to Stockton, which I wasn't happy about," Jennifer said later. When asked what Bruce had said to this, she quoted him saying, once again, "It's nobody's fucking business."

What Jennifer did not tell Bruce was that she had told a friend at the Mountain Women's Resource Center in Sonora that she was going to stay with her "uncle." Doubtless Jennifer also told this friend, Marlene Leach, about Jana's disappearance, as well as the fact that Bruce was a suspect. The way things turned out, Jennifer's briefing of Marlene in advance of the trip suggested that one of her main objectives in going with Bruce was to obtain incriminating information from him. Later, it would be Leach who contacted the Los Angeles County Sheriff's Department with the particulars of Jennifer's story.

Bruce and Jennifer headed south and west down Highway 108, eventually striking Highway 99, one of the main routes back to southern California. They stopped in Merced at a Marie Callender's restaurant for lunch. During the drive, Jennifer asked Bruce about the oil the police had found under the car—meaning Jana's SUV.

Granted that Jennifer was naturally curious about Bruce's predicament, this was still an odd question. Indeed, almost from the outset it appears that she was trying to pump him for information about Jana. Given what happened later between Bruce and his "niece," and particularly the way she ultimately came to the attention of the investigators, the possibility exists that Jennifer may have decided to try to obtain information on her "uncle" to relay to the police.

Jennifer eventually would in fact obtain the assistance of the police in February 2003 when she was pulled out of a jail in Sonora by Detective Sheehy before she could take the witness stand to give devastating testimony against her uncle.

As a result, a good part of Jennifer's story has to be carefully scrutinized as to her possible motives. By the time she testified against Bruce, more than two years later, it was in her interest to make Bruce look as bad as possible.

Jennifer's question about the oil that had supposedly been found by police also indicates that she and the rest of the Titchenals had been discussing Bruce's predicament among themselves. It appears that she had heard about this from her father, who may have had the story somewhat garbled, possibly from something that Bruce himself may have said while he was visiting on September 9. Likely, this was a conflation of information about the search of the oil field on August 31, which Bruce may have mentioned to Dan and Dave, the police search of the undercarriage of Jana's SUV, and Dan's recollection that Bruce had once worked for an oil company. But there was no indication that the criminalists had found any suspicious oil under the SUV.

Bruce now told Jennifer that he didn't know what she was talking about. Jennifer persisted: well, what about the fact that Bruce had once worked in oil fields? Dan had told her so, she added.

"That was twenty years ago," Bruce said.

"Did you tell the police about it?"

"No," Bruce said, "I didn't. They aren't going to find out about it."

Just before they reached the Grapevine, the long climb over the mountains separating the Los Angeles basin from California's Central Valley, Bruce steered the conversation around to sex, Jennifer said.

"What did he say?" Jennifer was asked later.

"That he wanted our—basically he wanted to have a sexual relationship with me."

"And what was your response?"

"My response was that I didn't want to have a sexual relationship with him."

Bruce made another reference to Jennifer going out with him to "pick up girls," Jennifer said. But when Bruce brought this up again, she realized "he didn't take it as a joke."

Bruce and Jennifer reached the Lakewood house just after 4 P.M. that day. According to Jennifer, Bruce pulled all the blinds shut and told her not to use the telephone. She said he told her he didn't want anyone to see her in the house. He told her that the telephone might be tapped.

Bruce then left to go to the office. He returned a few hours later, and changed clothes. He put on "a crop top, a blue netted jersey and black shorts," Jennifer said, suggesting that he was attempting to dress for seduction.

They began to play pool, Jennifer said. Bruce fixed her a drink. He asked her again to have sex with him.

"I told him I was pregnant to get him off my back," Jennifer said.

At that point, Jennifer said, Bruce got upset. He told her he thought it was very unfair of her not to have told him this first. If she thought that she could come to freeload off him while having a baby, she was very mistaken, she said Bruce told her.

Bruce calmed down after a few minutes. Then he invited her to watch TV with him in his room.

"He told me to hop up on the bed and watch MTV with him, which I don't normally watch, MTV," Jennifer said.

"Did he ask you to sleep in his bed with him?"

"Yes." But Bruce persisted, she said, and after a while she rolled over on her side and began crying. "I'm eighteen years old," she said, "and I'm stuck in this house . . . I went down there to better my life, and now I have my uncle pressuring me for sex."

The tone was therefore set for the next four days, with Bruce clumsily attempting to seduce his stepbrother's daughter, and Jennifer fending him off with excuses, with crying jags, and eventually, when those didn't work, by diving into Bruce's amply stocked liquor cabinet.

While all this was transpiring, Sheehy was tracking down Michael Freeman, the 18-year-old who had split the money from Jana's purse with young Rayray.

"He knew we were looking for him," Sheehy said later. "It was just a matter of time before we found him."

Sheehy was pretty sure that it had been Bruce who had dumped the car on Lewis Avenue, but until he had Freeman's version of the events of August 20, he couldn't completely rule out the possibility that Freeman might have been involved. When he finally caught up with him, Freeman readily admitted swiping the purse and taking the money.

"When did you first find out that the car had been involved in the disappearance of a woman?" Sheehy asked.

"Two days later," Freeman said. But by that time, Freeman added, the SUV had disappeared again. It was only the following week that he heard it had been found in the garage. He'd seen it on television.

Sheehy hadn't been a cop for twenty years without being able to recognize a streetwise kid, which Michael Freeman definitely was. But that didn't mean he'd had anything to do with what happened to Jana. Otherwise, Sheehy knew, he never would've caught up with him.

Bruce continued his pursuit of Jennifer with all the grace and charm of a slobbery Komodo dragon. He told her she could wear any of Jana's clothes she liked; Jennifer thought this was weird. He kept plying her with liquor; being an "alternate addict," Jennifer drank it.

On the day after her arrival in Lakewood, Bruce took her to a restaurant for lunch, a place called Fuddruckers. It so happened that this restaurant was directly across the street from the Lakewood sheriff's station. Bruce seemed amused by the proximity, Jennifer recalled.

"He said that they were looking all over for him, and here he was right across the street." At one point, she said, Bruce draped his jacket over her. Jennifer could feel the weight of his pistol in the side pocket. It seemed that he wanted to give her the idea that he was some sort of desperado.

After lunch, Bruce took Jennifer to a nearby juice stand so she could see about getting a job. There didn't seem to be any openings, so they drove on to a nearby drugstore,

where Jennifer picked up a home pregnancy test kit. Bruce
drove her back to the house and returned to work.

That evening, he came back from work and told her
they would go to the Mighty Ducks hockey game in Anaheim. Bruce had season tickets. At the game, Jennifer informed him that the test had shown she wasn't pregnant
after all.

"Oh, good," Bruce told her. "Now you can have my
baby."

After the game, Bruce kept pressuring her to have sex
with him, Jennifer said. "He said he hadn't gotten it in
over a month and he was horny."

Jennifer protested that Bruce was her uncle.

"Not by blood," Bruce told her.

But Jennifer burst into tears again, once more refusing
Bruce's advances.

Jennifer said she spent the night in the guest room. When
she awoke, Bruce had already left for work. She'd been
asking him to take her to the office; she had hoped that he
would give her a job there. But Bruce had told her he
didn't want her in the office. "He said I look like a little
Jana," Jennifer said.

When he returned from work, the argument over sex
began once more, with Bruce doing his best [or worst] to
persuade her, and Jennifer refusing. Finally she asked
him to drop her off at a nearby shopping mall. She had no
clothes other than what she was wearing, and no money,
either. Bruce gave Jennifer one of his credit cards to buy
$400 in clothes.

That night, Bruce and Jennifer attended a rock concert
at the Pond. He bought her "a number of cranberry and
vodka drinks," she remembered. "And maybe some beer."
On the way back from the concert, they stopped at the
drugstore again. Bruce bought a package of condoms.

When they got back to the house, he made another drink for Jennifer.

"What did he make for you?" Jennifer was asked.

"A blow job."

"And what is that?"

"I'm not exactly sure," Jennifer said later. "It's a mixed drink."

"How do you know it's called a blow job?"

"That's what Bruce told me."

Jennifer said she didn't drink the "blow job," at least not then.

The next day, Bruce again went off to work, while Jennifer slept in. At noon, Bruce returned to the house. "He came home for his lunch," Jennifer recalled, "and we had gotten into an argument over me not wanting to have sex with him for, like, about the hundredth time."

Bruce left to go back to work. Jennifer espied the "blow job" that had not been consumed the night before. She drank it. Then she began to find other things to drink.

"I continued to drink a large portion of alcohol to not deal with the situation," she recalled.

Jennifer was wearing a bikini and sunning herself by the pool in the rear of the house. By her own count, she had had four beers, "and maybe, if you were to pour all the hard alcohol, it would probably add up to one full bottle. Maybe, you know a couple of quarts or something."

The hard alcohol, on top of the "blow job," whatever that was, came from four or five rum and cokes, a wine cooler, and six glasses of peach schnapps.

Jennifer, who weighed about 140 pounds, soon passed out.

The next thing she knew, she was lying on her stomach on the bed in the guest room. As she came to, Jennifer thought that her bikini bottoms had been pushed to one side. She had no recollection of getting from the pool to the bed. She got up to go to the bathroom, and encountered Bruce in the hallway.

"He was across the hall in his boxers with an erection," Jennifer recalled. "He was talking on the phone."

Jennifer had an inkling that Bruce might have been fondling her while she was passed out. She went into the bathroom and violently vomited.

When she felt better, Jennifer asked Bruce to take her to a nightspot in Newport Beach. As she put it later, she wanted to get out of the house, to be around more people her own age. They drove to Sharkeez, a restaurant and bar. There Jennifer drank beer, while Bruce wrapped his legs around her bar stool in a possessive, seductive fashion, she recalled. She got a telephone number from a younger man; she wanted an escape route if it became necessary. Later, Jennifer arranged to have someone take a picture of her with Bruce.

"At that point," she said, "I didn't know who Bruce was, exactly . . . after all that had taken place, so I wanted a picture to show that I was there, because I didn't feel comfortable."

Of course, the photograph would be proof that she had been with Bruce, which raises the question of Jennifer's motives for being with him at all—it would later come in handy.

After Sharkeez, Bruce took her to a condominium in nearby Huntington Beach. He told her that a friend had offered the use of the condo "in his time of grieving."

"Like I'm really grieving," Bruce said, laughing, according to Jennifer.

Late that night, they returned to the Lakewood house.

"Did he ask for sex from you again?"

"Yeah," Jennifer said. "I was emotionally a wreck, and I told him, what do you think he would think—my family would think, about, you know, if my grandma was alive, what would my grandma think? What would my dad think? What would the rest of the family think about him? And I was asking him why he was doing this, because I didn't understand why family would do this to each other."

Bruce told her that no one would believe her. He cajoled her some more, asking her for "a cute little blow job," Jennifer said. She again refused.

"I was just plain sick, period." Weeping, she went back to the guest room. "He told me our relationship was over. Because I wouldn't have sex with him, which I didn't even know it was a relationship."

Bruce said he'd take her back to Sonora in the morning.

Don't Get Mad—Get Even

In between his attempts to seduce Jennifer, Bruce had apparently decided that Clive Martin was right—he *was* still a suspect in Jana's disappearance. But he decided to jettison Martin. Instead, Bruce retained Henry Salcido, a highly regarded criminal defense attorney in Long Beach. They would later have a falling out, but not until two separate trials had been held to determine Bruce's guilt or innocence in the matter of Jana's disappearance.[11]

Salcido was apparently on the job in the third week of September, because on September 22, even as Bruce was driving Jennifer back to Sonora, a new private investigator, Larry Kallestad, was hired by Salcido to investigate Jana's disappearance. It would be Kallestad's job to find someone other than Bruce who might have been responsible.

Kallestad, a retired Los Angeles Police Department detective, had investigated a number of homicides while with LAPD. He began with Arrita LePire, who had told both sides that she and her husband, Allen Radcliffe, thought they'd seen Jana on Sunday morning, August 19.

---

[11] Salcido repeatedly declined to be interviewed for this book.

Arrita and Radcliffe told Kallestad the same story they'd told everyone else: they'd seen a blonde woman come out the backdoor of the Koklich office and cross the parking lot in the direction of an SUV. When they left their own business a second later, they'd seen the SUV heading north in the alley. They had assumed it was Jana. "She was near the corner of her shop," Kallestad reported to Salcido later, "when she saw the white Pathfinder . . . drive forward and arc left to proceed northbound in the parking lot.

"In her mind it was Jana, as she has seen Jana and Bruce and their cars, in the lot for years."

Granted that Arrita later admitted she hadn't seen the blonde woman's face, and that her husband, Allen, who had seen the face but didn't know Jana from Jane Pauley, the specificity of the color of the SUV—"white"—would turn out to be critical. Eventually, the sheriff's department would turn up another blonde woman, Sandy Baressi, who would say that she'd left the Koklich offices at about that same time, and driven off in her own car. However, Sandy Baressi drove a blue minivan, not a white SUV.

Part of the trouble here seemed to have been a lack of precision on the part of those who interviewed Arrita and Radcliffe. When first accepting the assertion that the person they'd seen was possibly Jana, everyone who interviewed them assumed the vehicle they'd seen had been a white SUV, because that's what Jana drove. It was only later, when Sandy Baressi was interviewed, that the color and type of the vehicle became important. As a result, it was possible that the vehicle was mistakenly established as a white SUV in the very beginning. And while Arrita in Bruce's first trial swore that the vehicle was white, by the second trial she was no longer so sure. It didn't help matters any that Arrita was blind in one eye.

Over the next month, Kallestad would concentrate his investigative efforts on the Koklich office staff. By October 15, in fact, Kallestad had narrowed his search for possible alternative suspects to one man: Chris Botosan.

But by then, a lot of other things had happened, not the least of which was that Bruce was investigated for the possible rape of his "niece," Jennifer Titchenal.

Bruce had dropped Jennifer off at her father's house in Sonora sometime in the morning of September 22. They had arisen about 4 A.M. to make the drive north, which didn't give Jennifer a lot of time to sleep after her last night on the town with Bruce. Bruce seemed to have been anxious to be rid of her. "It just wasn't working out," he said later.

Based on a later reconstruction of the sequence of events, it appears that after she got home, Jennifer told her father and mother that Bruce had molested her. Neither believed her.

Two days later, Jennifer decided to go back to the Mountain Women's Resource Center, which operated a crisis clinic. "I had done some volunteer work there before," Jennifer said, "and I had a girlfriend there who worked with crises such as mine, so I went to have a conversation with her. Because I haven't had much in life, but I thought I had my family to help me—or not to help me, but to at least be supportive of me." When Dan and Jill both scoffed at her assertions about Bruce's behavior, Jennifer said, "I needed somebody to talk about it, because it was eating me up."

And, she added, "I wasn't so sure that it was appropriate for me to hold all of it on myself and not to tell the authorities." For proof of her four days with Bruce, Jennifer had kept a diary, which included a rather unflattering drawing of her "uncle."

At the resource center, Jennifer recounted her four-day excursion in southern California to her friend, Marlene Leach, and told Marlene that she was sore in the vaginal area. After this, things became a bit murkier, but it appears, based on various law enforcement reports, that Leach called the Los Angeles County Sheriff's Department, and was put in touch with Detective Joe Sheehy. From this, one can surmise that Jennifer had told Leach that her uncle, the man she suspected of raping her, was also being investigated for the disappearance and possible murder of his wife, and that a sheriff's detective named Joe Sheehy was working on the case. In other words, Leach now sought out Sheehy specifically to tell him of Jennifer's allegations about Bruce, rather than simply make an independent complaint of sexual assault, which ordinarily would not have come to Sheehy's attention.

Sheehy, in turn, called the Sonora Police Department, which sent Sonora officer Steve Marino to the Mountain Women's Resource Center. Although Sheehy was later to say his department first heard of Jennifer's allegation against Bruce from the Sonora police, Marino's report indicates it was Sheehy who told him about Jennifer, not the other way around:

> On September 25, 2001, I spoke with Investigator Sheelay [sic] of the LA County SO [sheriff's office]. He related that Jane Doe, 18 years old, was a victim of a sexual assault. He explained that the suspect was Doe's uncle, Bruce Koklich. Koklich was also a suspect in the murder of his wife, Jenna [sic] Koklich. Jenna's body has not been recovered. Sheelay requested that I interview Doe.

Marino's written report thus makes it clear that he first heard of Jennifer, and Bruce, from Sheehy. The sequence of who knew what first suggests that Jennifer had all along planned to be an informant against Bruce, and was now putting this plan into action.

> She felt he knew his wife was dead. She stayed with him at his home for five days . . . during her stay he would not allow her to answer or use his phone. When Koklich came into contact with his friends, his demeanor would immediately change to one of sorrow (because of the loss of his wife). As soon as they were alone, his demeanor would immediately change back to normal . . .
>
> She was convinced Koklich was responsible for the death of his wife.

After finishing his report, Marino called a detective in the Los Angeles County Sheriff's Department's sex crimes detail, Dina Black. He faxed Detective Black a copy of his report, and gave her Jennifer's telephone number. After Black talked with Jennifer over the telephone and consulted with Sheehy, it was decided to send a sheriff's department airplane to Sonora to pick up Jennifer, posthaste, and fly her back to Los Angeles.

Sheehy and Davis now had a potential witness who could provide useable evidence—that is to say, contemporary evidence—on Bruce's possible motive for murdering his still-missing wife: sex.

The sheriff's airplane flew into the Long Beach Airport on the next afternoon, Wednesday, September 26. The urgency and importance of lassoing Jennifer as a witness against Bruce was illustrated by the decision to go to the expense of using the sheriff's air force to bring her back to southern California. Davis, Sheehy and Black checked Jennifer into the Marriott hotel near the airport, and paid for her room and dinner. Afterward they conducted an hour-long interview. Jennifer filled them in on her four days with her "uncle." But it soon became clear that, despite her initial suspicions in Sonora, she couldn't say positively that she'd been abused or raped.

Sheehy and Davis were particularly interested to find out what Bruce had told her about Jana. After Jennifer told them that he didn't want to take her to the office because she looked "like a little Jana," but that he had told her she could have any of Jana's clothes she wanted, Jennifer said that Bruce had told her the police had found DNA in Jana's SUV. Bruce told her that he believed Jana was gone—that she was dead—and Bruce had told her that if someone isn't found within the first seventy-two hours after being reported missing, the chances were they were deceased.

The next day Black took Jennifer to a nearby hospital for a sexual assault examination. The examination did not produce evidence of rape. But there was another way to get this kind of evidence: an unwitting statement from Bruce himself might do the trick. That same afternoon, Detective Black had Jennifer telephone Bruce at the office. This was a so-called "pretext call," in which the victim of a sexual assault calls the alleged perpetrator in an effort to get him to admit his actions. The pretext: the victim claims that she may have been infected with a venereal disease. This usually elicits some sort of reaction from the supposed perpetrator. The call is always surreptitiously taped.

"Bruce appeared to be very hesitant in his responses to Jennifer," Davis wrote in his notes at the time of the call, "and also appeared to be very suspicious, as if he knew the conversation was being recorded."

But Jennifer's call to Bruce, in which she claimed that she had genital warts, provoked no useful response from him. Indeed, it appears that Bruce knew he wasn't also infected because he hadn't had intercourse with Jennifer.

Still, armed with Jennifer's assertions, the detectives went to court and obtained another search warrant for the Koklich house. After getting this warrant, the detectives went to the office, where they told Bruce they had a new warrant, this one alleging sexual assault on Jennifer. "We contacted him at his business and had him drive from his business with two deputies in his car to his home so we didn't have to damage the door," Dina Black said later. Without Bruce there to open it with his key, they would have had to smash it in.

During this search, the deputies found the unused box of condoms, and an opened box of tampons, along with the photograph Jennifer had taken with Bruce at Sharkeez. This was a very slim haul—all this proved was that Jennifer had been in the house and at Sharkeez with Bruce, and that Bruce had purchased some condoms. When Black interviewed him, Bruce denied having had sex with Jennifer. He told Black that he'd hoped to be able to help his "niece" out, but that she'd done nothing but drink like a fish, so he'd had to take her home.

Given the paucity of evidence that any crime had occurred, at least with respect to Jennifer, there may have been other reasons for this search. It seemed likely that the real reason for it was to embarrass Bruce—to drive a wedge between him and Janie, as well as him and Paul. To that end, publicity was very useful.

KOKLICH RESIDENCE SEARCHED, the Long Beach *Press-Telegram* headlined the next day.

Quoting from a press release issued by the Lakewood sheriff's station, the paper reported with a straight face that the search had "no connection and is not related to the disappearance of Jana Koklich."

Bruce spoke to a reporter for the newspaper and

vehemently denied Jennifer's allegation. It was embar-
rassing, Bruce acknowledged. "But the only thing that
matters to me is getting my wife back."

Now Bruce had to explain what was going on to Janie,
Paul and all of Jana's friends, not to mention his own office staff.

Just after speaking with the reporter from the newspaper, and before the story was published, Bruce called
Chris Botosan aside in the office, and told him there was
going to be a story in the paper the following day that
would say he was being investigated for a sexual assault,
on a complaint from his own niece.

This was the first time he'd heard that Bruce's niece
had been staying at the house, Chris said later. Afterward,
Bruce held a meeting of the office staff, and told them
there would be an unflattering story about him in the
newspaper the next day. "I haven't been thinking straight
lately," Bruce said. He went on to say he should have realized how it would look to have his niece stay with him
so soon after Jana's disappearance. But he again denied
doing anything wrong, and suggested that Jennifer had a
drinking problem.

After this, Bruce made tracks for Janie Carpenter's
house in Orange County. He wanted to tell her of this development before she heard it on the news. He explained
once more about Jennifer's conduct, and she accepted this
story. Bruce decided to spend the weekend with Janie.

But others' lingering doubts about Bruce flared up in the
wake of the publicity. Jan Baird, for one, had been suspicious of Bruce for several weeks. Just after Bruce had returned from taking Jennifer back to Sonora, he had called
Baird, Paul Carpenter's former office assistant, to try to
convince her that Jana had once missed an appointment
with her.

No, Bruce, Jan told him. That never happened. Bruce insisted that it had, but she was firm: Jana never, ever missed appointments. Jana was so disciplined about this as to be almost obsessive.

From this, it appears that Bruce's first lawyer, Clive Martin, and possibly Martin's replacement, Henry Salcido, had learned that one part of the sheriff's department's nascent case against Bruce was the unlikelihood of Jana missing her appointments on the Saturday and Sunday before she'd disappeared. From the middle of September on, Bruce continued calling Jana's friends and acquaintances, trying to demonstrate that she had missed appointments in the past. One by one, he'd called them all: Jana's hairstylist, her manicurist, her trainer, her friends. All said that Jana had never, ever missed an appointment—at least, not without having called them first to let them know she couldn't make it.

Bruce's seemingly desperate search to find someone to validate his contention that Jana had decided to ignore the weekend calls sparked Jan Baird's doubts. Even as the sheriff's department was winging its way to Sonora to grab Jennifer Titchenal, Jan Baird sent an email to Doris Morrow and Paul Carpenter in Texas. She wanted to let them know that Bruce had been trying to get her to say things about Jana that weren't true:

> I feel so bad for you, as it must be difficult being so far from all of this. However, being close doesn't seem to help either.
>
> Bruce called me yesterday [September 25] and asked me about the time, about six months ago—maybe eight—when Jana forgot to show up at the Cerritos Mall for dinner. I told him I was unaware of her ever forgetting to show up to meet me. He pressed me, stating that he knew for a fact she had forgotten to

> show up, and that I had called from the mall. I was
> sympathetic but never backed down. He went on to
> explain that the authorities were trying to pin this
> whole thing on him based on the fact that she never
> missed an appointment . . .

Jan added that she knew that Bruce had cited her to the
sheriff's department as an example of someone with
whom Jana had missed appointments. It just wasn't so,
she said.

The next day, after receiving this email, Paul Carpenter decided to tell Sheehy about it. He said that he'd had a
telephone call himself from Bruce a few days earlier, asking whether it was possible that someone from Paul's former life as a high-rolling legislator had decided to take
revenge on Paul by harming Jana. He had told Bruce that
was very unlikely.

But for some time Paul had been thinking like the *old*
Paul—the man who calculated all the angles. Even as he
returned to San Antonio from California, in the middle of
September, Paul began working out the probabilities.
Paul had to admit to himself that just about any way you
figured it, Bruce was the person who was most likely to
have done something to his youngest daughter. In the
middle of the month, even before the Jennifer situation
had been splashed all over the newspapers and airwaves,
Paul decided to tell Joe Sheehy that he'd reconsidered
about Bruce.

Told that Paul had called him from Texas, wanting to
speak to him, Sheehy called back. In his notes from the
middle of the month, Sheehy recorded:

> *Paul informed me he had a change of heart since go-*
> *ing back to Texas.*
>   *Paul said he has put the pieces together and started*

thinking using his brain and not his heart. Paul said
he no longer believes Bruce is innocent, and is now
guilty. Paul based this on the following:
1—Bruce is not the type of person who can sit still
and relax for more than an hour, let alone a whole
weekend.
2—Bruce can't explain the missing sheets, towel and
pillow.
3—Jana would never stand up her mother and espe-
cially not call her if there was a change in plans.
4—Neither Jana or Bruce would go the whole week-
end without using the phone.

He might be dying, Paul said later, but if there was any
justice left in the world, he'd stay alive to see Bruce arrested for his crime—and more important, made to tell
exactly what he'd done to Jana Carpenter Koklich, who'd
never done anyone any harm, and whose disappearance
threatened to take the last glimmer of light from Paul's
own fading life.

And as his candle burned down to the stub, Paul recalled another ancient political maxim: Don't get mad—
get even.

The Informant

In the wake of the publicity over the Jennifer search warrant, the first obvious schisms began to appear in the pro-Bruce front. Paul Carpenter had already expressed his doubts about Bruce to Sheehy, as had Jan Baird. Perhaps sensing that these supporters were beginning to slip away from him, especially now that he'd been investigated for allegedly assaulting his own niece, Bruce tried to explain himself.

On Saturday, September 29, Bruce decided to call Jan Baird while he was still at Janie's house. Janie, at least, was still on his side. It was Janie who suggested he call the Bairds to explain the circumstances of the search warrant. But Bruce also knew that the Bairds were close to Paul Carpenter and Doris Morrow. If he had any chance of keeping Paul and Doris on his side, Bruce may have believed, it might be useful to make sure that the Bairds were still on the team. He didn't yet realize that it was too late, that Paul was already convinced that his son-in-law was guilty.

Bruce told Jan Baird that the only reason his niece had leveled charges against him was that he had reneged on a promise to take her to another rock concert. When he'd instead taken her back to Sonora because of her drinking, Bruce indicated, Jennifer had decided to get even with him. Jan Baird thought this was pretty lame.

That same afternoon, Sheehy called Chris Botosan for at least the sixth time. Chris told Sheehy that when Bruce had explained the circumstances of the Jennifer search warrant to his office staff the preceding week, Bruce had taken great pains to make himself appear to be innocent. Chris added that several of the employees had mentioned that "it appeared to be an overkill of an explanation," Sheehy would note in his report. "I knew it might hurt him," Chris said later, "but it was the truth."

Chris added another bit of information that never made it into Sheehy's subsequent formal report on the conversation, however. He told Sheehy that Mike Bowden, who had first introduced Chris to Bruce in Florida years before, and re-introduced them in 2001, had telephoned him on the previous Friday. Chris told Sheehy that Bowden had told him that "someone will be coming forward within the next day or so with information as to Jana's disappearance." And, Chris said, Bowden told him that the person with the information, whoever he was, "was possibly with Bruce within the last week when Bruce saw something—"

What was this? It appears as though Chris Botosan was telling Sheehy that Mike Bowden in Florida knew someone who knew something about Jana's disappearance, and that person would soon be coming forward with this information. But Sheehy's notes, which were later filed in court by Bruce's lawyer Henry Salcido, were cut off at this point, and only partially disclosed. Sheehy later said he had no recollection of Botosan providing this information to him, or any idea what it meant. Nor do the notes of Sheehy's interview of Bowden reflect any questions on this topic. And since Salcido never raised the matter when he later defended Bruce, one can only conclude that whatever it was, it wasn't very helpful to Bruce, even if it did seem to point the finger in another direction.[12] So what was Botosan trying to tell Sheehy? Was it some sort of baseless concoction, one that dragged in Mike Bowden without his knowledge? And if so, why?

It appears that at this point in the game, Sheehy and Davis had already eliminated Botosan as a potential suspect in Jana's disappearance. They hadn't taken his DNA—not that it would do any good, since they had no suspect DNA to compare it to—and they hadn't searched his apartment. Indeed, they hadn't even yet verified Chris's whereabouts for the weekend that Jana had disappeared. But Chris didn't know this at the time Sheehy called him. It therefore appears that Chris was trying to direct Sheehy's attention away from himself by raising the specter of a Florida mystery man.

Why would Chris try to do this? It's not at all clear, even at this point. But by October of 2001, the AMOS project was in jeopardy, notwithstanding the creation of its "shell" brother, AAMOS. By early October, Chris said later, the banks that had been interested in buying the software program were all backing off, mostly because of the notoriety surrounding Jana's disappearance. When asked if the "scandal" surrounding the disappearance had driven potential customers away, he said, "Absolutely."

One of the problems, according to Chris, was that Jana owned a lot of stock in AMOS. And while NABUCO might be willing to broker a loan for AAMOS, the same could not be said for AMOS—not unless someone became

---

[12] Bowden, reached by the author at his office in Florida, had no recollection of ever telling anything like this to Chris; he also indicated that neither Sheehy nor Davis called to ask him about this tale, which only raises the question of why Chris told the detectives about it.

a trustee for Jana's share in the original software company, and agreed to the deal. After all, AMOS, not AAMOS, held the rights to the software that was to be the basis for any loan. For a while, Bruce tried to induce Janie to stand in for her daughter.

"They were concerned about having somebody be able to vote Jana's shares in the company that owned this software," Chris said later. "So they could take some action with regard to something." A meeting was held with Bruce, Chris, Henry Salcido, Janie and another lawyer. Bruce wanted Janie to vote Jana's shares. Janie said she didn't understand why Bruce couldn't do it himself.

"He told me that he couldn't do it, because he was under suspicion, and that, therefore, I was the next logical person," Janie said later.

Janie declined to act as her daughter's trustee, however—she may have read the proposed fee agreement between AMOS and NABUCO, and realized that if she became a trustee for Jana's stock, NABUCO might be able to get money from her as well as Bruce. Thwarted by Janie's decision, Bruce began to cast around for someone else to act as Jana's trustee.

As October wore on, the problems over control of the AMOS stock in effect relieved NABUCO from having to actually find real money for AAMOS. If Bruce pressed Chris to cajole NABUCO to come up with the promised millions, NABUCO could simply point to the problems over the stock ownership and say that no money would be coming until those were ironed out.

It's possible that as of October 1, 2001, Chris was concerned that the detectives' investigation would veer into the NABUCO area, and that by raising the prospect of some mystery man from Florida who would be "coming forward within the next day or so with information as to Jana's disappearance," he might have been trying to deflect such an inquiry, which would have inevitably led to questions about the Las Vegas group's intentions.

If that was Chris's motivation for telling Sheehy about the supposed Florida connection, he needn't have worried. By the first week of October, both Sheehy and Davis were convinced that Bruce had murdered his wife so that he could philander around to his heart's content.

It wasn't money that was the motive, Sheehy and Davis were sure. It was lust.

But if Sheehy and Davis were content to use Chris as a conduit into Bruce's camp, that wasn't the case with Henry Salcido, Bruce's new lawyer. On October 15, 2001, Salcido's private investigator, Larry Kallestad, sat down with Chris to find out what he knew about Jana's disappearance. Kallestad told Chris where he had to sit— as if he were still working for the LAPD, and was questioning a suspect. About five minutes into the discussion, Kallestad said he thought *Chris* might be responsible for Jana's disappearance. Chris later said Kallestad told him that he'd been hired by Salcido to "push the blame away" from Bruce, although it appears that Kallestad denied ever saying this. But any way Kallestad phrased it, Chris knew immediately what he meant: Kallestad and Salcido intended to make him the fall guy.

Chris instantly terminated the interview with Kallestad. "I became outraged by his mannerism and implication," he said later. He called Sheehy to tell him what Kallestad had said. What Sheehy said to Chris at this point is unrecorded, but it appears that Sheehy assured Chris that he wasn't a suspect and never had been.

By that point, in fact, Sheehy and Davis had assembled numerous tales of Bruce's penchant for chasing women other than his wife. They had Rosie Ritchie's "entertainment" episode, and Michelle McWhirter's cash-stuffed envelope. They had Jennifer Titchenal's story, and they kept hearing stories from people in the Long Beach real estate community that Bruce habitually propositioned women in crude fashion. Several of the women in the Wells Fargo portion of the office had complained to Larry Garcia about Bruce's behavior, both before and after Jana had disappeared. On October 9, Sheehy and Davis talked to a woman named Denise Brandenberg. She told them Bruce had called her on September 25— three days after he'd returned Jennifer to Sonora—and asked her for a date.

Denise was a travel agent in Long Beach, and had a casual acquaintance with both Bruce and Jana. When Bruce had called her to ask her out to a concert at the Pond, Denise had told him she wanted to think it over. She asked him about Jana's disappearance. Bruce talked about it for perhaps twenty minutes, she said, but his demeanor seemed "canned"—meaning, too rehearsed. It was, to Denise, as if Bruce had his story, and he was sticking to it.

Two days later, she said, Bruce called her again to see if she would go to the concert. This time she told him no. Bruce suggested that she was "stressed out," that maybe he could "unstress her." Denise was offended, but tried to put him off gently. Bruce had called her twice more since then, leaving messages on her answering machine, and still attempting to get her to agree to a date. Denise thought Bruce was getting pushy. "He was starting to yell and say that I was avoiding him, and not returning his phone calls, that I was scared of him, just like all of his other friends. It bothered me," she said later.

She didn't know what to make of Bruce, she told Davis and Sheehy, except that he was becoming an annoyance. The detectives asked her to wear a wire to tape-record Bruce.

No, Denise said, she would never do that. But Sheehy

and Davis kept after her, and eventually, she agreed to
tape Bruce surreptitiously the next time he called. When
this finally happened, however, Bruce said nothing of any
significance.

On October 9, it became official: The blood in the rear of
the SUV contained Jana's DNA. Sheehy and Davis drove
to Orange County the next day and gave the unhappy tid-
ings to Janie. Janie in turn called Bruce. Two days later,
the news appeared in the Long Beach paper.

KOKLICH'S BLOOD FOUND IN SUV, the *Press-Telegram*
headlined. The paper quoted Lieutenant Peavy: "Her
whereabouts are still unknown to us, but it is looking
more and more like something happened to her. We doubt
that we are going to find her alive."

The paper called Bruce for his reaction. Bruce said that
the investigators had notified Janie, who in turn told him.
That was interesting—if true, it implied that for some reason the detectives had decided not to call him with the information, but only Janie. Anyone reading between the
lines would infer that Bruce was the most logical suspect.

But, said Bruce, speaking for his alliance with Janie,
"We are both devastated." He said he was at work even
after hearing about the results of the testing, because it
didn't do any good to be "pacing the floor and crying . . .
I did that the first two weeks."

If they weren't talking directly with Bruce any
longer—they had Chris Botosan to tell them how Bruce
was behaving—the detectives were still questioning his
office staff. The next day they talked to Laura Roman and
Albert Canedo. This was when the detectives learned for
the first time that Laura and Albert had passed out flyers
on Lewis Avenue, and that they had talked to two women
with stories to tell: "Nicole" and "Star."

"Star" had told him, Albert said, that she knew of a

man who claimed to have seen a white man in a white shirt driving the Pathfinder in the Lewis Avenue area several days before it was found. Albert told Sheehy that he'd taken notes on the day they'd passed out the flyers. He was pretty sure he had notes with "Star's" telephone number on them. Sheehy and Davis asked Albert to look for the notes and turn them over to them. Albert said he would do that.

A bit later on the same day, Sheehy and Davis encountered Theresa Thornton—who had gone outside to pick up her newspaper on the morning of Monday, August 20, only to see a white SUV parked at the curb in front of her house. Theresa said she was pretty sure she'd seen the SUV as early as 7 or 8 A.M. Later that afternoon, she told the detectives, she'd seen a group of young African-American kids gathered around the car. Still later that day, she added, she'd seen someone get into the car and drive it off.

So, if Theresa was correct, that meant the SUV had been on Lewis Avenue as early as 7 or 8 Monday morning. That corroborated Rayray's and Freeman's stories. The only way the car could have gotten to Lewis Avenue by that time in the morning would be if Jana had left the house at, say 7 A.M., and was shortly thereafter carjacked and murdered, and her body stuffed in the SUV's cargo area. But that would still leave far too little time to dispose of her body—and even if it was possible, why would a carjacker leave her purse, her gun and her cellphone in plain sight—not to mention the keys in the ignition? It made absolutely no sense. Why commit the crime and then leave the fruits of it lying around for the likes of Rayray and Freeman to avail themselves of?

The far more reasonable explanation would be that (1) Bruce was lying when he'd told the detectives that he'd kissed his wife goodbye that morning; and (2) Bruce had planted the car on Lewis Avenue, with its "Steal Me"

flags, very early Monday morning in the hope that some
dupe would drive off with it and get himself arrested.

That raised another question, though: if Bruce had left
the car on Lewis Avenue at, say, 1 A.M., how did he get
home? The detectives weren't sure. One possibility was
that he had put one of the Koklich bicycles in the rear of
the SUV before starting off with Jana's body, and pedaled
himself back to Lakewood. Another was that he had simply walked the five miles back to his house. It was an unresolved loose end, but it didn't particularly trouble the
investigators.

Still, Reverand Bryant, who had done so much to help
the detectives find the purse and the gun, had his own theory: "I think somebody picked him up," Bryant said later.
"I just don't believe a single white man could walk
through this neighborhood at one in the morning without
somebody noticing him. I think he had help."

Meanwhile, Bruce's real estate business was sinking fast.
The sources of most of his listings, the banks, seemed to
be steering clear of the Koklich firm, apparently because
of the notoriety from Jana's disappearance. Cynthia Correa, for one, noted that the firm's inventory of foreclosed
properties was drastically diminished, almost down to
nothing, in fact. In October, she quit.

Sheehy and Davis kept finding people who had noticed
that things weren't going all that well between Bruce and
Jana just before her disappearance, either. Somehow they
tracked down a man who had installed a fireplace mantel
in the Lakewood house a year before. The Koklichs had
liked his work so much, said Baylor Maggenti, that Jana
had paid him a $1,500 deposit for a second mantel to be
built around the fireplace in the Koklich rec room. When
Maggenti returned to install it, shortly after the Koklichs
had returned from Dave Titchenal's wedding in Sonora in

late July, Jana seemed downcast and uninterested, in sharp contrast to her earlier behavior.

"It was apparent to him," Sheehy wrote later, "that Jana appeared to have something of importance on her mind, because she paid no attention to him or the job that was done. It was his opinion that she appeared to be disturbed about something, as she said nothing about the work and seemed not to care. [Maggenti's] daughter accompanied him on the job and had told him that Jana had discussions with her about going to a doctor's appointment . . ."

Here was still more evidence that something had been bothering Jana in the weeks immediately prior to her disappearance. If it wasn't the mystery caller—"Hiya, Jan, how you doin'?"—and Nini said Jana hadn't been that upset about the calls, what could it be? Jana's habitual reticence to discuss her private life led Sheehy and Davis to the conclusion that it had to be something about Bruce that was upsetting her.

And on October 18, they heard yet one more story of Bruce's attempts to find another woman. This was Dawn Bynum, a 27-year-old businesswoman whose grandmother lived just down the street from the Koklichs. Sometime in mid-September—apparently before the Jennifer interlude—Dawn found a note on the windshield of her car, which had been parked in front of her grandmother's house while she'd been visiting. The note was on Bruce's business stationery and contained a picture of him. Bruce wrote that he'd noticed Dawn in the neighborhood before, and wanted to know if she'd be interested in going to a concert with him.

Dawn said she'd laughed this invitation off; she'd never met Bruce and had no idea who he was. She crumpled the note up and tossed it into the back of her car. Eventually it was lost. But one day in October, Dawn mentioned the note to her grandmother, who then told her that Bruce was the man who was under investigation in the disappearance of his wife. A day or so later, Dawn called someone she knew in the Long Beach Police Department. She thought it was odd that Bruce was trying to get a date with her, under the circumstances. The Long Beach officer thought so, too, and passed the information on to Sheehy and Davis.

With this, the detectives were convinced—Bruce had gotten rid of Jana for the oldest of reasons: he wanted to fool around.

THE RUNDOWN

Son of AMOS

On Tuesday, October 16, Albert Canedo faxed over a copy of the notes he had taken while passing out Jana flyers in the Lewis Avenue area. The notes included a telephone number for "Star."

When Sheehy contacted "Star," she told him about a friend of hers, Ricardo Vargas. Vargas had told "Star" that he'd seen someone in a white SUV around Lewis Avenue, late at night, in mid-August. This second-hand account seemed to fit the picture, if one assumed that the SUV driver Vargas had seen was Bruce, dumping the car.

The following week, Sheehy met with Vargas. It turned out that Vargas' girlfriend lived in the apartments that were in front of the garages where the SUV had been found. Sometime in late August, Vargas said, his girlfriend had asked him to come over, because their small son was sick. Vargas recalled arriving after midnight, and pulling into the alley behind the apartments. While driving south through the alley, he said, he saw a smaller white SUV parked along the side of the alley with its lights off. Behind the wheel, he said, was an Anglo man wearing a white shirt. Ricardo recalled that the man's sleeves were pushed up.

As Vargas drove past, the white SUV suddenly shot forward, going northbound up the alley.

The incident stuck in his mind, Vargas told Sheehy, because he'd never before seen a white man driving in the alley so late at night.

Here was a witness who could offer evidence that it had been Bruce—or someone like him—who was in the area about the time the SUV had been dumped. True, Vargas couldn't positively identify Bruce—all he'd seen was the driver's arm with the shirtsleeve pushed up—and he couldn't say for sure that this had happened before August 20. But it fit. Sheehy could visualize it: Bruce, having dumped Jana's body someplace, wants to get rid of the SUV. After midnight, early on Monday August 20, Bruce drives the SUV into the alley, and is about to leave it there when Vargas drives past. The last thing Bruce wants is a witness to his dumping the car, so he shoots forward, exits the alley on the north end, goes around the block to Lewis Avenue, makes sure that no one's around, and pulls the SUV to a stop in front of Theresa Thornton's apartment, leaving the purse, cellphone and gun in plain view, the keys in the ignition and the windows rolled down— everything but the "Steal Me" sign on the windshield.

After getting this story from Vargas, Sheehy and Davis thought they might have enough to arrest Bruce. They drove downtown to talk to Deputy District Attorney Greg Dohi, a member of the prosecutor's Major Crimes Division. Dohi was convinced that Sheehy and Davis had the correct solution to Jana's disappearance, but before he took the case to court, he wanted a chance to evaluate the potential witnesses himself.

The case had one huge problem: There was no body. No body meant there was no physical evidence that a murder had occurred, except for the blood in the SUV and the drops found on the master bedroom carpet. There was no way to definitively tie Bruce to Jana's fate, whatever it had been, and even the blood evidence couldn't be used to prove that a murder had taken place—there simply wasn't enough of it for that. The entire case would have to be based on evidence from the circumstances, which, when taken together, would have to prove beyond a reasonable doubt that Bruce, and Bruce alone, had murdered his wife. Before embarking on such a potentially weak case, Dohi wanted to make sure he understood how the pieces might fit together. By meeting with each of the main witnesses himself, he could gauge how the case might play out before a jury.

On October 24, 2001, Dohi, Davis and Sheehy went to Jan and Jeff Baird's house in Whittier. Dohi took notes, which later formed the basis of a typewritten report he placed in the case file summarizing the testimony that might be expected if the case ever came to trial.

> Jan has known Jana Koklich for 27 years. Jan and Jana were like sisters. They met when Jan worked on one of Senator Carpenter's campaigns. Jan would see Jana about once a month. Jan would usually call Jana at Jana's office. Jana confided in Jan about Jana's father.
>
> Jana never missed appointments without calling first, Jan can only remember one time when Jana cancelled at the last minute. Jana was never more than 10 minutes late. Jana was extremely dependable.
>
> Jan has never known the Koklichs to spend an entire weekend relaxing. Bruce was obsessed with money. He was cheap and would suggest that Jan pick up the bill at restaurants.
>
> Jana said in March or April that she and Bruce were going to adopt a child.
>
> Bruce Koklich called Jan on 8/20 around 5:15 p.m.

When Jan asked if there was anything she could do, Bruce broke down and said, "You can tell me where Jana is." He then quit crying immediately, which struck Jan as odd.

Jan now recounted the substance of various telephone calls she'd had with Bruce in September and October, including the time that Bruce had tried to suggest that Jana had missed an appointment with her. Bruce had also called her to explain about Jennifer at Janie's urging, Jan said.

Jeff Baird, for his part, showed Dohi and the detectives copies of the deeds that Jana had executed, giving real estate to the marital community with Bruce in July before her disappearance. Baird suggested that the detectives talk to Harry Parrell for more background on Bruce.

"Although it doesn't appear in my written notes," Dohi reported, "at the end of the interview Jeff mentioned that about a week after Jana disappeared, Bruce asked him how long a person had to be missing in order to be declared dead."

Over the next two weeks, Dohi met more of the key witnesses: first, Consuelo Lopez, then Chris Botosan, followed by Nini Angelini. A week later, Dohi met with Botosan once more, and went with Sheehy and Davis to interview Bruce's stepbrothers, Dave and Dan Titchenal.

The critical testimony expected from Consuelo had to do with the sheets. "The sheets on the Koklichs' bed were not the same as those she had placed there on Tuesday," Dohi noted, after debriefing Consuelo at the Lakewood station. "Jana and Bruce had never changed the sheets before. The missing sheets had beautiful words in black letters . . . the pillowcases were also missing. The front doormat was missing." Three days later, she said, she'd discovered that Jana's long, flat pillow was gone. The pillow usually had traces of Jana's makeup on it, she said.

Consuelo added that Bruce's lawyer, Henry Salcido, wanted to talk to her. But Consuelo said she didn't want to talk to Salcido. She'd already quit working for Bruce, because she was afraid to be in the house alone.

The same afternoon, Dohi interviewed Chris; this was the first time he had met Bruce's computer expert. Chris told Dohi that he mostly worked for the Union Rescue Mission, spending only a couple of days a week at Bruce's business. "He has worked for a couple of computer software companies," Dohi wrote in his notes, "including STS in London, and has worked as a consultant to the U.S. Army Special forces."[13]

In his conversation with Dohi, Chris claimed that he had only met Bruce "eight months ago," contradicting Bruce's assertion to the detectives that they had actually first met in the 1980s in Florida in connection with Berkeley Federal Savings.

Chris sketched in some of the details about AMOS. "The Koklichs had formed Asset Management Origination Systems (AMOS)," Dohi recorded. "They held 22 million shares together. Botosan got one million shares, and was to receive 100,000 for every client he signed up. Bruce was looking at $50–100 million in 18 months. Botosan has all the financial documentation. The business should have a 72 percent profit margin. Bruce spent three-fourths of his time on AMOS. Jana spent only five percent of her time."

---

[13] Although Chris claimed to have consulted with Special Forces in Florida over ways to detect land mines, a spokesman for the Special Forces Command could not verify or deny that Chris had ever done any work there.

But, Chris told Dohi, "the scandal surrounding Jana's disappearance has driven off potential customers" for AMOS.

"NABUCO is issuing a $100 million bond," Dohi's notes continued, "from which AMOS was supposed to get $7.8 million. Botosan can't stop it."

This made it sound as though Chris was helpless to prevent NABUCO from financing AMOS, that this was some sort of transaction that he had nothing to do with. From Dohi's notes, it appears that Chris did not tell Dohi at that point that he had a financial interest in NABUCO.

Dohi's notes now indicated that "Botosan is trying to set up a trust to hold the Koklich shares." But Dohi didn't make clear which Koklich shares—Bruce's or Jana's?

Reviewing Dohi's notes on his talk with Chris, in retrospect it appears that Chris was playing a three-cornered game that fall—seeming to be Bruce's partner and confidant, while secretly informing on him to the authorities, and at the same time, trying to protect the NABUCO principals from falling into the abyss created by the investigation into Jana's disappearance. That was one reason why his varied explanations of NABUCO never made a lot of sense—the details, always somewhat vague, kept shifting. But as for Bruce's incriminatory behavior, Chris was quite specific.

"Bruce would often make suggestive comments [about various women]," Dohi noted. "Today, when Botosan said that he was going to get his car washed, Bruce said that he likes to take his car to where high school girls wash cars."

From the direction of the questions, it wasn't hard for Chris to deduce that the law believed that Bruce's motive for getting rid of Jana was sexual, not mercenary.

Even though the NABUCO proposal—or at least its promise—was a much stronger motive for Bruce to have

killed his wife, neither Dohi nor the detectives seemed
very interested in pursuing it. That may have been because advancing it to a jury meant that prosecutors would
have to undercut Botosan as one of their witnesses, and in
the process, might hand the defense a quasi-plausible alternative explanation for Jana's vanishing. It was much
simpler to avoid NABUCO altogether by attributing
Bruce's motive to his sexual shenanigans. It may not have
been the truth, the whole truth and nothing but the truth,
but it at least had the distinct advantage of making a conviction of Bruce much more likely.

A week later, Dohi and Sheehy met with Chris again.
Apparently they had decided they needed to make sure
that the NABUCO proposal wasn't critical to the prosecution of Bruce.

Dohi noted in a memo to the file dated November 11:

> We asked him to explain the real estate software ven-
> ture. Botosan showed us a number of documents and
> told us the following:
>
>   The deal had two components: (1)—the clearing-
> house taskmaster software service (Asset Manage-
> ment and Origination Service (AMOS)); and (2)—the
> financing package.
>
>   The real estate service:
>
>   Every client bank was going to sign two consecu-
> tive three-year contracts. The business was going to
> make $10 million a year, or $60–70 million over six
> years. The costs of running this business would be
> low, and 65 percent of its earnings would be profit.
> Botosan calculated the cash value of the venture at
> $600 million.
>
>   AMOS was planning to buy another company . . .
> which had 25 percent of the foreclosure market. [The
> other company] had 12 client banks, which would add

12 customers to the four banks already signed up with AMOS. Botosan conservatively estimates $600,000 in profit per client.

Botosan created a Nevada shell corporation called AAMOS to take over the functions of AMOS. AMOS is paralyzed because of Jana's disappearance. Directors for AAMOS have yet to be appointed. Bruce was pushing for his allies Jim Rivas and Larry Garcia.

The more interesting part of the business was the financing package.

Botosan has a close friend, Steve Boyers, who formerly sat on the SEC [federal Securities and Exchange Commission] committee [sic], and who is a high-ranking officer with a company called NABUCO.[14] NABUCO was set up to issue a $100 million bond for AAMOS at 8 percent.

NABUCO's assets are all tied up in Treasury bills. NABUCO was to loan $7.85 million to $14.85 million to AAMOS. The money won't get loaned until February [of 2002] at the soonest. That money was going into an account in a brokerage firm (Fiserv)[15] and earn interest at a rate of 5.5 percent a month. AAMOS was therefore guaranteed $431,750 a month against expenses of $67,000 a month to service the loan. Of that $67,000 payment, 35 percent would go to an account to pay off the loan. After 10 years, a $3.8 million balloon payment would become due, which NABUCO would forgive.

[14] A check of the former members of the SEC showed that Stephen Robert Boyers was not a former member of the commission. An SEC spokesman was unable to confirm or deny whether Boyers had ever worked for the SEC in some other capacity.

[15] An inquiry to Fiserv as to whether it had ever heard of NABUCO, or if it had ever paid 5.5 percent per month in interest on any account, generated no response from the well-known investment firm.

The deal works for NABUCO because NABUCO needs to get Treasury bills in small quantities but can't buy them directly. Fiserv uses client accounts to buy Treasury bills in convenient quantities. NABUCO was to get everything above the 5.5 percent. Botosan was going to get a piece (13 percent) of what NABUCO makes.

Under new arrangements recently made by Botosan, if Bruce is arrested, or if there's a finding of wrongful death, Bruce's money is held in trust. NABUCO will probably sue for it. Jana's money goes to her estate.

Steve Boyers has said that Bruce can't be in the company anymore.

Miscellany: NABUCO pushed for Janie to serve as Jana's conservator. Bruce went along.

The most astonishing thing about Dohi's memo is the fact that both the prosecutor and the detectives seemed to accept Chris' description of NABUCO and its proposed financing plan at face value. No one ever checked up in Las Vegas to determine NABUCO's antecedents, which would have turned up Piotrowski's connection to the old unsuccessful federal criminal prosecution from the alleged Aladdin hotel scam. Nor did anyone check with the SEC or Fiserv to see if there was any substance to Chris's tale.

And as previously noted, the proposed financing arrangement seems remarkably optimistic, to say the least: it's difficult to see how any brokerage firm could pay 5.5 percent interest per month, especially by investing in "Treasury bills." And from the perspective of the dwindling pro-Bruce contingent, there was even grist here for an alternative theory of the case. First Jana disappears, "paralyzing" AMOS. Then Botosan comes along, creates the shell AAMOS, and asserts that the control of

AAMOS is up for grabs. QED, Bruce's lawyers might argue: someone made away with Jana in order to take control of AMOS. Botosan adds that if Bruce should be arrested, Botosan has already made arrangements to create a trust that would have the effect of cutting Bruce out of the management of the company, and further asserts that "Steve Boyers has said that Bruce can't be in the company anymore." Again, QED: Bruce was being cut out of AMOS, giving a possible motive for Jana's disappearance to Chris.

This was all very interesting, and even a bit intriguing. But the problem was, what in the world did it have to do with the missing sheets? No matter what NABUCO and Botosan had been up to when they came on the scene, the single most damning fact of all was that only Bruce could have changed the sheets, and used the wrong kind, to boot.

Either it was Bruce, or it was someone fiendishly clever—clever enough to use the one piece of seemingly innocuous evidence that would mean that only Bruce could have done it.

And both Sheehy and Dohi knew from long years of experience that no matter how someone played with figures, no one was *that* clever. It simply wasn't very likely that someone could have surreptitiously gotten into the Koklich house, made away with Jana, and changed the sheets before they left. It was just too bizarre.

On November 13, Bruce called Linda Vargas in San Antonio. "My in-laws have turned against me," he told her. "They're trying to frame me."

By this point, Linda had talked to Paul Carpenter about Jana's disappearance. She knew about all the telephone calls neither Koklich had answered on the fateful weekend. She now asked Bruce about these calls. Bruce told her that he and Jana had decided to spend a quiet weekend together without distractions. Linda said she found this hard to believe—in her mind, Jana could have been prostrate with illness and she still would have called back. Bruce said nothing to this.

Dissatisfied with Bruce's story, Linda called Paul to tell him what Bruce had said. Paul urged her to call Detective Sheehy.

The following week, Linda Vargas did just that, telling Sheehy about the dinner conversation in San Antonio on July 27, in which Jana had told her that she and Bruce had been "in and out of love for the past fourteen years." Linda added that Bruce had called to invite her and her girlfriend to come stay with him in Lakewood. She said that the last time she'd talked to Bruce, about a week before, she'd pressed him to explain about the missed telephone calls, and that Bruce hadn't said anything when she'd told him that Jana would have returned calls even if she'd been bedridden.

On the same day, Sheehy and Davis returned to the Koklich office with another search warrant. They wanted the Koklich office computer to see if there was any evidence that records of Jana's schedule on the suspect weekend had been altered. Bruce answered the knock on the backdoor. Both he and Barbara Hauxhurst were detained outside the office while the searchers removed the computer's hard drive for laboratory analysis. Bruce was asked if he knew of any will or trust executed by Jana, and Bruce said he knew of none. Afterward, the detectives escorted Bruce to the Lakewood house. They wanted to take the Koklich bicycles in another search for evidence, presumably blood.

Following the search, Chris called the detectives to tell them that Bruce had been "very cocky" during the raid. Criticized later by Bruce's lawyer for this snitching, Chris defended himself: "It was information in a crime that had been committed," he said, "and this is not something that I took lightly. I believe it was a relevant fact."

That same afternoon, Sheehy met with a former employee of the Koklichs', Nilesh Solanki. It appears that Chris had provided this name to the detectives earlier. Solanki had worked for the Koklichs as an inspector in the late 1990s. He told Sheehy that on one occasion when he was inspecting a vacant property listed with the Koklichs, he had tried to open the front door, only to meet resistance from inside. He'd heard a woman inside saying, "Let me out," or words to that effect. When he finally got the door open, he discovered Bruce inside with his zipper pulled down. A woman—Solanki guessed she might have been a street person—brushed past him and left. "We were talking and I asked him what happened," Solanki said later. "He says he's going through some type of problem, and something to the [effect] that, you know, he does not receive this at home . . . he asked me not to tell anybody." But Solanki had told the others in the office, which was probably how Chris eventually learned of it.

Well, thought Sheehy, here's just another example of Bruce's proclivities. The case was simple, Sheehy decided—Jana had caught Bruce fooling around once too often, and Bruce had simply decided to do away with her.

Only he'd done it so well, no one could find her.

Totalities

HUSBAND FOCUS OF KOKLICH PROBE, headlined the *Press-Telegram* the morning of December 7, 2001.

Reporters Paul Young and Tracy Manzer, who had been covering the case almost from the outset, said that although the sheriff's detectives had followed dozens of leads in Jana's disappearance over the prior three months, "the one thing they haven't done is eliminate her husband, Bruce Koklich, as a suspect."

Lieutenant Peavy said his detectives had cleared all other suspects, and the only person left was Bruce.

But in preparing their story, the reporters interviewed Bruce and his lawyer, Henry Salcido. Bruce denied responsibility for Jana's disappearance, and told the reporters that she had received telephone calls from a man who had been "taunting" her in the weeks before she was last seen. He added that damage to the SUV's bumper showed that Jana might have been the victim of a carjacker.

Peavy said his detectives had investigated both of these claims and had ruled them out. The damage to the SUV was too slight, he said, to indicate a carjacking, and besides, what carjacker would have left Jana's purse, gun and cellphone in the car, along with the keys?

The most interesting thing about the newspaper's account of the Koklich case was the reporters' interview with Paul Carpenter. The newspaper noted that Paul was severely ill with cancer.

Paul, reached in San Antonio by telephone, told the reporters that he had never believed Bruce's claim that he'd spent a quiet weekend with Jana before she disappeared. He'd only told Bruce that, Paul said, in order to get Bruce's trust, and put him off his guard so he could get the goods on his son-in-law. It was nothing but a ruse on his part, Paul said—reminiscent of his old days at the Balboa Bay Club when he'd bluffed his way to a fortune. The bluff had worked so well, Paul added, that even Janie, his former wife, believed it.

The proof that Bruce was lying, Paul said, came from the fact that no one answered the telephone calls on August 18 and 19. "We believe," Paul told the reporters, "she couldn't pick up the phone because she was dead."

Doris Morrow added to this: "I can tell you that Jana Koklich was very close to her father. Considering her father's condition, she never would have not answered the phone. And if she were alive, and her fingers were working, she would have found some way to call her mother."

That was exactly what Sheehy, Davis and Dohi were doing on the day this story hit the streets: calling Janie Carpenter. Now, at last, Janie, too, believed that Bruce was responsible for Jana's disappearance. The detectives and Dohi went to Orange County to interview her.

Janie told them that when she'd arrived at the house on the afternoon of Monday, August 20, Jana's concert-going clothes from three nights earlier—Friday night—were still on the bed of the spare room, and the black shoes she'd worn were still on the floor. That casual strewing was so unlike Jana, Janie said, that it immediately caught her attention. Jana always put away her clothes, and especially her shoes, Janie said.

Like Nini, Janie had noticed the cosmetics case still in the bathroom. Jana never would have left voluntarily on a trip without taking it. Bruce kept playing the "mystery man" message to people that night, but Jana had never complained to her about any weird calls, Janie said.

The pillow business still bothered Janie, though. She explained that she'd slept on the long, flat pillow on Tuesday night, and that Chris had later said it was actually his own pillow. It was only three days later, when Consuelo reported that Jana's pillow was missing that Janie realized the pillow Chris had taken might actually have been Jana's.

"Janie said she is very suspicious of Chris, and was wondering if this pillow Chris took was the same pillow Jana always took with her . . ." the detectives noted.

Sheehy, Davis and Dohi asked Janie if she knew whether Jana had ever executed a will.

"Janie said she never saw one," the detectives reported, "nor was she ever told about one. However, she knew that her ex-husband Paul had his attorney (Jeff Baird), draw up some new papers regarding his, Paul's, will, while he was recently in town from Texas. Paul mentioned that Jana had named him as a beneficiary in her and Bruce's will, and due to his failing health, was reverting everything Jana had left to him back to Bruce."

But after Paul had decided that Bruce was responsible for Jana's disappearance, he had changed his will back, so Bruce would not get Jana's bequest to her father when he died.

That certainly made it sound as though Bruce and Jana had made wills. It was strange, the detectives thought, that Bruce kept insisting that there were none.

Janie told Dohi she'd recently received a letter from Bruce in which he had proclaimed his innocence. He'd also asked Janie to meet with him and Henry Salcido. But after reading the letter, Janie concluded that someone had written it for Bruce. She deduced that someone had advised him that it was critical to keep her on his side. It was too late, Janie indicated. She now agreed with Paul: Jana's disappearance had been Bruce's doing.

After talking with Janie, Davis decided to call Chris to get this pillow business ironed out once and for all.

"Investigator Davis spoke with Chris Botosan via telephone and confirmed that the pillow he took from the Koklich house on Tuesday (08-21-2001) [sic] was his and that he still has it. Chris said he has a hard time sleeping in strange beds and, like Jana, will travel with his personal pillow. On this particular occasion, he went home and got it."

Neither detective gave any serious thought to going over to Chris's apartment and seizing the pillow for forensic examination. Besides, what good would it do? Even if it had been Jana's pillow, with traces of her makeup on it, it almost certainly had been cleaned or even replaced by now.

The next day Bruce and his lawyer, Henry Salcido, struck back at the sheriff's department's fingering of him as the only remaining suspect by holding a press conference in front of the Long Beach City Hall. Bruce was backed by a number of his employees who'd come to attend the briefing.

"They're trying to drive a wedge between Bruce, his friends and his business acquaintances," Salcido said. "All we want is for them [the authorities] to join with us in conducting an unbiased, fair investigation."

Salcido said he would provide information to the sheriff's department that should be investigated. He was referring to the sighting of the woman in the rear of a Jeep by "Nicole," the account unearthed by Albert Canedo and

Laura Roman while they were passing out flyers the previous August. The police had never been able to interview "Nicole," it appears.

"We've given them the information," Salcido said, "but in spite of that, the message in the press is that we're not cooperating." It wasn't so, he added; the problem was, the police were looking in the wrong direction, and in so doing, they had poisoned Bruce's relationship with his in-laws, Paul and Janie Carpenter.

In the following week, Sheehy and Davis presented their case against Bruce to a full panel of lawyers from the District Attorney's Major Crimes Division. The purpose of these presentations was to allow the legal minds of the DA's office to evaluate the case—to see if it would fly.

One of the deputy district attorneys who was in attendance at this "case preview," as it was called, was Eleanor Hunter. A veteran prosecutor who had spent more than five years in the DA's Hard Core Gang unit, Hunter had long before learned to be skeptical of claims of innocence, especially when the evidence seemed to indicate otherwise. Sheehy and Davis ran through the circumstances of Jana's disappearance—the return from the concert, the missed appointments and unreturned telephone calls from the weekend, Bruce's behavior, and the sheets. The unreturned calls and the sheets caught Hunter's attention.

"The man had no explanation as to where she was over the weekend; that was the most glaring thing," Hunter recalled from the preview. "His story was completely suspect, and his demeanor, especially with eighteen calls unreturned, was unbelievable. It was pretty clear he committed the crime—especially after we heard about the sheets."

There were still some problems with the case, however—principally the lack of a body. That didn't deter

Hunter, or other members of the Major Crimes Division. All of them knew that other cases had been prosecuted and won when there was no body to prove that murder had occurred. A body wasn't actually needed, she said.

"The totality of the circumstances here indicated that a murder had happened," Hunter recalled. "There was the blood in the back of the SUV, *her* blood. How did it get there, if her body hadn't been there at one time? And this was a woman who was scrupulous about keeping in contact with her friends and family. All of a sudden, there's nothing? No appointments kept, no returned calls at all? There was only one reasonable conclusion, and that was that she was dead."

Beginning in September, shortly after Jana's disappearance, Sheehy and Davis had begun checking a large variety of sources, many of them computerized, to see if Jana was alive and well, or possibly dead and unidentified in some other part of the country. The detectives had checked the coroner/medical examiner offices in six southern California counties for a Jane Doe matching Jana's description, with negative results. They'd checked a database of driver's licenses that covered the whole country, to see if Jana had ever applied for a new license in another state; voter registration lists; changes of address with the U.S. Postal Service; the Social Security System to see if she'd taken a job someplace; an index of divorce cases; credit reports; a check of jails; the firearms tracking system; pawn shops; hospitals; criminal history records; and Canadian police records. They found no records of Jana Koklich, living or dead, after August 20, 2001.

Okay, said the reviewing panel of deputy district attorneys—you've convinced us that Jana Koklich *is* dead. There is, however, one other problem: The Koklich neighbor, school principal Donna Baker, has told everyone that she recalled seeing Jana's SUV in the garage, possibly around 8 A.M. on Monday morning. If that sighting stands up, then Bruce will be able to claim that he couldn't have killed his wife—he was out inspecting houses at the time, and was back in his office by 8:30 A.M.

If Donna Baker was right, there was no way Bruce could have killed Jana after 8 A.M. on Monday morning, disposed of her body someplace, driven the SUV to Lewis Avenue and gotten back to the office in time for Barbara Hauxhurst, Larry Garcia, Rosa Canedo and the others to see him. Somehow, the deputies said, that hole had to be plugged.

On January 9, 2002, Davis and Sheehy met with Ms. Baker, who reiterated that she thought she'd seen the white SUV in the Koklich garage on either Sunday morning, August 19, or Monday morning, August 20, between 8 and 8:30 A.M. But which day was it? If it was Sunday, Bruce could still have planted the car on Lewis Avenue early Monday morning. But if it was Monday, there had to be someone else involved.

"Donna continued, telling investigators she was unsure as to which day she saw the white SUV parked in the Koklich garage," the detectives reported later. But Donna now remembered that she'd told Bruce, when he'd canvassed the neighborhood back on August 21, that she'd noticed the SUV was parked on the left side of the garage. That was unusual, Donna now said, because typically Bruce parked his own white coupe on that side. And she remembered that the garage door of the house next door—the Rombergs'—was open by a foot or two.

This was a new problem: The detectives had already interviewed Dr. Romberg, the dentist. He told them he habitually raised his garage door a small amount in the early morning hours of his office days of Monday, Tuesday, Thursday and Friday, to let cool air in while he was working out inside the garage. He said he usually got up about 6 A.M. on his office days, opened the garage door slightly, worked out in the garage for thirty minutes, and then jogged around the neighborhood for another thirty minutes, leaving the garage door slightly ajar while on his run, so the space could cool down.

"Dr. Romberg said he closes the door around 8 A.M. when he leaves for the office," the detectives recorded.

This seemed to show that when Donna Baker noticed the white SUV parked on the wrong side of the Koklich garage, and also noticed the slightly opened garage door of Dr. Romberg, it had to have been on a Monday morning just before 8 A.M.

Just like Romberg's garage door, this was a slight crack in the case. Before everything was over, Bruce's lawyer Henry Salcido would try to shove that crack open as wide as he could, in order to create space for Bruce's innocence. He'd also try to put Chris Botosan firmly in the gap.

Opting Out

On January 24, 2002, Paul Carpenter died. His life story had described a classic tragic arc, from humble beginnings in Iowa, to highly successful politician, to criminal defendant, to a fugitive from justice, followed by the disappearance and presumed murder of his youngest child, possibly at the hands of his own son-in-law. Like the protagonist in a Greek myth, Paul had been raised to great heights by the gods, only to be shattered by his own hubris.

By the end he had become certain that Bruce had killed Jana. But as the weeks turned into months after her disappearance, and she remained missing, Paul's hope for a resolution, an answer, began to fade, and with it, his own bodily strength. There were some who thought that the disappearance of Jana had robbed him of his will to live. "I'm a fighter," Paul had said, just before going to prison. "I've been on some tough mountains before." But this—week after week, month upon month with no explanation—this was a mountain too tall to climb. It was the not knowing, nor having the hope of knowing, that was truly toxic. Paul died without ever finding out what had become of the daughter he had taken for granted for so long, and then had come to love in a way he had never anticipated.

But it was too bad Paul could not have lived just a little longer. One week after he died, Sheehy and Davis came to the Koklich office and arrested Bruce, charging him with the murder of his wife, Jana Carpenter Koklich.

KOKLICH ARRESTED, the *Press-Telegram* headlined the next day.

"I don't want to say he acted like he expected it," said Lieutenant Peavy, "but he did not seem shocked by the fact that he was being arrested." Bruce was booked at the Lakewood sheriff's station, and then transferred to the county's central jail in downtown Los Angeles. Bail, assuming that Bruce could qualify, was set at $1 million. Bruce's lawyer, Henry Salcido, told the newspaper that the authorities would never be able to convict Bruce.

"We have enough evidence to establish reasonable doubt," Salcido said, meaning the Donna Baker/Dr. Romberg accounts, and the LePire/Radcliffe supposed sightings of Jana at the office on Sunday, August 19, both of which tended to show that Jana was alive on both Sunday and Monday. In addition, he said, Bruce could easily establish his alibi for the time of Jana's reported disappearance on Monday morning.

"You'll see in court," he told the newspaper.

Janie said she was glad that something had finally been done.

"I'm glad they are closing in on the case," she said. "It's been a long time, and a long investigation. I hope they have a solid case."

The paper also resurrected some statements made by Paul just before he died. It was eerie, in a way, a bit like hearing from a ghost. Paul's words were prophetic, like the imprecations of a spirit who'd had foreknowledge of what was to come:

"That first week," Paul had told the newspaper a month before he died, "I was hoping he was innocent. But on my plane ride home [to Texas in September], I reviewed all the facts, and there's just so many holes in his story that there's not any way his story would hold up."

Bruce's motive, Paul had said, was "money, greed. I think she wanted a divorce, and rather than split your assets two ways, I think he wanted it all."

The next day, Bruce pleaded innocent to the murder charge. Salcido asked that he be granted a reduced bail, noting that if Bruce had wanted to flee, he could have done so long before. The judge, however, was unmoved: if Bruce wanted out pending trial, he had to come up with $1 million in hard cash. Bruce went back to jail, while Salcido and others scrambled around, trying to raise the money. It took about two weeks, with Bruce pledging real estate he owned separately, properties he held with others, and some assistance from his old real estate partner, Harry Parrell, but he finally got the $1 million together. He was released on bail on February 15, 2002.

That same day, the *Press-Telegram* was back, this time with a new story:

NOISE AT KOKLICHS' REPORTED, the paper's front page headlined on February 15, 2002.

"According to affidavits filed in support of a search warrant," the newspaper's account read, "a neighbor and her sister told investigators that they heard the noises at approximately the same time Jana Carpenter Koklich returned from the concert . . . the neighbor and her sister said it sounded as if someone were dragging furniture across a room and banging it into a wall. It appeared as if two people were arguing, then the sound suddenly stopped."

This information was contained in the affidavit supporting the September 5 search for blood in the bedroom, the one that had been conducted with luminol, and referred to the statements made by Marguerite Grinder and her sister, Catherine Eva Hansen. The affidavit had been sealed by the court since it was issued, but was unsealed after Bruce's arrest.

Asked for his comments about the allegations contained in the search warrant affidavit, Salcido said he would have to study the document further. But, he said, the investigators may have "tainted" some witness who had provided information for the search warrant. He seemed to be referring to the "noises in the night" assertion of Marguerite and her sister. The detectives, Salcido suggested, had fueled the sisters' recollections by telling them that Bruce had to be guilty.

"I know for a fact that they are attempting to poison [witnesses] against Bruce," Salcido told the newspaper. "They are hinting that they have evidence that proves Bruce did it." This only encouraged witnesses to come forward with half-baked or unfounded conclusions, Salcido implied.

The worst thing about all the publicity was its spillover effect. Somewhere along the line, the Union Rescue Mission had discovered that Chris was using one of their computers to help Bruce with the AMOS project. In the wake of Bruce's arrest, they'd called Chris and demanded that he return their computer forthwith. And by the way, the Mission added, your services are no longer needed— you're fired. Chris immediately went to the Koklich office and removed the Union Rescue Mission's Macintosh computer, and returned it to them. Larry Garcia saw what he was doing and tried to stop him, but Chris insisted that the computer—with all its AMOS software—had to be returned as soon as possible.

Apparently this dire development had been communicated to Bruce, because almost as soon as he was out of jail, he started looking for Chris to find out what was going on. He called NABUCO's Joe Heller to see if Heller knew where Chris was. Heller called Chris to tell him Bruce was trying to track him down.

One can imagine what was going through Chris's mind when he heard that Bruce was looking for him. After four months of secretly informing on Bruce, Chris had to guess that Bruce had finally tumbled to the fact that his partner had played him for a fool. The DA's office had already explained that Bruce would soon learn of Chris's role as an informant against him. Now Chris was forced to wonder if Bruce wasn't gunning for him.

"I'm a gun nut," Bruce had told Chris months earlier. And Chris knew for a fact that Bruce liked to pack a pistol. Now that he was out and looking for Chris, who was to say that Bruce might not shoot him for ratting him out?

Chris called Joe Sheehy. Sheehy called Dohi. Dohi had been under the impression that a condition of Bruce's release was that he not contact any witnesses. The court's order, however, did allow Bruce to contact "business associates." In Bruce's mind, that's all Chris was at that point—a business associate. Bruce still hadn't realized that Botosan was two-timing him. Or possibly even three-timing him, if one counts NABUCO. He had no idea that Chris had been snitching all those months, that he was more a witness than a partner.

Sheehy and Dohi now figured they might be able to get Bruce back in jail for his violation of the no-contact-with-witnesses order. They told Chris to call Bruce back, and tape the call.

Nervously, not knowing whether Bruce had finally figured out what his true role had been during all the months of the investigation, and was about to threaten to blow his head off the next time he saw him, Chris returned Bruce's call, and switched on his tape recorder.

Bruce's receptionist answered the telephone, and Chris identified himself. Within a few seconds, Bruce came on the line.

"Hey," Bruce said.

"Hey," Chris responded.

"How you doing?" Bruce asked, as if it had been Chris who'd been in jail, not him.

"I'm all right."

"Good. Well, I'm out of the can."

"Yeah," Chris said. "Finally."

"A lot of work to get me out. If the DA had his way I'd still be in there."

"So you saw the Macintosh?" Chris asked.

"Yeah," Bruce said. "I was pretty upset."

"Well, as you saw, I got fired."

"I can't believe that. How could they do it?"

"They did it, regardless."

"Is there any way we can get the computer back?"

"I can get a copy of it, probably," Chris said, meaning a copy of the hard drive's contents. He'd have to check to see if he could find a way to get data off the returned computer.

"All right," Bruce said. "So how are you doing?"

"I'm okay."

"Okay," Bruce said. "Well, hopefully, you're still hanging in there with me."

What? Bruce still hadn't figured out that Chris had been informing on him? Chris could hardly believe his ears.

"Yeah," Chris said, noncommittally. Bruce's avowal of

faith in his "partner" either showed he didn't know that Chris had been cooperating with the police, or was some sort of trick. Chris opted for a tentative response to see which way the shadow was being cast.

"So what's next?" he asked.

Bruce said that he wasn't supposed to contact witnesses, but was allowed to talk to business associates. He wanted to know which Chris was, at that point: witness or associate? Because, Bruce added, he could talk to Chris if he was an associate; he couldn't talk to Chris if he was a witness. In which case, the judge would send him back to jail, "which, you know, I don't want to do," Bruce added.

This was it: Chris had to choose which side he was on, Bruce seemed to be saying. Chris had to be wondering what Bruce really knew about his role up until then. Was this some sort of test? If he lied and Bruce knew it, would Bruce come after him? "I'm a gun nut," Chris heard again in his mind. He knew that Bruce was an excellent shot.

"Yeah, all right," Chris said. "Right now I'm concerned and I don't think that it's—you know, there's too much stuff. So I don't know."

Bruce didn't seem to hear Chris. Or perhaps he thought that Chris was only saying he wasn't ready to decide. This declaration of loyalties by Chris *was* pretty wishy-washy.

"Okey-doke," Bruce said. "Well, I can just say what I've been telling everybody else . . . you know how the press works, and they're creating shit that just isn't there. I mean, that crap about, you know, fucking noises in my house on Friday night. I mean, there were two sets of investigators who talked to that woman [Marguerite Grinder] two days after Jana was missing and none of that shit came up. I don't know where the hell it came from. It's ridiculous. It's crap."

"Yeah," Chris said, still striving for neutrality.

"Anyway," Bruce continued, "let me know what you decide . . . I'm hoping you'll stay in the game . . . Let me know where you stand."

"Okay," Chris said. "All right. Bye."

After he hung up, Chris realized that Bruce *still* didn't know that he'd been the detectives' most consistent source, almost from the beginning. It was amazing, in a way: Bruce was so focused on what he thought Chris could do *for* him that he'd never considered what Chris could do *to* him.

Four days later, Sheehy and Davis met with Chris. Chris gave them the tape recording, and Dohi began efforts to put Bruce back in jail for violating the no-contact order. Once Dohi told Salcido he intended to ask for the revocation of Bruce's bail, and that he had a tape recording to prove that Bruce had violated the no-contact order, Chris was finally, irretrievably exposed as the police informant he had been, almost from the beginning.

Bruce's reaction to this news went unrecorded.

Not long after Bruce had been arrested, and apparently while he was still trying to arrange bail, Detective Longshore had a call from Kellee, his East Coast psychic, who happened to be visiting her grandmother in southern California. He asked her if she was interested in seeing some of the locations involved in the case. Kellee said she'd be very interested. The only time Longshore could meet with her was well after midnight.

"So I took her down to Bruce's house," Longshore recalled, "and we parked in front of the house. And I said, 'Okay, this is Bruce's house, what do you see?' And she goes, 'Well . . . gosh, my throat's hurting . . .' And she goes, 'If this is the house, I'd guess that the master bedroom must be in the front of the house . . . but I don't see anything there. But in the bedroom behind, there's something. I'm not sure what.'

"The way the house is set up, the master bedroom is in the back of the house, and that's where we found the blood. And she goes, 'I'm getting— Gosh, my throat's hurting . . . I'm getting a real strong feeling from this garage.' Well, that's where Jana's car is . . . and that's, of course, where the blood was, in the car.

"So then I said, 'Should we go to the oil field?' 'Sure.' So we drove up there and walked around. It's not my idea of a good time, walking around this oil field in the middle of the night, but okay. And she goes, 'She was here. But she's not anymore.' And she says, 'I can see her. We're close. She's talking to me. She says we're close, don't give up.'

"So then we went down to the garage, where we found the car. And I say, 'This is where we found the car.' And she says, 'This is what I saw, but whoever put it here had nothing to do with it, they had no idea of what was going on.'

"I said, 'Okay.' And I said, 'Let's go down to this other street,' down on Lewis. I parked the car just where Jana's car had been parked. And she said, 'What happened here?' And I said, 'No, it doesn't work that way—you tell me.' She sat there for a minute, and then she looked up, and said, 'What happened on top of that building?' And that's where we found the purse."

Despite his best efforts, Dohi's attempt to put Bruce back in the slammer was rebuffed by the court, which found that as far as Bruce was concerned, Chris, to him, *had* been a business associate. Which only showed that Bruce was as willfully unaware as he had ever been, even going back to the days when NABUCO first arrived on the scene with their promise of millions in big money.

It wasn't long before the true dimensions of Chris's informing on Bruce became apparent to Salcido, however. Someone, presumably Salcido, soon put Bruce straight as to Chris's role as the detectives' prized informant. By the end of February 2002, Chris was asked to clean out his desk at the AMOS office. A little more than two months after that, he received a formal letter from the new chief technology officer for AMOS, Kraig Newkirk, demanding that Chris cease claiming to have designed critical parts of the AMOS software, of which Chris apparently thought he owned at least a portion. But Newkirk said he and Bruce, along with others, had developed the software code, not Chris.

"I am offended," Newkirk wrote, appending a copy of his letter to lawyer Steve Boyers, who apparently claimed to represent Chris,[16] "by your attempts to falsely take credit and claim ownership of technology that you did not design and/or develop. You must immediately cease making these false statements. As for your claims of ownership of my personal code, I will initiate legal action if you make any additional claims of ownership."

A month later, Newkirk demanded that Chris return all software he might have taken from the AMOS offices before he was kicked out of the company. When he left, Chris had removed software from AMOS computers, causing the entire system to crash, according to Newkirk.

Newkirk addressed his letter to Chris's new business, "The Christopher Group," located in an apartment

---

[16] Stephen Robert Boyers, a Pacific Palisades, California, lawyer, was contacted by the author during the research for this book. He initially acknowledged familiarity with NABUCO and the Koklich case, but declined to be interviewed. A letter dated December 16, 2004, was received from Mr. Boyers, asserting that Chris Botosan had declined to be interviewed. Mr. Boyers never responded to the author's initial inquiry as to whether he also represented NABUCO.

complex in Downey, just north of Lakewood. Newkirk believed Chris was still trying to flog the AMOS software, or at least a portion of it, in search of the elusive $600 million payday.

NABUCO, meanwhile, had faded entirely from the scene.

Sex and Money

The case of the *People of the State of California* versus *Bruce David Koklich* came to trial a little over one year after Bruce had been arrested, in February of 2003. By that time, Dohi as prosecutor had given way to Eleanor Hunter, in part because the possible case against actor Robert Blake, which Dohi had also been supervising, was beginning to take more and more of his time.

For Hunter, the task was to weave together the various strands of known facts about Jana's disappearance with the mostly anecdotal evidence of Bruce's lecherous behavior. Hunter believed she had evidence to show that Bruce, and only Bruce, had caused the disappearance and presumed murder of Jana: She had the sheets, and she had the unreturned weekend telephone calls as major facts in her favor. She also had the blood in the SUV, along with its obvious planting by the presumed perpetrator on Lewis Avenue, in the hope that someone easily prosecutable would run off with it.

What Hunter did not have was a body, with its capacity to give tell-tale evidence of who, how, what, where and when. And while Hunter thought she had a motive—Bruce's penchant for trying to induce women other than his wife to have sex with him—Bruce's singular lack of success in this field, over years and years, suggested that this theory of the case could be vigorously attacked as the main reason for Jana's disappearance.

Bruce might be a boorish cad, but that alone was hardly enough to prove he was a callous murderer. And Hunter knew, although she did not express this publicly, that murders without bodies often need clear and powerful motives to make any sense to a jury: you say he killed her, even though you can't show us a body; okay, a jury may think, tell us *why* he did it, and then maybe we'll believe you.

So Hunter knew her sex motive was pretty wobbly. She would try, if possible, to suggest that Jana, frustrated by the decision not to adopt a child, and tired of Bruce's controlling ways, was contemplating leaving him; but in the absence of any hard evidence of Jana's thinking—her inferred but unexpressed unhappiness with Bruce—this could only be hinted at.

As a result, Hunter decided to double up on Bruce's motive: Not only did Bruce want Jana gone so he could hop into the sack with other women, he also wanted to get rid of her so he could, as Paul had asserted before he died, have all the money.

Sex and money: that's what it came down to, in Hunter's view of the case, or at least the view she would present to the jury. It would be Hunter's task to try to convince the jury that *all* the factors, taken together, showed that Bruce had to be the person who had killed his wife, even though the only evidence showing Jana was dead was almost purely circumstantial.

Salcido's problem was even more complex. His goal was to establish reasonable doubt that Bruce had committed any crime. This involved assuming that a murder had taken place without conceding that it was a proven fact. *If* a murder had occurred, Salcido had to argue, it wasn't Bruce who had committed it. It was someone else— maybe, he would suggest, Chris Botosan. That required Salcido to present evidence of "third-party culpability," a the-other-guy-did-it defense, and it meant he had to attack Chris Botosan's motives for informing on Bruce.

The way to do this, Salcido perceived, was to suggest that Chris's actions had been motivated by his ambition to take over AMOS, edging first Jana, then Bruce, out of the picture. Thus, Salcido would suggest that Chris himself had made Jana vanish, and then had pointed the finger of blame at Bruce. Once Jana was gone and Bruce was blamed for the crime, the way would be clear for Chris to move in and get all the riches AMOS was supposed to generate.

This was by far the most tricky part of Salcido's defense. He had to show that Chris's motive was money— the money Chris had told the authorities that AMOS could expect to earn, the supposed $600 million. To that end, Salcido had to show just enough of the NABUCO deal to give Chris a plausible motive—$600 million—but not enough to suggest that these future riches might be ephemeral, part of some pie-in-the-sky plan.

Delving deeply into NABUCO's roots and exposing the apparent fallacies of the proposed loan and business plan only undercut Salcido's effort to paint Chris as the killer, however—it would make it plain that while Chris might have been part of some attempt to get loan fees from Bruce and Jana, killing Jana would have been the *worst* thing Chris could have done, since it would inevitably bring attention to the rickety NABUCO proposal.

Exposing the details of NABUCO's shortcomings would only bring the jury's attention back to Bruce, it seemed clear.

Salcido's defense of Bruce would thus be centered on trying to expose Chris as a fabricator who'd been bent on incriminating Bruce for his own benefit. Salcido had to destroy Chris on the witness stand—his motives, and his veracity. Then, if needed, Salcido would put Bruce himself on the stand to demonstrate that he not only had no motive to kill Jana, but he had an alibi as well.

An alibi, Salcido would strenuously attempt to show, that Chris did *not* have.

Any criminal trial—any trial, really—requires storytelling ability from the lawyer, whether prosecuting or defending. A trial is like a movie, or more exactly, a stage play. The lawyer is partly a director and partly an actor—his or her gestures, demeanor, tone and expression serve as the underlying narration, the voice-over, so to speak. The other actors are the witnesses.

Skillfully done, the audience—the jury—follows each actor's point of view as it is related, coordinated by the actor-director, the lawyer. It's only when all the roles are played out, under intense questioning from both sides, that the jury has the total picture. Or at least the picture permitted by the judge. In this trial, the judge was Robert J. Higa. Higa would make a number of rulings that gave Bruce every chance to defend himself. But Higa also steadfastly refused to limit the evidence the prosecution wanted to present against Bruce, particularly testimony about his character. In Hunter's view, his behavior was powerful evidence that Bruce knew for a fact that Jana was dead, and that he didn't really care.

Hunter began with the basics: Jana's character and reputation for reliability, especially as to keeping appointments. She called Kathy Ensign, Jan Baird, Jana's hairdresser, her manicurist, and trainer Dean Costales to demonstrate that Jana had never, ever simply skipped an appointment without calling to let the other person know. This also gave Hunter a chance to sketch in the events of August 20 and 21, particularly Bruce's behavior on those two critical days. There was little that Salcido could do with this testimony, except to get the witnesses to admit that they'd never heard Jana complain about Bruce, or otherwise say she was unhappy in her marriage.

Hunter followed this with testimony from Janie, who told of the unreturned calls over the weekend, her worries, and Bruce's behavior after Jana's disappearance. Hunter next called Nini Angelini, Consuelo Lopez, and then Howard Cooper, thereby setting the stage for Jana's disappearance, and Bruce's reaction to it.

She soon reached Jennifer Titchenal.

Here Salcido entered his most vigorous objection. The charge that Bruce had attempted to have sex with his niece was so inflammatory as to be prejudicial to Bruce's right to a fair trial, Salcido argued. More importantly, it had nothing to do with the issue at hand, Jana's disappearance and presumed murder.

"The prosecution is really presenting this to dirty him up," Salcido told Judge Higa. "The court can well imagine that if this jury [the jury was out of the room at that point] hears any of these things as it pertains to his eighteen-year-old niece, they are going to find it reprehensible. They absolutely are going to be prejudiced against Mr. Koklich. They are not going to like him, and beyond that, they might even hate him . . .

"I would anticipate," Salcido continued, " if the court lets this in, we can forget about the murder trial, because all they're going to be doing is focusing on this kind of reprehensible conduct, and Mr. Koklich will *not* be receiving a fair trial."

Not only was it prejudicial, Salcido argued again, it wasn't even relevant.

On the contrary, said Hunter. It *was* relevant.

"It shows consciousness of guilt," she said. Bruce had imported Jennifer to be his housemate, and hopefully his bedmate, less than a month after Jana had vanished. That showed he *knew* Jana wasn't coming back.

"This is a circumstantial case," Hunter said, "and in a circumstantial case, I think it's fair to say you have to look at everything." Everything in this case included evidence about Bruce's behavior, she said.

"The defendant protested that he was grieving, that [Jana] was the love of his life, and yet he goes out, and he brings the eighteen-year-old into the house."

Judge Higa ruled that Jennifer's story was admissible; the jury would be allowed to hear it.

Salcido immediately moved for a mistrial because of this ruling. The judge denied the motion, but Salcido at least had preserved the issue for later appeal.

Jennifer then told her story; there wasn't much Salcido could do to mitigate the damage, except to try to show that she had troubles with drugs, alcohol and memory, thereby suggesting that she wasn't a reliable witness. But the damage was done—Bruce *did* look reprehensible.

To drive the point home, Hunter next called Michelle McWhirter to tell the story of the cash-stuffed envelope, and Rosie Ritchie, who recounted Bruce's long-ago request for "entertainment."

Hunter then turned to the technical part of her case, the blood evidence. Using testimony from the criminalists, she showed how blood samples had been collected and typed from the SUV and the bedroom carpet. While the amount of blood was less than one might expect, it showed that at one point Jana—or more likely, her dead body—had been in the rear cargo area of the SUV. That showed that the SUV was used in the crime.

Hunter went next to the recovery of the SUV, calling

Michael Freeman and Theresa Thornton to demonstrate that the SUV had been on Lewis Avenue by 8 A.M. on Monday morning, August 20.

Here Salcido had to push the clock backwards. He already had information from Raesean that the time he and Freeman had swiped the purse was closer to 10 A.M., not an hour or two earlier, as Freeman had always insisted. Salcido hoped to show that Raesean and Freeman had really first noticed the SUV closer to 10 A.M., not before 8. Salcido also knew that Freeman was in jail on a recent burglary arrest, and guessed he could attack Freeman's reputation for honesty. Salcido had already noticed that Hunter hadn't called Raesean as her witness; he realized it was because Raesean's recollection of the time of the purse grabbing differed from Freeman's. These discrepancies, albeit minor, were helpful to Bruce.

On his cross-examination, Salcido aggressively pressed Theresa and Freeman on their accounts. He wanted to make the window of time around the first observation of the SUV as large as possible. His plan was presumably to suggest, later, that it was possible that *Chris* had been the one who had planted the car, and this at a time when Bruce's own whereabouts were accounted for back at the office. The larger the window of time the car could have been planted, the greater the possibility was that someone other than Bruce had done it.

But Theresa and Freeman doggedly insisted that they had seen the car early that morning.

Now Hunter turned to the money motive: She established that Bruce and Jana had twin $1-million life insurance policies, that it appeared the Koklichs were short on cash that summer, and that Bruce had asked Jeff Baird how long it took for someone to be declared "legally dead."

By February 26, after a week of trial, Hunter was

ready to move on to one of her most important witnesses: Chris Botosan.

In putting Chris on the witness stand, Hunter had several objectives. She wanted to show that Bruce had been such a fanatic about work that he frequently called Chris on the weekends—but hadn't made a single call to Chris on the weekend of August 18–19. She wanted to show that the Koklichs had been short of money during the summer, that AMOS was consuming resources. But mostly, she wanted to show that Bruce's behavior from August 20 forward was not what one might expect from a loving husband whose wife had just gone missing. She especially wanted Chris to testify about Bruce's actions when they'd gone back to the house to look for Jana, and again that evening when everyone had gathered at the house, and the remark that Bruce had supposedly made a few days later: "There, I cried for you on national television."

After Chris had established these points for Hunter on direct examination, it was Salcido's turn. This is what he had been waiting for: He wanted to show that Chris had every bit as much of a motive to get rid of Jana as Bruce ever had, maybe even more so. Salcido wanted to use Chris's role as the detectives' prized secret informant to show that every chance he got, Chris had something bad to say about Bruce—as if Chris were trying to get Sheehy and Davis to go after Bruce, not him. If he could establish this, Salcido would try to give the jury the idea that Chris was the killer, not Bruce. He would use his leading questions on cross-examination to make Chris look as dishonest, untrustworthy and as sinister as possible.

Salcido began by establishing that Chris had had a financial interest in AMOS. Chris said he had had 100,000 shares in the company when Jana disappeared, and had been promised up to 1 million, based on the number of banks he could get signed up. Salcido asked if Chris had been trying to arrange financing for the company; Chris said yes.

"Is that a company by the name of NABUCO?" Salcido asked.

"Yes."

"What kind of company is NABUCO?"

"NABUCO is a company that arranges financing and holds securities," Chris said.

"How much capital, how much money were you going to obtain from or through NABUCO?"

"About $8 million."

"Now, assuming something happened to Bruce Koklich, based on your knowledge, your involvement, everything you had done, obtaining the financing, you could complete the project—you could have completed that project yourself, could you not?"

"No," Chris said.

Salcido found Bruce's copy of the NABUCO application.

"You've seen that before, haven't you?" he asked, handing it to Chris. "And where it says, 'If you become incapacitated, given name and address of person to complete the project,' you see 'Christopher Botosan,' right there?"

"Yes, I see where Mr. Koklich put in 'Christopher Botosan,'" Chris responded, neatly throwing it back onto Bruce.

After Chris explained that he had helped Bruce set up AAMOS in Nevada, Salcido asked, "The funding was going to come from NABUCO through AAMOS to AMOS?"

"That's correct," Chris said.

Salcido asked about the briefing Chris had given Sheehy, Davis and Dohi on the last day of October 2001.

"Do you recall telling them that Bruce was looking at

fifty to one hundred million [dollars] in 18 months?" Salcido asked.

"No," Chris said.

"Do you recall telling them that you had all the financial documentation?"

"No, I don't."

"Do you recall telling these gentlemen that it should have a profit margin of 72 percent?"

"No, I do not."

"Does that figure, Bruce reaping fifty to one hundred million in 18 months, does that sound outrageous to you?"

"Depending on market conditions, just about anything could happen," Chris said. "No, it doesn't sound ridiculous."

"In November of 2001, did you calculate the cash value of the venture at $600 million?"

"No," Chris said, "I don't believe that I did."

Now that he was under oath, Chris seemed to be running away as fast as he could from the statements Dohi had recorded in his notes to the file in October and November 2001. If everything broke right, he said, AMOS might be worth somewhere between 3 and 8 million dollars. This was good for Salcido: He was trying to show that either Chris was lying then, or lying now, if one assumed that Dohi had recorded Chris's information accurately at the time.

Salcido pressed on. Wasn't it true that Chris had told Dohi, Sheehy and Davis that the company was going to make $600,000 a year in profit from each bank?

"I honestly don't recall what that number would be," Chris said.

Salcido asked about the loan that was to be brokered by NABUCO.

"And that money," he said, "however much it was going to be, it was going to go into an account in a brokerage firm and earn interest at the rate of 5.5 percent a month, is that right?"

"There were no arrangements made to do that, no."

Salcido asked if that wasn't what Chris had told Dohi and the detectives on November 6, 2001.

"I would—I would have to agree with that," Chris said.

"Is it true that AMOS is, therefore, guaranteed $431,750 a month against expenses of $67,000 a month to service the loan?"

"I would have to agree with that," Chris said again.

This was obviously a very lucrative profit potential, wasn't it? Salcido asked.

"Yes," Chris said.

"Isn't it true that at the present time you're involved in disagreements with other people about raiding and ripping off AMOS?"

"No."

"Isn't it true you took some software that belonged to AMOS?"

"No."

Salcido suddenly threw a curve at Chris.

"The week before Jana's disappearance, you and Jana spent, what, four to five hours alone on the road?" He meant Chris and Jana's drive to Las Vegas for the trade show.

Chris said that was so.

"And you and Jana were alone in the Koklich home, correct?"

"I don't believe I even stepped in the home, no," Chris said. Salcido was trying to show that Chris had been in the Lakewood house before, that he could have known where the sheets were, that he could have put the wrong sheet on the bed in order to frame Bruce. But Chris wouldn't admit to ever having been in the house, before going with Bruce to look for Jana on August 20.

Salcido turned next to Chris's informing on Bruce.

"From the time Jana disappeared, up to the present time, you've had approximately 20 contacts with the detectives assigned to the case?"

"I don't know," Chris said.

Chris would call the detectives with derogatory information about Bruce, wasn't that so? Salcido persisted.

"I would call them with information, that's correct," Chris said.

"And certainly," Salcido said, "if Bruce and Jana were out of the way, with your knowledge of AMOS, you certainly could reap millions. Isn't that correct, sir?"

Hunter objected, saying the question called for speculation on Chris's part. He did not have to answer.

Salcido asked Chris about his accompanying Bruce throughout the first two days, to the point he'd spent the night at the Lakewood house. Chris had told Hunter on direct examination that Bruce "appeared to be fine" on the Monday when Jana had first been reported missing— in other words, Bruce hadn't looked upset.

"If he appeared to be fine, why was there a need on your part, to literally go everywhere with him?" Salcido asked.

"It's part of how I am," Chris said. "I'm a very caring person, Mr. Salcido. I think you know that about my background."

"No, I don't know that about your background, thank you," Salcido shot back.

Salcido zeroed in on the early hours of Monday, August 20.

"What time did you wake up on Monday morning?"

Chris said he didn't know. Nor could he remember when he'd left his apartment.

With this, Salcido tried to pry the door open a little far-
ther, attempting to establish that Chris had no alibi for
Monday morning after the time Bruce had claimed he
had last seen Jana in bed. Before he was finished, Salcido
would imply that Chris had gone over to the Koklich
house between 6:30 in the morning just after Bruce had
departed, had killed Jana, stuffed her sheet-wrapped body
into the back of the SUV, disposed of the remains someplace, planted the car on Lewis Avenue, and then went to
the Koklich office.

Of course, that still left the same question that police
could not answer about Bruce: How had Chris managed
to get back to his own car after leaving the SUV on Lewis
Avenue? But Salcido was less interested in answering that
question than in trying to cast a shadow of reasonable
doubt about Bruce's culpability: After all, he only needed
one steadfast vote for acquittal, to run away to fight another day—in case there was a hung jury.

And in this he seemed to be succeeding, at least so far.

No Baby, No Dog

Now that Salcido had portrayed Chris as someone with a possible motive and opportunity to have done something to Jana, he was ready to move on to his next phase: He wanted to be able to present evidence in support of Chris's viability as an alternative suspect to the jury. Hunter wanted to head this off, if she could. From her point of view, it would only confuse the issues, and confusion meant those dreaded words to a prosecutor, "reasonable doubt."

She filed a motion with Judge Higa asking him to forbid Salcido from presenting any evidence of "third-party culpability," meaning any suggestion that some specific person other than Bruce might have done the deed.

But Salcido filed his own motion, asking the judge to permit this presentation of evidence. Indeed, Salcido said, without it Bruce's rights would be prejudiced. If the defense weren't permitted to present this alternative theory of the crime, Salcido said in his motion, any conviction of Bruce would have to be reversed on appeal.

After summarizing the case so far against Bruce, Salcido tried to turn it around to fit Chris, telling the court:

The incriminating evidence as to Chris Botosan's culpability is equally as compelling as the evidence against the defendant, given the fact no witness has testified as to how Jana disappeared, the nature of any injuries Jana suffered, or how the alleged crime occurred.

In this case, there is circumstantial evidence linking the third person [Chris Botosan] to the actual perpetration of the crime. Circumstantial evidence includes the fact that Botosan had a substantial financial motive to remove Jana and Bruce from participating in AMOS. The defendant and Jana had started the software company, and Botosan had a financial stake in the company and was in charge of software and software development. He was also in charge of financing, and in the process of obtaining financing for NABUCO, which would have made AMOS financially secure. While Bruce was in custody, Botosan removed the computer that housed the AMOS software without anyone's permission. By removing the computer without Bruce's consent or others involved with AMOS, he [Botosan] stole the software for AMOS and refused to either return the software, or provide a back-up copy of the software essential to AMOS. For the entire period of time Botosan knew the Koklichs, he spent only one night at the Koklich residence, and that was the night that Jana disappeared. Botosan removed a pillow from the Koklich residence after he stayed there, and did not tell the police. Botosan lied to detectives about renting a movie the weekend before Jana's disappearance. Botosan drove to Las Vegas with Jana the week before her disappearance. Botosan acted in control of the investigation after Jana's disappearance and told co-workers he was in charge. The defense anticipates the evidence will show that Bruce [sic] acted very nervous and strange after Jana's disappearance. On Monday morning, Botosan had the opportunity to commit the crime which caused Jana's disappearance.

Law enforcement made no effort to include or exclude Botosan as a suspect. No one ever checked Botosan's apartment for evidence relating to Jana's disappearance. No one ever obtained a DNA sample from Botosan.

There is no direct evidence supporting the actual perpetration of the crime by Bruce Koklich. There is as much circumstantial evidence against Botosan as there is against Bruce Koklich.

Bruce's right to a fair trial, Salcido concluded, demanded that the court permit the defense to present evidence allegedly implicating Chris.

After a brief hearing, Judge Higa said Salcido could present the evidence about Chris.

Hunter finished the rest of her case by calling Joe Sheehy and Doris Morrow. Sheehy described the outlines of the investigation, and told how Jana's purse had been recovered from the rooftop. Salcido asked only a few questions on cross-examination, and then reserved the remainder of his questions for his own case.

"Your Honor," he said, "just so the court will know, I will have a great number of questions for Mr. Sheehy, but instead . . . [I'm] reserving my right to cross-examine . . . I'd prefer not to ask any more questions at this point in time." It appeared that he intended to use Sheehy to demonstrate that Chris Botosan could have been a suspect, and that Botosan had manipulated Sheehy, as well as the entire investigation.

Salcido's abrupt termination of his cross-examination

seemed to have caught Hunter by surprise. She realized that she hadn't asked Sheehy about the detectives' "due diligence," which was crucial to establishing that Jana was actually dead, if still undiscovered. Without this evidence, the defense could later say that the prosecution hadn't proved the most important part of the charge against Bruce, that someone in fact had been murdered. Hunter re-called Sheehy to the witness stand, and he explained all the things that he and Davis had done to look for Jana.

For her final witness, Hunter called Doris Morrow. Doris told about the last time she'd seen Jana, the trip to San Antonio in late July, when Jana had appeared to be crying, but not wanting anyone to know. That was when Jana had told Paul, "I think he's trying to ease me out of the decision-making process for the new company."

"At one point," Hunter asked, "did you become aware that she was not able to have children?"

"Yes," Doris said.

"Do you recall a comment the defendant made concerning her wanting a dog?"

"Yes," Doris said. It had happened a few years before Jana disappeared, Doris said.

"And this was after the time that Jana knew she couldn't have a child?"

"Yes."

"And how did that come up, the conversation about the dog?"

"Well, she was playing with our dog," Doris said, "and when we were down in the family room, I suggested we get a dog [for Bruce and Jana]."

"And what was the defendant's response?"

"He said, 'She's not getting a dog until she produces a baby.' "

With that, Hunter rested her case.

Due Diligence

As soon as Hunter rested, Salcido asked Judge Higa to dismiss the charge against Bruce. The law permitted a defendant to ask for a dismissal if the evidence put on by the prosecution was insufficient to withstand an appeal.

"I'm not going to go through the evidence in the case, other than to say it's rather clear that, at this juncture, they have presented absolutely nothing to indicate that Mr. Koklich was responsible for the death of his wife. There's no evidence at all as to how anything occurred."

That was hardly the case, said Hunter. She said they'd established a motive, that Bruce might have killed Jana because he was losing his ability to control her; moreover, she said, Bruce was the last person to see her alive—by his own admission. The fact that the usually obsessively punctual Jana had missed her weekend appointments without even calling indicated that she was dead, and the fact that Bruce had not reported her missing until two days later was evidence of his guilt.

Higa denied Salcido's motion to dismiss the charge, so now it would be Salcido's turn to present evidence. His objective was to turn all the suspicion he could in Chris

Botosan's direction, while getting Bruce off the hook. He started with school principal Donna Baker, trying to show that Jana's SUV had been in the Koklich garage between 8 and 8:30 Monday morning. Baker said she still couldn't be sure it wasn't Sunday she had seen the SUV, rather than Monday. But Dr. Romberg, the dentist, had already testified that he routinely opened his garage door between 6:30 and 8 A.M. on weekdays; since Baker remembered seeing the Romberg garage door open the morning she'd seen Jana's SUV, that seemed to prove that Baker had seen Jana's car on Monday morning.

If he could only show beyond a doubt that Jana's car had been in the Koklich garage on Monday morning, Salcido could get Bruce off the hook. It simply wasn't possible for Bruce to have killed Jana and dumped her car in time to be back in the office at 8:30. And the later Salcido could place Baker's sighting of the SUV on that Monday, the wider the opportunity to blame Chris for committing the crime.

But then Baker told Salcido that she could have actually seen Jana's car on the previous *Friday* morning, and repeated the statement when she was cross-examined by Hunter. This information wasn't at all helpful to Bruce.

Salcido pressed ahead, regardless. He called Dr. Romberg, who said he routinely opened his garage door slightly between 6 and 8 A.M. on Mondays, Tuesdays, Thursdays and Fridays.

"On the weekends, would the garage door be up in that manner, ajar?" Salcido asked.

"Probably not," Romberg said.

Salcido moved on to his next defense witness, Arrita LePire. Salcido asked if she'd been at her hair salon on Sunday, August 19, and if she'd seen a vehicle in the rear parking lot. Arrita said she had indeed.

"What vehicle did you see, ma'am?" Salcido asked.

"A white SUV," Arrita said. "A white Pathfinder."

She'd seen a woman in the car, Arrita said. "I saw blonde hair. I assumed it was Jana."

Salcido now called Allen Radcliffe, Arrita's husband.

"Would you please describe the woman you saw behind the building?" Salcido asked.

"I believe she was blonde, approximately five-six, 120, 125 pounds. She had a white blouse, black skirt, and, I believe, black heels." The woman had shapely legs, Radcliffe added. She walking toward a white SUV.

Salcido moved to the critical Monday morning period. He called Rosa Canedo, who testified that Bruce had been in the office that morning, and that he'd given her a list of properties he said he'd inspected. If one believed that Donna Baker had in fact seen the SUV in the Koklich garage that morning at just before 8 A.M., and if Bruce was in the office at 8:30 A.M. giving Rosa a list, that seemed to show that Bruce couldn't possibly have killed Jana.

Next, Salcido called Raesean Hollie. Rayray said he was pretty sure that he'd first seen the white SUV parked at the curb on Lewis Avenue about 10 A.M. This seemed to contradict Michael Freeman and Theresa Thornton, who said they'd first seen the white SUV between 7 and 8 A.M. Salcido was trying to show that Thornton and Freeman were simply mistaken as to the time or even day; he wanted to show that someone could have planted the SUV on Lewis Avenue later that morning, while Bruce was at his office or on his way to the funeral.

Over the next two days, Salcido called more witnesses, trying to establish that Bruce and Jana had a positive, loving relationship, while at the same time casting suspicion on Chris Botosan. He called Melinda McBride, Chris's former girlfriend, who testified that contrary to Chris's assertion, she had not been at his apartment on Monday morning. Salcido wanted the jury to wonder where Chris had been during the crucial post–7 A.M. period.

Eventually, Salcido worked his way back to Detective Sheehy. His plan had always been to poke holes in the sheriff's investigation, to buttress his later argument that the detectives had fastened on Bruce from the very start, ignoring anything that didn't fit their preconception of the case.

Salcido pressed Sheehy on small inconsistencies in the detectives' reports, and suggested that both investigators had skewed the information from various witnesses by providing them beforehand with bits of critical information, such as dates and times certain events happened. The detectives had biased the witnesses, Salcido suggested—particularly Theresa Thornton and Michael Freeman.

He turned to the subject of Chris Botosan, asking how many contacts had been made between law enforcement and Bruce's former business partner.

"It would be safe to say at least 25 or so," Sheehy said.

Salcido asked Sheehy if the detectives had "enter[ed] into some understanding or agreement with Chris Botosan that he was to continue working for Bruce Koklich, and try to get information that might help you with your investigation in this case?"

Salcido's implication was that Chris had become an informant for the detectives out of some sort of consideration, such as money or immunity from prosecution.

"No," Sheehy said.

Under Salcido's questioning, Sheehy admitted that Chris had told them things about his own activities on Friday and Saturday that weren't true when they first began the investigation, although later he had been more accurate. As for the critical Monday morning period, Sheehy admitted that Chris hadn't initially told them he was with Melinda McBride, as Chris had testified he was. Salcido wanted to use this omission to suggest that Chris was lying under oath, for some reason, when he claimed that he'd been with Melinda at the time the SUV was supposedly seen by Donna Baker in the Koklich garage. Salcido wanted the jury to see that Chris was trying to use Melinda as *his* alibi for the critical time period—an alibi that Salcido would soon contradict.

Chris had told them, Sheehy said, that he'd awakened around 6:30 A.M. on that Monday morning.

"He said he awoke, and he did some computer work for the Rescue Mission," Sheehy said.

"What time did he tell you he got to the office?"

"About 9:30," Sheehy said. Chris had testified that he'd gotten to the office about 8:30. Salcido wanted the jury to note the discrepancy.

"Did you ask him if there were any witnesses who could corroborate his time between 6:30 and 9:30, other than his claim to you that he was at his apartment before he got to the office?"

"No," Sheehy said.

"Did he offer the names of anyone who could explain his activities that Monday morning before he got to the office?"

"Melinda McBride," Sheehy said.

"Well," Salcido retorted, "in regard to your report, there's no reference whatsoever to Melinda McBride [being present at Chris's apartment] on Monday morning, correct?"

"Correct," Sheehy conceded.

Salcido asked Sheehy if it was true that Chris had told him, Davis and Greg Dohi that he had at least 100,000 shares of stock in AMOS, and that AMOS expected a profit margin of 72 percent.

"Yes," Sheehy said.

"When he told you that he had all the financial documentation to verify what he was telling you about all these figures, did you ask him to give you those documents, so you could verify that, to test him?"

"I don't think I did, personally, no," Sheehy said.

Salcido turned to the pillow issue. Chris had already testified about taking his pillow to the Koklich house, and removing it the following day—before Janie would have slept on it that night, so Chris's recollection had to be wrong. But Salcido wanted to demonstrate that the detectives had been sloppy in letting Chris take the pillow. Of course, at the time, no one knew that two feathers, presumably from a pillow, would be found five days later in Jana's just-recovered SUV.

"At any point in time," Salcido demanded, "did you tell Chris Botosan, 'That pillow you took out of the Koklich residence, where is it?'"

"No, sir," Sheehy said.

"Did you ever ask him to turn it over to you?"

"No, I didn't."

Nor had he ever compared any feathers from Chris's pillow to the feathers found in the SUV, Sheehy admitted.

Hadn't Chris told the detectives that he'd been to Bruce and Jana's house "five or six times," rather than the one time that Chris had testified to?

"Yes, he did," Sheehy said.

"Did you ask him what his reason was for going to the Koklich home?"

"No."

"Did you ask him for the dates that he'd been there?"

"I don't believe so."

Salcido asked Sheehy about the searches of the Koklich residence and the office.

"Now," he said, "was Botosan's apartment ever

searched for any evidence having to do with Jana's disappearance?"

"No," Sheehy said.

"Were any of Botosan's clothes or his car ever examined for the presence of blood?"

"No, sir."

"Was his vehicle ever searched for any evidence of Jana's belongings?"

"No, sir."

"Did you ever compare Botosan's DNA to the DNA found in the blood drops on the master bedroom carpeting?"

"No, sir."

"Did you ever get a DNA sample from Botosan?"

"No."

"Did you ever conduct secret surveillance of Botosan?"

"No."

"Ever check his banking records?"

"No."

After getting Sheehy to admit that Bruce had voluntarily consented to the first search, and that it had been Bruce who first called about the missing sheets, Salcido moved to conclude his examination of Sheehy.

"Now," Salcido said, "you were in on the investigation basically from day one, the 21st, correct?"

"Yes, sir."

"Now, from your investigation, can you say what the exact injury was that Jana sustained?"

"No."

"Can you say where on the body the injury was?"

"No."

"Can you say what caused the injury?"

"No."

"As far as a specific time, can you say for a fact when it may have occurred?"

"No."

"Can you say for a fact that the injury she sustained was not an accidental one, or an unintended one?"

"No, I cannot."

"Do you know for a fact exactly in which room of the house the injury may have occurred?"

"No, sir."

"In regard to how Jana's body may have gotten into the back of the Pathfinder, can you say for a fact that only one person carried her and placed her in that Pathfinder?"

"No."

"Can you say for a fact that only one person might have unloaded her body from that Pathfinder?"

"No."

"Can you say for a fact that the sheets on that bed were not gathered up by some unidentified person or persons who did not want to leave any potential DNA evidence there in the house?"

"No."

"Can you say for a fact that you know the reason why this happened to Jana?"

"No."

Bruce Speaks

Now Salcido was ready for his own key witness—Bruce.

This was the critical moment of the trial. For more than two weeks, the jury had been hearing all about Bruce—from Janie, Doris, Kathy Ensign, Jan Baird, and Nini; from Chris, Jennifer, Michelle McWhirter, Rosie Ritchie, Denise Brandenberg, and Dawn Bynum. But everyone had been talking *about* Bruce. Now the jury would get to hear the man himself, for better or worse.

Salcido's objective was to take the sting out of the allegations about Bruce's philandering, and try to show that Bruce and Jana had had a loving relationship, that there was no motive for Bruce to have killed his wife. Bruce admitted that he had patronized massage parlors "five or six times." He didn't deny the accounts of Rosie Ritchie and Michelle McWhirter. But he said he'd never had sex with Jennifer Titchenal.

Salcido asked Bruce how he would characterize Jana at the time she disappeared.

"Wonderful person," Bruce said. "Committed person. Things that I've said this whole time, the love of my life. I mean, there's nobody I love more than her.

"We work together," he added. "We live together. We vacation together. We do business together. And [it is a] very close relationship and very precious one to me . . . we had a very caring relationship. I always brought her flowers and tried to do special things for her, and she was one for really doing surprises on me."

"Until Jana disappeared," Salcido asked, "how would you best characterize your relationship at that point in time?"

"Excellent."

"Was it stable?"

"Very."

Salcido asked Bruce about AMOS. Bruce said he and Jana hoped to expand the company to go national, to get clients in all 50 states.

"Now, when you say it could go nationally, you heard the figure of $600 million being mentioned?"

"Yeah," Bruce said.

"Was that reality or a stretch—"

"Not in my mind," Bruce said.

"Did you ever mention $600 million to Chris Botosan?"

"No."

Not only had he never told Chris that AMOS could be worth that amount, he had never even dreamed it, Bruce said.

Salcido walked Bruce through the Koklich finances to demonstrate that there had been no cash crunch in the summer of 2001. He turned to Doris Morrow's anecdote about the baby and the dog. Bruce said it wasn't like that, at all, the way Doris had made it sound. He said he only meant that when they had a child, they could also get a dog, because then they would be more tied down—but until then, having neither dog nor child, they could be free to travel whenever they wanted.

Salcido turned to Botosan. He asked why Bruce had gotten involved with him.

"He had a background of software engineer," Bruce said. "He designed a program for a bank that we worked for back in West Palm Beach called Berkeley Federal Savings. He designed that program. He also managed a crew of programmers to design another software program, so he had technical expertise that far exceeded mine . . . he brought things to the table that I really didn't have any experience in, insofar as handling programmers, the finance side. He had a background with— I shouldn't say *background*. Maybe connections with insurance companies and some bond finance companies.

"He felt the company was at a stage to where it was being hindered by the [lack of] ability to expand rapidly, because it doesn't have the capital that it needs, and so he came up with a financing package through connections of his, to basically bring in lots of capital for the company to expand the software user base."

Salcido asked Bruce to explain about NABUCO.

"NABUCO is basically the paperwork person," Bruce said. "There's underwriters. There's all kinds of due diligence people, attorneys that look at the whole bond finance package, and AMOS would issue a bond. [A Denver bank] would issue a bond. AMOS' bond would be a higher interest rate. The [bank] bond is a lower interest rate, but there's a discount because of the low interest rate, and that discount in the bond would pay the interest. It's a little bit complicated, but that's the best I can explain it." Just how a bank's lower interest rate would pay for AMOS' higher interest wasn't at all clear.

"All right," Salcido said. "Now, who knew more about the financing, you or Chris?"

"Oh, Chris."

"Who had the connections as far as that finance—"

"Chris had all the bond connections, the insurance company connections, all that stuff."

Salcido showed Bruce the NABUCO loan application, the one that had Chris Botosan's name on it as the person who would complete the project if Bruce became incapacitated.

"This application is pre–filled out by NABUCO," Bruce said. "There was a $10,000 retainer fee that was paid to NABUCO prior to us getting the application, and once we executed that $10,000 check to NABUCO, they forwarded this application for processing, and it was basically completed by them."

Bruce suggested that Chris's name had been put on the application by NABUCO, not him.

Salcido returned to the subject of Bruce's marriage with Jana.

"As of August of the year 2001, was there anything wrong with your marriage at all?"

"No," Bruce said.

"Was there anything wrong with your financial situation?"

"No."

"Were you financially stable?"

"Yes."

"Did you kill Jana?"

"Never."

"Did you have anything to do with her death or disappearance?"

"No."

Now Hunter would come face-to-face with her quarry at the trial's important moment of truth. She had noticed—and hoped the jury had, too—that Salcido hadn't asked a single question about the bedsheets.

. . .

Hunter had heard enough about Bruce from her witnesses that she had already formed an idea of how he would respond under cross-examination. She believed Bruce at heart was a sexist—that he had contempt for women. She intended to get up close to him, get under his skin, make him expose this streak of misogyny by sneering at him, pricking his vanity. In this strategy, she would turn out to be very effective.

She began by pointing out that Bruce had told the police back on August 21 that he had no relationships with other women. That was a lie, wasn't it? she asked.

No, Bruce said. He thought the police meant if he had a girlfriend on the side, or an ongoing affair. He didn't. The police had asked him if there were other love interests, Bruce said, and he'd truthfully answered that there were no other "love interests." That didn't mean he didn't try to have sex with women he met. But that wasn't a love interest, not in his mind.

Hunter suggested that Jana had begun to get away from Bruce, that she was changing, taking more control over her life under the influence of her friend Nini. She suggested that Bruce was angry at Jana for going to the concert with her friend.

"You didn't like Nini, did you?" Hunter asked.

"I liked Nini," Bruce said. "She was a lot of fun."

"Well, she was a very independent person, correct?"

Bruce said that was accurate—Nini *was* an independent person.

"She was encouraging Jana to kind of come out of your shadow, correct?"

"No, that's not correct," Bruce said.

"And the last person to see Jana alive before that weekend was Nini, correct?"

"No."

Noting that Bruce had told the police that he'd left the house alarm off when he left for work on Monday, Hunter asked if it had been on when he and Chris Botosan had gone back to the house to look for Jana. That was a key point, because Bruce had always said it showed that Jana herself had set the alarm before leaving. Of course, if Jana was already dead and her body disposed of, Bruce could have set the alarm himself that morning.

"So whoever killed Jana must have been kind enough to set the alarm after they removed her from the home?"

"That's possible," Bruce said.

"How likely is that?"

"Very," Bruce said.

"It's very likely?"

"That's right."

"That somebody comes in, kills your wife, takes her, puts her in the car, takes off, before doing that, sets the house alarm?"

"That's what happened," Bruce said.

Hunter's peppering of questions at Bruce was having her desired effect: Bruce was starting to get rattled. With this answer, he'd just contradicted his own defense—that Jana had left the house voluntarily and had been carjacked on the way to work, sometime before 10 A.M. And the notion that an intruder would take the time to set the alarm was ludicrous, even assuming that the killer knew the code.

"Let's go on to the sheets," Hunter said. "We've had a lot of discussion about the sheets. You never make your bed, do you?"

"No."

He hadn't changed the sheets over the crucial weekend, had he? Hunter asked. Bruce agreed that he had not. And

Jana hadn't changed them? No, said Bruce, he hadn't seen Jana change them.

If the sheets the detectives found on the bed on Tuesday were different from those that had been on the bed when Consuelo last saw them on Friday, how did it happen? Hunter asked.

"I didn't pay attention to the sheets, ma'am," Bruce said. "I mean, when I talked to the officers, they asked me, 'Well, what about the sheets?' And I'll tell you what I told them. I am not paying attention to what sheets are on the bed when I sleep in it. It's just not something that I pay attention to."

"What explanation can you give us for the fact that the sheets that were on your bed on Friday are not on there on Monday or Tuesday? What explanation can you give for that?"

"I can't give you one," Bruce said.

In all, Bruce was on the witness stand for the better part of two days, answering Hunter's questions. She walked Bruce through everything he said had happened that weekend—sleeping late on both Saturday and Sunday, the walks and bicycle ride, the reading and television watching. She asked how it was possible for Jana to have been in bed next to him on Sunday at the same time Bruce was claiming she might have been at the office to be seen by Allen Radcliffe and Arrita LePire. Bruce said it was possible that Jana might have gone to the office, then returned to the house and gotten back into bed.

At length, Hunter turned to all the telephone messages left by Dean Costales, Nini, Janie and others. Bruce insisted that they'd decided to simply ignore the telephone that weekend, in part because of the mystery caller.

Hunter pointed out that Paul was dying in Texas. Surely Jana would have wanted to know if Doris were calling about Paul's condition, she said. And Bruce knew that Jana had promised to be at his bedside when the time came, didn't he?

"I never heard that conversation," Bruce said, evading the question.

"So essentially, because of this one phone caller, you're saying that the fear of that one phone caller outweighed everything else?"

"No, I'm not saying that."

"Well, you're saying she didn't pick up the phone because she was afraid?"

"We were trying to escape, okay? We were trying to regenerate. We were—"

"The weekend that she decides not to answer the phone and shut herself off just happens to be the weekend before you report her missing, correct?"

"Correct."

Hunter played one of Janie's messages left on the answering machine from Sunday. Bruce said he'd heard the messages as they were left that evening. Hunter asked him why Jana hadn't heard them, too, with the answering machine right next to the bed.

"I think she was downstairs," Bruce said.

"Didn't you just testify that she was in bed as of *Sixty Minutes,* and then reading a book in bed until she fell asleep?"

"I may have said that. I was wrong."

"Did you purposefully try to hide it from her?"

"No."

"I'm sorry, what?" Hunter asked, showing her disbelief.

"No."

"Didn't you tell police that . . . you made it a point to listen to them so Jana wouldn't hear them, because she might have been afraid about that one caller?"

"Yeah," Bruce said.

"So you purposely did it so she wouldn't hear."

"Yeah."

"So when you said 'No' you were wrong?"

"Correct."

"You heard that poor old woman calling for her daughter, asking where her daughter was?"

"I was reading. I wasn't focused in on the call. I basically overlooked the call. I mean, I heard it. That's what happened."

"You just spaced out and didn't call [out] or tell Jana?"

"That's the facts," Bruce insisted.

Hunter now tried to get Bruce to explain how Jana's SUV could be in the Koklich garage at 6:30 A.M. when he left to go to work, and be seen more than four miles away on Lewis Avenue just half an hour later.

"So somewhere between 6:30 and 7 or 7:30, someone came into your house, killed your wife, set the alarm and left?" Hunter asked.

"Correct."

"The sheets were missing?"

"Correct."

"So in addition to doing all these other things that I just mentioned, somebody took the sheets?"

"Yes."

"And somebody made up the bed?"

"Probably."

"So not only did somebody come in, take the wife, take the car, set the alarm, was able to set the code for the garage door to shut, they also took the sheets?"

"That's possible."

Hunter asked if Bruce had ever looked for the missing sheets himself. Bruce said he had.

"Couldn't find them, could you?" Hunter asked, her sarcasm obvious.

"No," Bruce said.

Hunter asked Bruce if he'd seen the sheets when he cleaned up the house before selling it, when he was raising his bail money. Bruce said he wasn't sure.

"Oh, so you might still have them?" Hunter asked, clearly disbelieving.

"There's a bunch of sheets. It's hard to tell what it is. There's a huge plethora of stuff, okay? So it's hard to tell what is what . . ." Bruce said he wasn't sure he'd even recognize the sheets if he did find them.

But, Hunter said, Bruce had known for more than a year that the sheets were key evidence in the case. "Are you trying to tell us you might have them in your possession?"

"It's possible," Bruce said.

"You just haven't *looked*?"

Bruce said he'd tried to get Consuelo to come back to the house to check the sheets he did have, but she wouldn't come. It was possible that the sheets had simply been overlooked, even by the detectives who had searched the house three different times.

"I don't know how good they did their search," Bruce said.

"So somebody came into your house, killed your wife, took the sheets, changed the bed, put her in the back of the car, set the alarm, went out of the garage, closed the garage with the code key, correct?"

"Correct," Bruce said.

"And they were able to do all this between the time of 6:30 and 7 o'clock in the morning?"

Bruce said the Lewis Avenue witnesses might have been wrong about when they first saw the SUV.

Hunter turned to the financial motive.

"Hypothetically, if Jana were to leave you, you would have lost 51 percent of your real estate business, correct?"

"I probably would have lost more than that," Bruce said.

"[She would] take half of the software company?"

"Not necessarily," Bruce said. "That doesn't mean she *is* going to take it. Doesn't mean she is going to split the company up and rip the software apart and put the company in the tank. She'll own half of it, yeah."

Hunter asked him about the $1 million insurance policy.

"Based on case law that I've seen," Bruce said, "I may never collect."

"So you've researched it?"

Bruce admitted that he'd asked people to look into the issue. He wouldn't waive any right to it. "I think that would be pretty foolish," he said.

"Because money is important to you, isn't it, Mr. Koklich?"

"It's important to all of us," Bruce said. "It *is* a capitalistic society."

Not for Money

After Bruce had finished his testimony, Salcido called George Miller, a financial expert. Miller said he'd looked over the Koklich financial records, including the books for AMOS, and had concluded that there was no such thing as a cash crunch for Jana and Bruce in the summer of 2001. Among other things, they had nearly $100,000 in cash in a local bank, along with about $4 million in real estate equity. If they had to, Miller said, Bruce and Jana could have put their hands on almost $600,000 in liquid assets at the time of Jana's disappearance. There was no need to borrow money from Janie and Paul, certainly no "cash crunch." And, said Miller, Jana's disappearance had been a financial disaster for Bruce—his income from the real estate operation had dropped by more than half since she had vanished.

Salcido also called a man who claimed to be an expert on sexual behavior, Warren Farrell. Farrell held a doctorate in political science, and was a professor at Montclair State University in New Jersey. Farrell also said he was a "sex counselor." The author of several popular books on sex and relationships, Farrell was accepted by the court as an expert on male sexual behavior over Hunter's objections. Farrell asserted that just because a man liked to chase women, it didn't necessarily mean he had a bad marriage. In fact, Farrell said, a lot of "high achieving men" chased women who were not their wives. Then Farrell went too far: He claimed that men didn't kill women for financial reasons, but emotional ones.

"I'm almost completely unaware of a man killing [women] just for money," Farrell said.[17] "Even that being a significant part of his motivation. He'll kill other men for money, but he will not kill a woman for money." But Farrell also admitted that in present-day America, men tended to have the money, not women. He also contended that women have sex to get economic security, while men wanted sex for emotional reasons.

With that, Salcido was finished. He asked Judge Higa to dismiss the case once more, and for the second time, Higa declined to do it.

Now Hunter called two witnesses in an effort to demolish Bruce's version of the events. She called Bruce's next-door neighbor Dr. Romberg back to the stand.

"Let me ask you this," Hunter said. "After you testified [the first time, for Bruce] did you re-contact me?"

"Yes, I did," Romberg said. "I was reading an account in the paper, and I felt that my testimony was either misleading or incomplete."

"Okay. Would you like to take this opportunity to complete your testimony?"

Romberg now said it was possible that on Sunday, August 19, he *had* opened his garage door a bit before 8 A.M.

That meant Donna Baker could have seen Jana's SUV in the Koklich garage on Sunday morning, as well as Friday

---

[17] The author has written six different books on men who killed their wives, mothers, sisters or daughters for money.

and Monday. It was therefore still possible that Bruce had planted the car on Lewis Avenue very early Monday morning.

Romberg's alteration had the effect of letting some of the air out of Bruce's Monday morning alibi. Salcido tried to pump it back up a bit.

He asked how Romberg had decided to contact the authorities with his new information, and Romberg said he had an acquaintance who was a judge, and the judge had advised him to call the district attorney's office right away. He hadn't called Salcido because he didn't think Salcido wanted to know.

Salcido fished out a copy of the report of the conversation that his investigator, Larry Kallestad, had held with Romberg on October 13, 2001. Salcido read from the report:

" 'Romberg states he only does this [raises the garage door slightly] when the weather is warm and only on weekdays, not on Saturday or Sunday.' "

"If I said that, and I may have," Romberg now said, "I don't know if the correct word is 'recant,' but I misspoke. I was thinking of the weekdays, and I wasn't thinking the weekends were any big deal, and that's why it was kind of glossed over . . . If I said that, then I said something that's incorrect, because it's just not true."

Hunter had one more rebuttal witness. She called Sandy Baressi, a blonde woman who worked in the Wells Fargo office adjacent to the Koklich office. Sandy said she'd been at the Wells Fargo office at 11 A.M. on Sunday, August 19. She'd left shortly thereafter, she said. That suggested that the woman Arrita LePire and Allen Radcliffe had partially seen on Sunday was in fact Sandy, not Jana.

But under Salcido's cross-examination, Sandy admitted her minivan was blue, not white, and where Jana was about 5-foot-6, Sandy was 5-foot-1. She also said that while she was in the office, she thought she'd heard a noise in the Koklich office next door. That opened the door to the possibility that while Sandy had been in the Wells Fargo office, Jana had in fact been next door in the Koklich office, and that Allen and Arrita had in fact seen *two* different blondes—Jana as she was driving away, and seconds later, Sandy in her own car. That idea was bolstered when Sandy said that when she left the office, she drove south in the alley, not north; Allen and Arrita had consistently said the "white SUV" they'd seen had gone north, the way back to the Koklich house.

Hunter was convinced that Arrita and Allen were simply mistaken in their observations—that they had to have seen Sandy Baressi. Baressi's mere presence at the office at the critical time was enough: Hunter suggested to the jury that the woman Arrita and Allen had seen was actually Sandy, not Jana.

Lies and Motives

By March 13, 2003, both sides were ready for their closing arguments.

As the prosecutor, Hunter went first.

"I think we've all learned one thing," she told the jury, "and that one thing is, things are not always as they appear. I'm sure family and friends of Jana are thinking that very thing. The 'what ifs' that must be going through their minds—what *if* we just asked more questions, what *if* we just listened a little bit more, what *if* Jana just opened up a little bit? Maybe then they would be able to see that in fact, the marriage [that], from the outside, looked pretty stable, in reality was not."

The reality, Hunter said, was that Bruce had committed an unspeakable act—he had murdered his wife and hidden her body so that, to that day, it still had not been found.

"We got to see this defendant," Hunter said. "We got to hear about this defendant. We got to see how this defendant truly is, what type of person he is, what type of character he is, what type of morals he has. We also had the extra benefit of actually seeing him on the stand. We got to see the ultimate arrogance of a man, who, in his mind, feels justified in killing his wife. He gets up there and plays with words, plays semantic games. Ladies and gentlemen, he got up on that stand and he lied to you. He lied to the police back on August 21, and he's lied ever since."

Hunter described Jana as a woman who was changing, who was coming into her own, in part under the influence of Nini Angelini.

"Nini is a strong woman," Hunter said. "She owns her own business. And you saw her up on the stand. You saw her demeanor, and basically, she was an influence on Jana, an example . . . you can live your life. It's okay to be a strong woman. You don't have to live in the shadow of a man, and it's okay. It's acceptable.

"Nini encouraged her to maybe dress a little different, maybe get her hair a little different, and also, Nini encouraged her to please herself. It doesn't always have to coincide with what your husband wants. Live your life. Live it to enjoy yourself. If your husband likes it, fine. If not, that's his problem, not yours.

"You know what? Nini was a thorn in this defendant's side. She was an influence that he just didn't like. You've got to think about it. For many, many years, he had a pretty good thing going. He had a wife who was incredibly dedicated to him. She did not challenge him. As Nini said, everything went okay as long as they did what Bruce wanted to do."

Hunter claimed the defense had shifted its strategy. First they'd claimed that Jana and Bruce had a perfect marriage, but when evidence came in that Bruce was fooling around, Bruce had to admit it, but also claim it didn't mean anything. Well, Hunter suggested, they only had Bruce's word for *that*.

"In August, just think of what the defendant was facing," Hunter continued. "He had a wife who possibly no longer wanted to be just the little woman around the house, that she wanted to be more independent, wanted him to take up the slack, you know, wanted him to take care of himself. She was coming into her own. She was a woman who was starting to look better, feel better, become more confident about herself. She was also a woman who was desperately wanting a child, but had just been told no. She was a woman and a wife who was not acting like herself. She was distracted. She was sad. She also was a woman who had a husband who was cheating on her."

Hunter pointed to Bruce's claim that he and Jana were tired from the trip to Las Vegas, and planned as early as Thursday before the disappearance to spend a quiet weekend at home.

"That was a lie," Hunter said. "Why do we know that? Because on Thursday, did she call Dean [Costales, the trainer] and cancel her appointment? No. Did she call Nini and cancel that appointment? No. Did she call her mother and cancel an appointment? No. In fact there were emails back and forth between the mother and her during this time period, where they talked about still going [to the movie] on Sunday."

And Jana had had plenty of time on Friday night to tell Nini that she and Bruce were going to spend a quiet weekend together, and to cancel her appointment for the following day. She, who was so meticulous about keeping her appointments, failed to do this? It simply wasn't credible, Hunter said.

Hunter took the jury through the events that Bruce claimed had taken place on Saturday and Sunday, and tried to show they could not have happened—"because Jana was dead by 7 A.M." She pointed out that Bruce had said that he and Jana had slept in on Sunday morning. But when Arrita LePire and Allen Radcliffe said they thought they might have seen Jana, Bruce then said it was possible that Jana had gone to the office while he was still sleeping.

"Now, there is an issue about the car," Hunter admitted. "They believe they saw a white SUV, but Sandy says she has a blue minivan. I submit to you that they're just mistaken, because there's other evidence to support that Jana was not there at the business . . ."

For example, Hunter said, there was no evidence that Jana had left any instructions for anyone while she was supposedly at the office. Usually it was her habit to leave lists of things to do for the staff. There weren't any from August 19. Nor was there any evidence that Jana had used one of the computers, or made any telephone calls. "There's nothing to show that she was at work that day," Hunter said, "and the reason is, because she wasn't." Not only that, but Jana's meticulously kept, handwritten calendar, in which she habitually noted what she ate, where she went, her workout results, what she'd brought to Bruce for lunch—there wasn't a single entry showing she'd been at the office that day.

And, Hunter added, Jana hadn't used the office telephone to call her mother, or Nini or Dean. A living Jana certainly would have used the telephone for this purpose if she'd missed or planned to miss her appointments, Hunter said.

Even Bruce's description of their Sunday morning at home showed that Jana couldn't have gone to the office, Hunter continued.

"Just think about it," she said. "The defendant says they're sleeping in the same bed on Sunday . . . we're talking about ten in the morning. She gets out of bed, takes off her nightie, puts on her clothes, walks downstairs, goes out the door, opens up the garage door, starts her car, pulls out, closes the garage door, drives all the way to work, gets out, goes into work, stays for a period of time, comes out, drives back to the house, opens the garage door, comes into the garage, closes the garage door, walks upstairs.

"Now, what does he say she's wearing when he woke up, and she was next to him? He says he woke up first, and she woke up afterward. He wants you to believe that she did all these activities, started her day, [and] that when she came back to the house, she not only fell asleep again, but she changed out of her street clothes and got back into the nightie . . . How preposterous is that?"

Bruce had planned the crime, Hunter said. "The defendant was desperate with Jana. And he had to murder her. He couldn't afford to lose half of his assets. And in this case, he's desperate with you, and he had to lie to you.

"He wanted [the] Long Beach [police] to investigate this crime. He was hoping, praying, that the car would be found quickly, and that Long Beach would be the investigating agency. Why? Because he had the connections there. He was a good guy with those people. That's where his connections were. There was no coincidence that the car was planted in the area where this defendant had connections."

This was an overstatement by Hunter—Signal Hill was *not* under the jurisdiction of the Long Beach police, and Bruce had no inside connections with the Signal Hill Police Department. But Hunter went on to make her point: It was Bruce who had urged the police to find the car to get a clue on what had happened to his wife. His plan had been to get the police to believe there had been a carjacking, Hunter contended.

"Consuelo Lopez was the key to this case," Hunter said. "Why? Because it put the focus back inside the house. It wasn't a carjacking. It wasn't a robbery, it wasn't a kidnaping." The sheets—the changing of the sheets showed that the crime had occurred inside the Koklich house. This had caused Bruce to scramble for a new explanation.

"Now we [Bruce] shift to Plan B. *Now* the problem is,

she gets killed inside the house. Now the scenario is, someone came into the house after he left at 6 or 6:30, killed his wife, cleaned up, took the sheets, remade the bed, brought Jana downstairs, put her in the car, set the alarm, found out where the garage buttons were, brought her outside, drove to Lewis Avenue, dumped the body so that nobody could find her, left the car there, all within a span of about a half an hour to an hour or so. That's his scenario. Show me any evidence that was presented that substantiates that."

The facts—the facts, not the lies, Hunter said—showed that Bruce Koklich had killed his wife, and had hidden her body in a place where it still had not been found.

Hunter's argument was powerful simply because of its logic. The clock alone seemed to show that Bruce *had* to have been his wife's killer. The time frames seemed to show that only Bruce could have done it. But Salcido still had some reasonable doubt to work with. His task was to make sure it took root in the minds of the jurors. After all, he only needed one person among the twelve to insist to the others that Hunter hadn't proved her case. He tried to use the legal instructions to the jury to show how the law *required* jurors to vote against conviction, regardless of how they might feel about Bruce personally.

The state had tried to prove that Bruce was guilty of killing Jana, not with evidence of a crime, but by making him look bad, Salcido said. Jennifer Titchenal, Rosie Ritchie, Michelle McWhirter, the only reason for their testimonies was to smear Bruce, he said. The same was true of the testimony about Bruce's unlicensed guns, or accepting $5,000 from Paul Carpenter, "a dying man," as Hunter had described him.

"The district attorney knows she cannot prove that he had a motive to kill Jana," Salcido said. Instead, Hunter had presented a smorgasbord of motives, a repast of un-proven possibilities. "I call it her wandering theory of motives," Salcido said. Hunter had tried money, she'd tried sex, she'd tried resentment of Nini, she'd tried con-trol issues, and she'd tried the adoption, all in an effort to explain just why Bruce would have killed Jana. None of them stood up to scrutiny, Salcido said.

"She knows that she's got a major problem with mo-tive . . . she hopes that by dirtying up Bruce, you will not like him and find him guilty on dislike, or hate. The D.A. wants a conviction based on character assassination."

But that wasn't the law, Salcido said: The jury couldn't convict Bruce just because they thought he might be a reprehensible person. They had to base their decision on facts, and the most important fact was, there *were* no facts.

"Motive, motive, motive," Salcido said. "A reason—a reason to do something." While the law didn't require the prosecution to prove a motive to prove guilt, if it didn't, the jury could consider that as a fact that tended to show a person was *not* guilty.

"And so we have to ask ourselves," Salcido said, "why would Bruce have any reason at all to kill Jana? Why?"

It wasn't Jana wanting to be independent, Salcido said. The prosecution hadn't shown a single piece of evidence that proved that she wanted to leave Bruce because of that. Nini may have *thought* that, but that was Nini's idea, it wasn't necessarily Jana's. Even Nini admitted that Jana had never said anything like that to her.

What about money? Salcido asked. The prosecution had failed to prove that money was a motive.

"You know why they didn't prove it? Because they didn't do their homework, that's why. And they never would have been able to prove it. Because if they had done their homework, they would have known there was no cash-poor position. So Bruce had no financial motive or reason to kill Jana."

More than that, Salcido went on, Jana's disappearance was economically devastating to Bruce. Financial expert George Miller had testified that the lost value of Jana's contribution to the Koklich business far exceeded the $1 million in life insurance.

"You do not kill the goose that lays the golden egg," Salcido said. "You just don't do that. You saw what happened after she disappeared. I mean, those earnings *plummeted*. And Bruce is not an idiot. He understands that. So do you think for a second that he's going to be premeditating and deliberating on *killing* her? No way. No way."

Aside from Nini, Salcido said, virtually everyone had said that they thought Jana got along well with Bruce, that the marriage seemed happy. There was no evidence that Jana intended to divorce him. And there was proof of that: just before she disappeared, Jana had deeded two pieces of her separate property over to the marital community, Salcido pointed out. If Jana were really going to leave Bruce, divorce him, would she have done this? No, said Salcido.

"Jana is telling the world, she's telling the world, by executing those deeds, 'I love my husband. We are a team. We are one. This is our future, and I'm combining our future.' That doesn't sound like there's anything wrong with their relationship at all." For those who said, like Nini, that Bruce was a controller, the evidence was that Jana enjoyed caring for Bruce.

"Nini," said Salcido. "You talk about a controller. *Nini* is a controller."

The evidence was that Bruce and Jana had spent a quiet weekend together, Salcido said. They'd done it before—it wasn't that unusual, not nearly as odd as the D.A. claimed. And the evidence showed that it *was* Jana

who had come to the office on Sunday. Arrita had seen a
white Pathfinder, not a blue minivan. She'd seen Jana
hundreds of times, and certainly knew what she looked
like, and more importantly, knew what her car looked
like. No one could possibly have mistaken Sandy Baressi
for Jana, even if they were blind in one eye.

Donna Baker, Salcido said, had surely seen Jana's
SUV on Monday morning—after Bruce had left for
work. As for Romberg, the dentist, Salcido added, he'd
changed his testimony after talking to a judge.

"Whatever happened to Dr. Romberg—who is a friend
of Detective Cooper—whatever happened between the
first time he [testified] and his coming back to enlighten
us, I don't know what it is, but I can speculate like anybody else, and that is, Cooper is over at his house. They
are having their [church] meetings there. So did Cooper
whisper in his ear? I'll never know. All I know is that he
[Romberg] comes in here trying to change [his testi-
mony], because, you know why? Because it is not benefit-
ting the prosecution."

And, said Salcido, young Raesean, Rayray, had said he
first saw the white SUV on Lewis Avenue at 10 A.M. That
meant Theresa Thornton and Michael Freeman had to be
wrong when they said they saw the car before 8 A.M. It
couldn't have been before 8 A.M., because Donna Baker
had seen it in the Koklich garage at that same time.

"Remember, this is proof *beyond* a reasonable doubt,"
Salcido said. "No guesswork here."

What about Consuelo? Salcido pointed out that Consuelo had in fact picked up dishes from the upstairs bedroom floor on Tuesday morning. That showed that Bruce
and Jana had been together at home over the weekend, he
said.

"Now, Chris Botosan. What we know about Chris Botosan is that—very bright, very clever—early on, wanted to

do everything he could to dirty up Bruce. He had the opportunity, the motive, and the knowledge to kill Jana and try to shift the blame to Bruce. A financial motive. He would become more indispensable to Bruce with Jana out of the way. With Bruce out of the way as well, he could have the company to himself."

Here was where Salcido tried to reap the benefit of not demolishing the uncertain validity of the NABUCO proposal. The idea that a capitalized AMOS could be worth many millions, even if it wasn't, only helped establish his scapegoat's motive. Exposing the shifting uncertainties of the NABUCO proposal would also expose the poverty of Salcido's argument as to Chris's supposed motive. He slipped over this part quickly and went on to the remainder of his effort to implicate Chris as the real culprit.

"The opportunity. He lied to the police to cover up his opportunity. Melinda McBride, you heard her testimony. Spent the night with him, according to him, spent the night with him on Sunday, leaving Monday in the A.M. A flat-out lie.

"Melinda McBride told you that, if she spent the night with him, it was Friday and it was Saturday. It was not on Sunday. See, the reason for that is, he has to have somewhat of an alibi for Monday morning."

Chris had stumbled when he testified he'd only been to the Koklich house once, when he'd actually told the detectives he'd been there four or five times, Salcido said.

"Why would he do that? And if he was there four or five times, the question, of course, is when? What was he doing there? Obviously Bruce didn't know about it."

Salcido seemed to be on the verge of suggesting that Chris had been having some sort of secret relationship with Jana, and that *Chris* had been in the house often enough to know where the sheets were kept. But he did not go there.

"He lied about what he told Dohi and Sheehy regarding AMOS and the value of the company," Salcido continued. "It was Botosan who was handling the financial aspect of the corporation with NABUCO . . . Botosan's interest in AMOS is currently in dispute."

It was peculiar that Chris couldn't remember telling Sheehy and Dohi about the multiple millions AMOS was set to make, Salcido said. "It boggles your mind. Comes in here and says between three and eight million, and he's telling the detectives . . . between 50 and 100 million."

Chris's activities on Monday morning "have never been investigated by anyone," Salcido said.

"Chris had the opportunity in the A.M.," Salcido continued. "His movements, his whereabouts, have never been explained to anyone. He had the knowledge of Bruce and Jana. He had the motive to take over that company. And we don't have to prove that Chris killed Jana. That's not *our* burden. We don't have to prove that. That is for the prosecution."

Chris's statements to Dohi and the detectives were bizarre, Salcido suggested.

"Botosan, who . . . he says [the company might be worth] 3 to 8 million here [when Chris had testified] and 600 million to the detectives. I mean, that's outrageous. I mean, where do you fish that out of?"

Salcido went back over all of his points, again and again, apparently trying to make sure that he hadn't missed any, or possibly hoping, by sheer dint of repetition, that he could make an impression on the jury.

Finally he seemed to be nearing the end.

"What this forum is all about, it's all about 'prove it,' " he said. "And only one side has the burden of proving it. Bruce is presumed to be innocent." And the simple facts were, he said, that the prosecution hadn't even been able to prove that a person was dead, let alone that she had been murdered. As for the proposition that Bruce had done it—forget it.

"All of that equals not guilty," Salcido said. The evidence was too insubstantial to support conviction on the charge of murder.

Any Suggestions?

By noon on Monday, March 17, the jury had deliberated for seven hours. As they broke for lunch, they sent a note to Judge Higa:

We are unable to reach a verdict.

Higa called the lawyers back to the courtroom early that afternoon.

"Did you see the note?" he asked.

Salcido and Hunter said, yes, they'd seen it.

"Well, any suggestions, anybody?"

The jury had only been deliberating for seven hours, Hunter said. She thought the court should tell the jury to keep trying. Salcido wanted to find out how the jury was split. If it was 11 to 1 for acquittal, he'd probably side with Hunter. But if it was the other way, he'd want to see if there was any prospect of calling a mistrial, and starting all over again.

"I'd certainly like to know how many ballots they've taken," Salcido said. "And whether there's been any shift at all from the first ballot."

Hunter wasn't in favor of that. She suggested that the judge ask if the jurors wanted any of the testimony read back to them. Maybe, if they were stuck, a "readback" might clarify things.

"I think I have to ask them whether they feel additional deliberations would assist in reaching a verdict," Higa said. The fact that the jury had sent a note indicating they couldn't reach a verdict after only seven hours of deliberation seemed to be a strong indication that the split was both hard and irreversible.

Hunter didn't want the jurors polled, at least not right away. She suggested that Higa might want to read the law to the jury on manslaughter. Manslaughter was the unlawful taking of human life without intent; murder was taking human life intentionally. By suggesting that Higa read the instruction on manslaughter, she was suggesting that if the jury couldn't agree on murder, maybe it could vote for manslaughter. She noted that Salcido had discussed the theory of manslaughter in his closing argument, especially when he'd pointed out that the prosecution had never presented any evidence that Bruce intended to kill his wife. Without a body, intent could only be inferred. Hunter at this point thought a manslaughter possibility might move the jury to come up with a verdict. It wasn't murder, but it was better than an acquittal or a hung jury, at least for Hunter.

Higa thought he'd wait a while on the manslaughter instruction. Going too fast at this point was no help, he knew.

The jury was brought out. Higa told them if they needed any testimony read back, they could ask for it. The jury nodded, and went back into their deliberation room. But the early declaration of impasse seemed very ominous to Hunter.

Over the next week, the jury asked to listen to the tapes of various interviews the detectives had conducted, including the two interviews with Bruce, as well as the one with Consuelo. There was also an audiotape of Michael Freeman. Later they asked for the reading of the testimony of Freeman, Theresa Thornton and Raesean Hollie "pertaining to the exact time when the Pathfinder was found on Lewis Avenue."

Higa ordered *all* the testimony from these witnesses to be read back. It wasn't possible to narrow this down to the "exact time." The trouble was, the "exact time" was in dispute. He thought the jury should sort out the conflicts about the timing of when the SUV had first appeared for themselves; it was up to the jurors to assign credibility to the witnesses, and decide what was true. From this, Hunter had to realize that the state's version of the case was in serious trouble.

The following day, the jury asked for Bruce's complete testimony to be read back.

The Monday after that, after six days of deliberating, the jury sent another note to the judge:

> There has been no movement and we are absolutely
> deadlocked, and could not reach a verdict.

Salcido had convinced five of the twelve jurors that there was reasonable doubt.

Judge Higa formally declared a mistrial.

Retrial

Six months passed, with Bruce still free on bail, still trying to get AMOS off the ground, and in September of 2003, more than two years after Jana had mysteriously vanished, another trial of Bruce Koklich began.

This time, however, there would be some significant changes. Hunter, for one, was joined by Michael Latin, another deputy district attorney in the Major Crimes Unit; Latin and Hunter had previously been assigned to try accused SLA fugitive Sara Jane Olson, but when Olson entered a guilty plea, that left Latin free to assist Hunter.

By September, Hunter and Latin had gone over their case carefully, particularly the testimony from the first trial. One of their decisions was that Chris Botosan had to go. They decided not to call Chris as a witness in the second trial.

And on reflection, both Latin and Hunter thought the sex material had been too distracting. They thought it could best be used in rebuttal—in case Bruce took the stand again, and only if the defense tried to convince a new jury that he was a fine, morally upstanding man.

Mostly, however, they decided to junk the search for

motives entirely. They intended to present a stripped-down version of the case that would show that Bruce and only Bruce could have made Jana disappear. The timing—the Monday clock—was crucial here.

"I always think you learn something from a first trial," Hunter said later. "We decided to cut the fat, narrow the case. It was something like a chess game . . . we had to think, if we do this, they'll do that. Or, if we don't do this, how will they respond?"

Making the case leaner, Hunter said, helped the new jury focus more on the evidence and less on the distractions.

Besides excluding Chris, Hunter and Latin decided to include several witnesses they hadn't used at the first trial, including Marguerite Grinder and, most notably, Ricardo Vargas, who'd told detectives he'd seen a white SUV in the alley behind Lewis Avenue "three or four days" before it was found in the garage.

Otherwise, the new trial proceeded pretty much as the first one had, with the same witnesses giving substantially the same testimony. But this time, the prosecutors decided to jazz up their presentation with a mixed-media presentation comprised of still photos, tape from the interviews of Bruce and Consuelo, footage from Bruce's press conferences, and charts and diagrams, all controlled by a computerized PowerPoint presentation. Assembling these materials seemed to give the prosecution case a visual potency that hadn't been apparent in the first trial.

From the outset, Hunter told the jury that they could not prove Bruce's motive. But it wasn't necessary, she said, any more than it was necessary to have a body to prove that a murder occurred.

"The evidence will show that when you put all the pieces of the puzzle together," Hunter told the jury, "only one person is responsible. And that person is Bruce Koklich."

After demonstrating Jana's penchant for always keeping her appointments, showing that none of the telephone calls over the weekend had been returned, Hunter and Latin established once more that the white SUV had been seen on Lewis Avenue early Monday morning.

That set the stage for Vargas. Although he had told detectives that he'd seen the white SUV in the alley "a few days" before it was recovered from the garage—he'd seen that event on television—Vargas also thought he'd seen it in the alley on "a Sunday leading into a Monday." That suggested that it might have been during the early morning hours prior to Raesean's seeing the SUV on Lewis Avenue Monday morning.

This was critical testimony, but it did not go well for Salcido. Since the SUV had been found in the garage off the alley on the *following* Monday morning, August 27, it was possible that Vargas had seen the unknown man who had moved it from Lewis Avenue and put it into the garage, rather than Bruce. Vargas' inability to be precise about the night he'd seen the vehicle could cut two ways. Because Vargas said that he'd been in the area to visit his girlfriend and sick child, one way to verify the day would have been to call the girlfriend as a witness, to see if she could confirm the date and time her child had been sick. That neither side called her suggests that she had no useful information.

Hunter and Latin rested their case on September 25, 2003, after once again focusing on the mystery of the sheets. Now Salcido had to make a decision: to call Bruce as a witness for himself, or not?

Hunter and Latin were both hoping that Salcido would put Bruce on the stand again. They were convinced his arrogant demeanor, obvious during his testimony at the first trial, would come out once more. And if he did testify,

Hunter and Latin hoped he would once again claim that he loved his wife. Then they could summon witnesses like Rosie Ritchie and Michelle McWhirter to show Bruce's tawdry side.

But Salcido decided not to put Bruce on the stand a second time. It seemed a calculated risk—the jury would not hear from Bruce's own lips that he had not committed the crime, but on the other hand, it wouldn't hear about the "entertain me" demand, or the cash-stuffed envelope, and likely, any other character-debilitating evidence.

Salcido's other main problem was the prosecution's decision to drop Chris Botosan as a witness. But Salcido wasn't about to let his designated scapegoat go without trying once more to pin the crime on him. He decided to call Chris as a witness for the defense. Once again, he asked that he be permitted to raise a the-other-guy-did-it, third-party culpability defense. But this time, the judge, Philip Hickok, denied Salcido's motion. Salcido had to present substantial evidence to show that another person had *actually* committed the crime, Hickok ruled, not just that it was theoretically possible.

Salcido thought he might still accomplish his goal, however, by having the judge designate Chris as a hostile witness, which would permit Salcido to use leading questions, as if he were cross-examining Chris. But Hickok denied this too. The prosecution's decision not to call Chris as a witness for the state paid off.

Before Chris took the stand as Bruce's witness on October 3, Salcido complained that his cross-examination of Chris in the first trial was "a WWF wrestling match," meaning that Chris had been extremely wiggly under questioning. But if Salcido had learned something from the first trial, so had Chris: he learned to keep his answers truthful but short. That way, he could prevent Salcido from demonstrating that he was "hostile" to Bruce. Before his testimony was over, even Judge Hickok would observe that Chris seemed to know when Salcido's questions were legally objectionable. In short, he was well-prepared to testify.

Before this, however, Salcido started him off with a zinger, doubtless thinking it would put Chris on the defensive from the outset.

"Mr. Botosan," Salcido said, "did the police officers in this case ever instruct you to leave town and not be available for this trial?"

"No," Chris said.

"Did you ever tell anyone that you had been instructed by the police to leave town?"

"Yes."

The trial had been a frequent topic of conversation at his apartment complex, Chris said, and he'd only told people that so they wouldn't ask him any more questions about the case. He did leave town, he said, but when he found out that Salcido wanted to call him as a witness, he'd voluntarily submitted himself for questioning.

Salcido turned to AMOS. Chris said that he had 100,000 shares of AMOS in his possession, and that he'd been promised up to 1 million shares. Salcido had hoped he would fall into the trap of claiming ownership of 1 million shares, but Chris avoided it adroitly by telling the truth. Salcido moved on to NABUCO.

"What was your relationship with NABUCO?" Salcido asked.

"At the beginning it was a company that was owned by some people I knew. And I was further involved and became a part of that company, getting eleven percent of the stock of that company."

"Who were the people?"

"The directors of that company are— I can name some of the directors, I'm not sure I can be accurate with all of them. It's Benet Heller."

"Who else?"

"Dennis Piotrowski. I don't know any other directors besides those two. I am named, I believe, as a director also."

"Did you know a Joe Heller?"

"Yes."

"Who is he?"

"He does consulting work for the NABUCO company."

Salcido asked how long Chris had known Joe Heller as of August 2001. About three or four years, Chris said.

Salcido asked when Chris had introduced Bruce to Joe Heller.

"I believe it might have been July," Chris said—before Jana disappeared.

Salcido asked Chris where Joe Heller lived, but Hunter objected to the relevancy of the question, and Hickok sustained her.

Salcido next wanted to show that Chris, by November of 2001, three months after Jana had disappeared, believed that AMOS had the potential to be worth up to $600 million. He asked Chris if he'd ever used that figure with the detectives and Dohi.

"At the point of 10 years, given all the extrapolations that I had given [to the detectives] previously, that they had 100 percent performance, of 100 separate banks, doing all their business through the company, and being satisfied over a six-year period, absolutely," Chris said. In other words, if everything happened perfectly, and 100 banks were signed up, $600 million was attainable.

Salcido turned to the proposed loan to be brokered by NABUCO.

"How many meetings did you have with Bruce Koklich and any apparent representative from NABUCO in regard to this funding?"

Chris said he didn't recall.

"Isn't it true that whatever meetings that you had, they were held in coffee shops somewhere?"

"I believe so, yes."

Salcido asked about the supposed $100 million bond that NABUCO was going to somehow be involved in.

"So they were going to fund $100 million, and out of the $100 million, $7.5 million was going to go to AAMOS?"

"It's their vehicle for the funding of the monies that were going to be available to the client," Chris said. It appears from this response that Chris was suggesting that NABUCO would find a financial institution to underwrite a $100 million bond, and that interest on the bond proceeds, when deposited or invested, would amount to $7.5 million, and that *that* money would be loaned to AAMOS, to be passed on to AMOS. In other words, NABUCO would get the interest, then loan that amount to AMOS, via AAMOS.

"It's their vehicle for funding the monies the net proceeds to the client," Chris said again.

"Who were you dealing or negotiating with that represented NABUCO?"

"I believe at that time it was Dennis Piotrowski," Chris said.

"Who is Dennis Piotrowski?" Salcido asked.

"He's one of the officers of NABUCO."

The next logical question might have been something related to the old Aladdin hotel controversy, the one in which Piotrowski was indicted by the federal government before being eventually acquitted. If Salcido had wanted to cast doubt on the legitimacy of the NABUCO deal, this was the time to do it. But Salcido did not go into the old Aladdin controversy.

Chris said he couldn't recall how many times he'd met with Piotrowski, or where.

"During the early months of the year 2001, did Bruce

Koklich pay $10,000 to somebody regarding getting money from NABUCO?"

"Yes, he did."

"Who was that money paid to?"

"It was paid to NABUCO."

"Wasn't it paid to Joe Heller?"

"I don't believe so."

"Wasn't there a check made out to Joe Heller for $10,000?"

Here Salcido was closing in on the nut of the issue—the advance fee paid to get the proposed loan process started. But Hunter quickly objected, saying Salcido was asking a leading question—not permitted, since Chris was Salcido's own witness. Hickok sustained her.

Salcido tried again. Had Chris seen the $10,000 check? Was it given to Chris, or someone else?

"I don't recall," Chris said.

Salcido asked what Chris was going to get from the deal with NABUCO.

"I don't recall," Chris said.

Salcido asked if Chris had ever received any money from NABUCO—it seems that he was trying to suggest that Chris had obtained $10,000 from Bruce, given the money to Heller, and then had Heller give all or part of the money back to him. But Hunter headed this off with another objection, which was once more sustained by Hickok.

Salcido was getting frustrated.

"Isn't it true that NABUCO was just a sham? Isn't that right?"

Hunter objected once more, Hickok sustained her and Chris did not have to answer.

Salcido tried the direct approach.

"Of that $10,000 that Bruce Koklich paid, did you receive any part of that $10,000?"

"No," Chris said.

That was the end of Salcido's attempt to get to the bottom of the NABUCO situation. It was enough to suggest that the entire transaction was unusual, certainly that there was more to the deal than met the eye. But the problem had always been: getting too deep into the deal could only show that Chris had every reason *not* to have killed Jana—because of the scrutiny it would bring on him and the others involved in NABUCO—and that Bruce had every reason to kill Jana himself, if Jana had opposed the deal.

And after all, who was the Koklich company's expert on loans and financing? It wasn't Bruce, that's for sure.

The Verdict

The Koklich case went to a jury for a second time on October 7, 2003.

Three hours later, they came back with a verdict:

> "We the jury in the above-entitled action, find the defendant, Bruce Koklich, guilty of the crime of murder."

But there was some positive news for Bruce in this abrupt turnaround of fortune: The murder was of the second degree, not first. In the absence of any evidence that the crime had been premeditated, Bruce could not be convicted of the stiffer charge. That was the difference between a sentence of 15 years to life, and a minimum of 25 years to life in prison.

Without a motive, premeditation was impossible to prove.

AFTERMATH

To Save a Life

About four months later, Bruce parted company from Henry Salcido, and hired a new lawyer, Ed George of Long Beach, to prepare a motion for a new trial. George's motion was voluminous—nearly a thousand pages that dissected the evidence presented at both trials, and which excoriated the prosecution for its conduct in the second trial.

Hickok denied the motion for a new trial.

On March 26, 2004, Hickok sentenced Bruce to a term in state prison of 15 years to life. Bruce showed no emotion, even when Janie read her victim-impact statement to the court.

"I lost my only child when she was in the prime of her life," Janie said. "There is a permanent hole in my heart. It will be there for the rest of my life."

She hadn't wanted to believe that Bruce had done this thing, Janie said.

"But now I have just one question: *What did you do with her body?*"

But Bruce didn't answer.

• • •

So ended a case that had taken more than two-and-a-half years to resolve, and even then, it ended with a question: Where was Jana Carpenter Koklich?

Detective Sheehy came to believe that Bruce had taken Jana's body to a Dumpster early on Monday morning, someplace on the way to the Lewis Avenue area. There, Sheehy believed, Bruce had disposed of her remains. Later the Dumpster would have been emptied of its contents in some landfill, just as later would happen with Salt Lake City's Lori Hacking.

Sergeant Longshore, however, believed that Bruce had originally left the body at the oil field near Lewis Avenue, the one that had been fruitlessly searched, the same one where Longshore's psychic friend, Kellee, had told him that "She was here . . . She says we're close, don't give up . . ." But, Longshore said, he believed that once Consuelo had pinpointed the problem of the sheets, Bruce had realized that he had to hide the body and so returned to the oil field one dark night, and moved it to another, still unknown location.

Bruce still denies that he killed Jana. His appeal is now working its way through the appellate courts. He claims he was framed.

There was one final development in the Koklich case: the money. Jana's survivors—principally, Janie and Doris, the two women loved by Paul Carpenter, eventually filed a wrongful death suit against Bruce, in order to prevent him from using any funds from the marital community. If they prevail, Bruce would be left with nothing, exactly the way he had started out so many years before.

Jana's mysterious disappearance never received the notoriety that other, similar cases got. It never had hours upon hours of talking heads on *Larry King*, dissecting every nuance. Her smiling face never became the staple of the evening news, coast to coast. But if she did not deserve to die—and she did not—neither does she deserve to be forgotten.

She was quiet and polite, probably too quiet and polite. And if there's a lesson anywhere in this, any sort of moral to this story, it's that, for women, standing up for yourself isn't a bad thing, and neither is telling someone how you really feel. It might even save your life.

Notes and Acknowledgments

This book was based on more than 8,000 pages of trial transcripts in the matter of *People* v. *Bruce David Koklich*, along with several thousand additional pages of court records, including exhibits, briefs and declarations, police notes and reports encompassing the findings of the Los Angeles County Sheriff's Department's investigation into the disappearance and presumed murder of Jana Carpenter Koklich.

In addition, this narrative was based on a number of interviews with principals in the case, including Los Angeles County Sheriff Department Detective Joseph Sheehy, Sergeant Richard Longshore, Detective Delores Scott, Deputy District Attorneys Eleanor Hunter and Greg Dohi, associates and relatives of Bruce David Koklich, his present legal counsel, Jana's friend Nini Angelini, and especially, the Reverend. H. A. Bryant, of the Great Deliverance Church of God in Christ in Signal Hill, California. Other interviews included Sacramento attorneys Charles Bloodgood and Mathew Jacobs, along with news reporters and columnists Wendy Thomas Russell of the Long Beach *Press-Telegram*, Mark Goldstein of the

San Jose Mercury News, George Skelton of the *Los Angeles Times*, Bill Boyarsky, formerly of the *Times*, and John Smith of the *Las Vegas Review-Journal*.

Records from the California State Archives, the California State Library, the California Fair Political Practices Commission, and the corporate record archives of the states of California, Nevada and Delaware were vital, along with various accounts of the history of California politics, especially that of former State Senator James R. Mills. So too were records from the United States Courts of the Districts of Wisconsin and Nevada.

Some principals in the case nevertheless declined interviews. Apparently because of concerns about still unresolved litigation related to the wrongful death lawsuit against Bruce Koklich, important sources such as Jan and Jeff Baird, Doris Morrow and Janie Koklich either declined to be interviewed or did not respond to interview requests. As noted in a footnote in the text, Christopher Botosan and Stephen R. Boyers also declined interviews. Former Koklich attorney Henry Salcido likewise declined to be interviewed, despite repeated requests.

Finally, the narrative includes various facts and assertions from Bruce Koklich, in response to a written request from the author for comment.

In addition to those named above, the author wishes to thank a number of others for their assistance in this endeavor, among them Nini Angelini, Harry Parrell, Barbara Hauxhurst, Steve Marino, Dave Titchenal, Kraig Newkirk, as well as several others who, familiar with some of those involved in the events recounted herein, asked not to be named.

Special thanks for assistance above and beyond the call of duty are due to Betty Fletcher of the Superior Court, Southeast District, for her assistance in organizing exhibits from the Koklich trial for inspection and copying.

Betty, who is now retired from the court, is one of the increasingly few of the judicial bureaucracy who recognize that court documents are *public documents*—and a vital part of our democratic capacity to hold our governmental institutions accountable.

Carlton Smith
South Pasadena, California
December 2004